INTERPRETING WOMEN'S LIVES

INTERPRETING WOMEN'S LIVES

Feminist Theory and Personal Narratives

EDITED BY THE

PERSONAL NARRATIVES GROUP

Joy Webster Barbre
Amy Farrell
Shirley Nelson Garner
Susan Geiger
Ruth-Ellen Boetcher Joeres

Susan M-A Lyons
Mary Jo Maynes
Pamela Mittlefehldt
Riv-Ellen Prell
Virginia Steinhagen

INDIANA UNIVERSITY PRESS
Bloomington and Indianapolis

Manufactured in the United States of America

Library of Congress Cataloging-in-Publication Data
Interpreting women's lives.
Includes index.
1. Women's studies—Biographical methods. 2. Auto-
biography—Women authors—History and criticism.
3. Feminist criticism. I. Personal Narratives Group.
HQ1185   1989   305.4'2   88-45445
ISBN 0-253-33070-X
ISBN 0-253-20501-8 (pbk.)

2 3 4 5   93 92 91 90

CONTENTS

Acknowledgments

The members of the Personal Narratives Group thank the many University of Minnesota colleagues whose efforts, interest, and support made possible both our May 1986 conference, "Autobiographies, Biographies, and Life Histories of Women: Interdisciplinary Perspectives," and this book. Without the Center for Advanced Feminist Studies as a receptive space and institutional base for cross-disciplinary feminist research, our working group would have been difficult, if not impossible, to sustain. To the Center itself, then, and to former Center Director Ruth-Ellen B. Joeres, who originally brought us together, we owe a debt of thanks. We are grateful as well to current Center Director Sara Evans, who has continued to encourage our project. The Center's secretary Karen Seefeldt Moon also deserves thanks for her efficiency, patience, and good humor in handling additional phone calls and mail, the biweekly traffic related to our meetings, and the periodic outbursts of frenzied activity and celebration accompanying the progress of our book.

For generous support of our conference, we would like to acknowledge and thank the following units of the University of Minnesota: American Studies, Anthropology, Concerts and Lectures, English, German, History, Spanish and Portuguese, Center for Humanistic Studies, College of Liberal Arts, Scholarly Conference Committee, Continuing Education and Extension Program Innovation Fund, Graduate School, Office of International Education, Office of Vice President for Academic Affairs, Women's Studies, and Western European Area Studies. Judson Sheridan, who was the Associate Dean of the Graduate School at the time of our project, should be singled out for his generous support of our requests for a graduate research assistant. We should also like to acknowledge Lori Graven, of Professional Development and Conference Services at the University of Minnesota, who was an extremely able and congenial colleague in her capacity as conference coordinator.

In addition to those conference participants whose work is included in our volume, we wish to thank Celia Eckhardt, Gelya Frank, Katrin Lunde, Daphne Patai, and Luisa Pusch, who presented papers and contributed importantly to our thinking on the subject of personal narratives. As panel moderators, Susan Geiger, Ruth-Ellen B. Joeres, Toni McNaron, Pamela Mittlefehldt, and Winifred Woodhull raised questions that added a great deal to the formulation of ideas that have shaped this book. For their contribution to understanding and appreciating personal narrative as it is expressed in a variety of forms, we also want to thank Susan McClary for her performance piece, Linda Brooks for her photograph-lecture, and Elizabeth Kennedy, Madeline Davis, and Lisa Albrecht for their discussion of the Buffalo Oral History Project on lesbian relationships in the 1940s and 1950s. We are aware of the enormous difficulties that were involved in providing a final overview of the conference, and we thank Annette Kuhn for her effort in that respect.

Our colleagues Amy Kaminsky, George Lipsitz, Shula Marks, Toni McNaron, Janet Spector, and Julia Swindells served as discerning readers of an early version of our essay "Origins" and offered useful criticism that helped us formulate our final version. We are also grateful to Indiana University Press editor Joan Catapano for her thoughtful and efficient treatment of our manuscript.

Finally, we wish to single out one among us whose continuous contributions to the development and success of our efforts have been invaluable. Pamela Mittlefehldt, in addition to sharing collective authorship and editing with the rest of us, served as graduate research assistant to our project from the conference planning stage through to the completion of our book. Her voluminous correspondence with contributors, her lucid minutes of our biweekly meetings, and her efficient handling of every detail allowed us to function. But even more important than that mammoth effort on her part was her major presence: at critical and potentially chaotic moments she persistently reminded us of the invigorating intellectual pleasures and personal victories represented by this process, and we feel that without her we couldn't have written our book. We offer to Pamela our heartfelt thanks.

PART ONE
Origins

ORIGINS

Personal Narratives Group

Traditionally, knowledge, truth, and reality have been constructed as if men's experiences were normative, as if being human meant being male. *Interpreting Women's Lives* is part of the larger effort to undermine this partial construction and to create a more inclusive, more fully human conception of social reality. This process of reconstruction challenges what has been defined and taught as our common intellectual and cultural heritage. Throughout the world, participants in recent movements for social change have asserted that this heritage has excluded their experiences. They have argued, furthermore, that what had been presented as an objective view of the world was selectively the dominant white, male view. What was once accepted as normative was recognized as being the limited and limiting perspective of a particular gender, class, and race.

This political climate effected corresponding upheaval in the academic world. If experience was open for redefinition, a crisis in representation was inevitable. As this hegemonic world view was challenged, the canons of all fields were questioned. Scholars within both the humanities and the social sciences raised the question of *whose* lives had been made exemplary in contemporary and historical studies, and asked further what impact on our understanding of the human experience the inclusion of different life experiences would have.

In the study of literature, for example, scholars began to ask why the canon was dominated by the writings of a small group of literary men, and why some forms of literary expression were valued above others. Not only were new authors brought into the field of study, but the formal basis of the canon was exploded as critical scholars insisted that all forms of cultural expression, such as diaries, film, and popular novels, demanded analysis. In the field of historical study, both the new social history that attempted to reconstruct historical experience "from the bottom up" and the varieties of radical history that documented social conflict from the viewpoint of the oppressed attacked the theory and methods of the previously dominant "great man" history. Whether relying on collective biography based on quantitative sources or on first-person accounts of the experiences of ordinary people, the new studies redefined what it meant to write history. In anthropology, a younger generation questioned the absence of *people* in ethnographies. They noted the absence of either the ethnographer or the subject from anthropological accounts, claiming that gender, emotion,

3

informal power, and cultural conceptions of the self were absent. At the same time, they questioned why societies continually undergoing change and domination were pictured as "primitive" and isolated in an ahistorical ethnographic present. They reassessed the political implications of representing non-Western cultures for Western audiences, and the significance of relations between ethnographer and informant for the production of ethnographic texts.

The strongest challenge to the disciplines came from feminist theory, which we understand as part of a vital, necessary revolution in human comprehension. Certainly that is what philosopher Elizabeth Minnich asserts when she exposes androcentric thought as a "devastating conceptual error." This is the position historian Gerda Lerner takes in proclaiming for contemporary feminist scholarship a significance equal to that of the Copernican revolution.[1]

The fact that human experience is gendered is central to the radical implications of feminist theory. That recognition of the impact of gender and an insistence on the importance of the female experience have provided the vital common ground for feminist research and thought. Feminist theory emerges from and responds to the lives of women. The recovery and interpretation of women's lives have been central concerns of feminist scholarship from the earliest pioneering works to the present. Listening to women's voices, studying women's writings, and learning from women's experiences have been crucial to the feminist reconstruction of our understanding of the world.

Since feminist theory is grounded in women's lives and aims to analyze the role and meaning of gender in those lives and in society, women's personal narratives are essential primary documents for feminist research. These narratives present and interpret women's life experiences. They can take many forms, including biography, autobiography, life history—a life story told to a second person who records it—diaries, journals, and letters. Although some contributors build biographical accounts from diaries or letters, *Interpreting Women's Lives* focuses on autobiographies, biographies, and life histories. These personal narratives illuminate the course of a life over time and allow for its interpretation in its historical and. cultural context. The very act of giving form to a whole life—or a considerable portion of it—requires, at least implicitly, considering the meaning of the individual and social dynamics which seem to have been most significant in shaping the life. The act of constructing a life narrative forces the author to move from accounts of discrete experiences to an account of why and how the life took the shape it did. This why and how—the interpretive acts that shape a life, and a life narrative—need to take as high a place on the feminist agenda as the recording of women's experiences.

We are also particularly interested in women's personal narratives because the dynamics of gender emerge more clearly in the personal narratives of women than in those of men. Certainly, men are affected by the social construction of gender, but for men, gender has been an unmarked category.[2] For a woman, however, the story is rarely told without reference to the dynamics of gender. Women's personal narratives are, among other things, stories of how women negotiate their "exceptional" gender status both in their daily lives and over the course of a lifetime. They assume that one can understand the life only if one takes into account gender roles and gender expectations. Whether she has accepted the norms or defied them, a woman's life can never be written taking gender for granted.

If women's personal narratives both present and interpret the impact of gender roles on women's lives, they are especially suitable documents for illuminating several aspects of gender relations: the construction of a gendered self-identity, the relationship between the individual and society in the creation and perpetuation of gender norms, and the dynamics of power relations between women and men. Since women's biographies, autobiographies, and life stories all recount a process of construction of the self, these narratives are potentially rich sources for the exploration of the process of gendered self-identity. Such a venture will probably not settle the argument concerning the location of the self: whether it is there to be discovered or uncovered and relatively stable, or whether it is a construction of the mind and continually shifting. Yet because personal narratives are verbal reconstructions of developmental processes, they can well serve feminist psychologists interested in exploring the links between the evolution of subjectivity, the acquisition of language, and the development of a feminine identity.[3]

Women's personal narratives can also provide a vital entry point for examining the interaction between the individual and society in the construction of gender. Traditional explorations of social dynamics have tended to emphasize either the constraints of social structure or the power of individual agency. Only recently have social theorists begun to undermine this polarity. Our reading of women's personal narratives suggests the need to understand the dynamic interaction between the two. While social constructions of gender impinge on the individual, they are themselves shaped by human agency. A paraphrase of the often-cited phrase from Marx may illuminate this claim: Women make their own lives (and life histories), but they do so under conditions not of their own choosing.

Both individual agency and social structure must be considered. Certainly different kinds of questions need to be asked in order to understand a complex social system such as that accounting for gender relations. Some approaches aim essentially at understanding the gender system from the point of view of the individual actor and the logic of her action; hermeneutic, psychological, and microeconomic accounts, for example, can all begin with the individual and generalize from that standpoint. Other types of explanations focus on systemic-level accounts, on the context within which social action unfolds, such as analyses of the intersection of class and sex in the work force, or kinship systems and their gender rules.

Certainly, a full understanding of the dynamics of gender requires both kinds of analysis. Feminist theory postulates as a central tenet the reality of a socially structured gender hierarchy. The uncovering of women's oppression requires attention to systems of relationships in which individuals are embedded and whose boundaries go beyond the individual and her realm of vision. At the same time, individual agency is critical for feminist theory because it provides both the source of insight and the means of action which lead to social change.

We maintain that personal narratives are particularly rich sources because, attentively interpreted, they illuminate both the logic of individual courses of action and the effects of system-level constraints within which those courses evolve. Moreover, each life provides evidence of historical activity—the working out within a specific life situation of deliberate courses of action that in turn have the potential to undermine or perpetuate the conditions and relationships in which the life evolved. One example of a provocative analysis of gender through use of women's personal narratives is Barbara Taylor's use of individual biographies in *Eve and the New Jerusalem,* a history of women in the Utopian Socialist movement in early nineteenth-century England. Her construction and interpretation of biographies allow us to understand, for example, the logic of Emma Martin's conversion from a devout Baptist into a freethinker, a transformation that was central to her challenging the gender norms of her society.[4] In *Interpreting Women's Lives,* these themes of individual agency and social structure recur in several essays. Karen Sacks, in "What's a Life Story Got to Do with It?" makes clear that in order to understand activism in the workplace, she had to consider not only family life and working conditions but also the organizational activities of key individuals. Sandra Frieden's essay, "Transformative Subjectivity in the Writings of Christa Wolf," points out how the East German writer has used various forms of personal narrative to set up the individual against the political expectations of the state. In particular, Wolf's *The Quest for Christa T.* presents a life which is lived as an assertion of individuality amid the political structures in which it is immersed. Personal narratives such as these allow us to see lives as simultaneously individual and social creations, and to see individuals as simultaneously the changers and the changed.

Finally, the dynamics of power relations, and in particular the power inequalities between women and men, are a major concern of feminist theory. Some feminists focus on the direct formal power by which men control women, such as discriminatory marriage rights and property laws. Others explore more subtle inequalities such as the gender division of labor and gender norms and expectations. Certainly, analyses of hegemony—the maintenance of inequality and domination through both ideological and material means—have provided us with insights that have been useful in our interpretation of women's personal narratives.[5]

Women's personal narratives, we have come to see, are especially helpful in understanding androcentric hegemony because they document a variety of responses to it. Some women's narratives can be read as counter-narratives, because they reveal that the narrators do not think, feel, or act as they are "supposed to." Such narratives can serve to unmask claims that form the basis of domination (for example, the claim that men and women profit equally from the gender division of labor) or to provide an alternative understanding of the situation. Personal narratives of nondominant social groups (women in general, racially or ethnically oppressed people, lower-class people, lesbians) are often particularly effective sources of counterhegemonic insight because they expose the viewpoint embedded in dominant ideology as particularist rather than universal, and because they reveal the reality of a life that defies or contradicts the rules. Women's personal narratives can thus often reveal the rules of male domination even as they record rebellion against them.

Other forms of narrative can provide insights of a different nature. Many women's personal narratives unfold within the framework of an apparent acceptance of social norms and expectations but nevertheless describe strategies and activities that challenge those same norms. Thus, for example, the author of the *Daughter of Han*[6] refers continually to her helplessness in the face of her "fate" like a good Confucian ideologue even while she goes about creating her life according to her own requirements. In this volume, Faye Ginsburg's essay, "Dissonance and Harmony: The Symbolic Function of Abortion in Activists' Life Stories," also illustrates this principle. Antiabortion activists she interviewed described themselves as concerned with upholding traditional roles for women and strong family ties; yet their activities defy some of the prevalent expectations for women's reproductive and work roles.

Still others may allow us new insights into the lives of women who apparently thrive within the established norms and parameters or even assertively contribute to the maintenance of prevailing systems of gender domination. For example, in her memoir *To Live Again*, Catherine Marshall writes of her life as the "behind-the-scenes wife" of Senate Chaplain Peter Marshall, commenting that "in marriage I had found my identity, my answer to the question, 'Who am I'"[7] But even narratives such as these suggest the extent to which assent to prevailing norms must be constructed or negotiated. Elisa von der Recke, the subject of Katherine Goodman's essay in this book, "Poetry and Truth: Elisa von der Recke's Sentimental Autobiography," advocates the ideal of the virtuous, martyrlike heroine popular in romance novels of her time, and tells her life to fit this model. Yet she reconstructs the model to fit her needs, casting her husband as the villain while maintaining her image as dutiful wife and mother.

For those interested in the creation of a world liberated from androcentric hegemony, the counter-narratives are naturally the most inspirational. For a woman, claiming the truth of her life despite awareness of other versions of reality that contest this truth often produces both a heightened criticism of officially condoned untruths and a heightened sense of injustice. This criticism is central to the production of feminist theory; this sense of injustice is a critical impetus for feminist political action. But it would be shortsighted of us to ignore the narrative models of acceptance and conformity, since these, too, must be analyzed, interpreted, and understood. For, in effect, the personal narrative, whether it reveals an acceptance of or a challenge to the given rules, also documents on the individual level the very process of reproduction or undermining of those rules. In other words, women's personal narratives, whatever form they take, can be thought of as part of a dialogue of domination. Women's lives are lived within and in tension with systems of domination. Both narratives of acceptance and narratives of rebellion are responses to the system in which they originate and thus reveal its dynamics.

Interpreting Women's Lives is a collective endeavor. While it explores the role of women's personal narratives in the creation of feminist theory, it emerges from and reflects the intellectual histories of the members of the editorial group. As editors, we share a commitment to feminist scholarship and an interest in women's personal narratives. Yet each of us came to this project by a different path. Because we represent diverse disciplinary backgrounds, intellectual generations, and areas of expertise, the book has taken shape through protracted, sometimes difficult, but always enriching discussions. The particular themes, the selected cultures, and the time periods explored here have emerged from our respective research. Our work has pushed each of us beyond our individual boundaries and made the book different from and better than anything any one of us might have written individually.

The Personal Narratives Group is a research group affiliated with the Center for Advanced Feminist Studies at the University of Minnesota. The center was established in 1983 to facilitate and coordinate feminist scholarship, to serve as a gathering place for members of the large feminist community in the area, and to provide a place where individuals could work together on common problems.

As women's personal narratives were gaining critical importance in the development of a feminist critique of many academic disciplines, women's testimonies about their lives were playing an increasingly prominent role in the scholarship and teaching of feminists at Minnesota.[8] That shared interest and a series of joint projects brought together the individuals who now make up the editorial board for this book. Riv-Ellen Prell, an anthropologist, and Susan Geiger, a historian of Africa in the Women's Studies Department, had worked together on life histories of Third World women. As they examined published life histories of Third World women as sources for understanding women's activities and perceptions, they discovered the inadequacies of traditional theories about those societies which failed to acknowledge or account for women as conscious social actors. They developed a course and coauthored conference papers on that topic.

Their joint teaching stimulated further curricular development and research.

Riv-Ellen Prell also taught a three-quarter sequence on women's autobiographies in 1982–83 with Shirley Garner of the English Department and Ruth-Ellen B. Joeres of the German Department. Garner was studying women's personal narratives and writing her autobiography; Joeres was doing research on German women biographers and autobiographers. Both challenged the literary canon's general view of autobiographies as low-status texts not worthy of critical attention, unless they were autobiographies of great men. Their work on women's personal narratives contributed to the expansion of our knowledge of women writers and their work.

M. J. Maynes, a historian specializing in Europe, was examining French and German working-class autobiographies written in the nineteenth century, a project that caused her to question some of the prevailing assumptions and methods underlying social-historical research. In the spring of 1983, she and Ruth-Ellen B. Joeres organized an international conference on German women in the eighteenth and nineteenth centuries that featured several papers drawing on German women's personal narratives. They subsequently published one of the first collections of essays on German women's history.

After instituting a series of discussions in early November 1984, the Personal Narratives Group decided to organize its first meeting. In the course of our discussions, we decided to organize a conference to bring together scholars in our respective fields who were doing innovative work on women's personal narratives. We envisioned a gathering where the invited participants would join with us to discuss our works in progress and to discover ways to bridge disciplinary and cultural differences. After a year of organization and continued discussion, "Autobiographies, Biographies, and Life Histories of Women: Interdisciplinary Perspectives" was held at the University of Minnesota May 23–25, 1986.

We asked participants to prepare papers on their current research; these were circulated in advance of the conference and served as the basis for discussion. We structured panels to include individuals from different disciplinary backgrounds and different geographic areas of interest in order to encourage cross-cultural and cross-disciplinary dialogue. Panelists included scholars from the United States, England, West Germany, Tanzania, Italy, and Norway, representing the fields of history, anthropology, linguistics, and literary criticism.

After the conference, a number of interested graduate students joined the initial group to complete our editorial board. Pamela Mittlefehldt, in American Studies, who had been our administrative and research assistant throughout the planning stages of the conference, continued to play a central coordinating role. Her particular interest is in the interaction between the lives and the writing of women who approach literature as a tool of social change. Susan Lyons, Virginia Steinhagen, Joy Barbre, and Amy

Farrell, who had taken Ruth-Ellen B. Joeres's humanities course on autobiographies, biographies, and life histories, and who had attended the
conference, also joined the Personal Narratives Group. As graduate students in English, German, and American Studies, they are using the many
new perspectives on personal narratives generated during the conference
in their own research.

We worked together to create an innovative form and process for writing
a book about the interpretation of women's personal narratives. As our
discussions about the book proceeded, we were repeatedly surprised by the
tenacious hold of our traditional disciplines. Despite our shared interest,
we often found the gulf between the humanities and the social sciences to
be wide. Each group spoke its own language. While the social scientists
emphasized social structure and human agency, the humanities scholars
focused on textual interpretation and narrative structure. What most interested the social scientists was the integration of personal narratives into the
study of society and history; those in the humanities were far more involved with the formal analysis of narrative. Method and theory overlap-
ped, and questions about one frequently led to questioning the other. We
were often simultaneously enlightened and bewildered.

Our discussions were most successful when we focused on the role of the
canon in literary analysis and the role of power relations in social analysis.
As we came to see the parallels between these concepts, we could agree that
the androcentric assumptions which had excluded certain types of texts
from the study of literature were the same ones that excluded women's
experiences from the usual accounts of social structure and historical transformation. We learned that we communicated most effectively when we
were able to draw such parallels rather than reeducating each other in
entirely new vocabularies or problems. The parallels were not forced. They
drew us together at the outset. But the phrasing of the problems was so
different that we had to work with the patience of translators. This book is
thus a product of feminist collective interdisciplinary work. It did not grow
out of straightforward or quick consensus. Rather, it developed from a
shared passion for a good story and our desire to understand and interpret
it for ourselves and for others.

Interpreting Women's Lives is based on the conference format: cross-disciplinary, cross-cultural, and collective. But it is not based on the organizational themes of the conference. Initially, we had identified three themes:
the *construction,* the *interpretation,* and the *use* of women's personal narratives. *Construction* included consideration of the literary and cultural
models which help shape people's life stories, the social and historical
conditions affecting their life experiences, and the family relations in which
the life develops. *Interpretation* encompassed the relationship between the
individual life story and the particular society. *Use* focused on the ethical
implications of researchers' collecting and publishing life stories, as well as

the search for new forms for the responsible presentation of research results.

As we reflected on discussions arising among conference participants, we began to redefine our categories and assumptions. Moderators at each session had asked panelists to address questions based on the papers. These questions often sparked debates and discussions, which have become the central themes of this book. For example, at the first session, moderator Toni McNaron's question about the ways that autobiography can function for "marginalized" women, such as black American, Third World, working-class, lesbian, or immigrant women, provoked lively reactions. While panelist Gelya Frank identified marginality as a recurrent theme in her interviews with Jewish women rabbis describing their religious experiences, some members of the audience objected strongly to using the concept of marginality in the analysis of women's lives. Several of the Africanists pointed out the problematic meaning of "marginality" when used in the Third World context because it assumes the colonial point of view rather than that of indigenous people. Elizabeth Kennedy, who had done extensive oral histories of lesbians in Buffalo, New York, stated that these women never characterized themselves as marginal, reminding us that we can use such concepts only when we are sensitive to self-definitions of the narrators of the lives.

Frequently, interdisciplinary exchange itself forced us to reformulate our thinking. For example, at a session on interpretation, members of the audience evoked an exchange between literary historian Julia Swindells and anthropologist Karen Sacks over the question of how the interpersonal context in which personal narratives were produced affected the narration. Is there an analogy between Arthur Munby, the Victorian man of letters whose peculiar fascination with the "dirty work" of housemaids prompted his encouragement of Hannah Cullwick's diary writing, and the contemporary feminist researcher who, in textual analysis of oral history, attempts to "liberate" women's voices? This "Arthur Munby problem," as it came to be termed, made it clear to us that the interpretation of women's personal narratives has to take into account the political and institutional context of the production and use of personal narratives—a central theme that would again be taken up in the fourth session.

Interaction between panelists and the audience often moved the discussion forward to new insights. One particularly fruitful exchange was sparked by Luisa Passerini's account of Italian working women, whose lives, on the surface at least, appeared quite orderly, but who in their interviews with her often described themselves as "always having been rebel girls." Members of the audience recognized the significance of this self-description of "rebel girl" in their own lives, which led to a discussion of the importance in women's lives of what we began to call "counter-narratives"—narrative elements in personal accounts which contrast self-image and experiences with dominant cultural models. This discussion also clarified connections between our earlier concerns about marginality and its role in self-definition, and the cultural models which inform life stories.

Discussions such as these made us increasingly aware that we were seeing women's personal narratives from new perspectives. We were repeatedly reminded of the importance of the narrators' own self-definitions as they talked about their lives, in contrast to definitions imposed by interpreters of personal narratives and by the narrators' own society. The importance of the political and institutional contexts of both the narrator and the interpreter of a personal narrative became increasingly obvious. We began to question the relationship between the form of a narrative and the interpretation of the life story told.

These issues exemplify our own intellectual transformation during the conference. While our initial categories of construction, interpretation, and use served as points of departure for discussion, we soon reconceptualized many of our ideas about their usefulness. A new constellation of issues arose around the complex interaction between context, narrative form, and interpreter-narrator relationships. *Interpreting Women's Lives* picks up where conference discussions left off and builds upon the thinking initiated there.

The organization of *Interpreting Women's Lives* reflects our intellectual struggle to locate useful interpretive frames for women's personal narratives. *Context, narrative form, narrator-interpreter relations,* and *truths* provide the framework for our ideas and for the book.

Our new focus on interpretation led us to direct our attention to *context.* Certainly we agreed that it was critical to understand the political and socioeconomic relations that shaped a life. Nevertheless, we approached contextualization with a new caution. We had learned, for example, that while black, Third World, or lesbian women might be defined as "marginal" from the perspective of a society's dominant norms and established power relations, the women so defined did not necessarily experience themselves as marginal. In other cases, a sense of deviation from the norm could be empowering. We concluded that context was an important interpretive framework for analysis, but agreed that its dimensions had to be considered from the standpoint of the subject of the personal narrative, as well as from the standpoint of the interpreter's analysis of a particular cultural or social system. Shula Marks's essay, "The Context of Personal Narrative: Reflections on *"Not Either an Experimental Doll"—The Separate Worlds of Three South African Women,"* provides a good illustration. Even as she assumes the race, class, and gender systems of South African society as the social context shaping Lily Moya's biography, it is nevertheless Lily's understanding of and efforts to manipulate those systems which are critical to Marks's interpretation.

Having settled on *context* as a term which accurately reflected our sense that women's lives, to be understood, had to be thoughtfully situated in time and space, we struggled with the need to comprehend and illuminate the forms which guided the logic by which women constructed their personal narratives. *Narrative forms,* therefore, was an interpretive framework which allowed us explicitly to understand how women themselves interpreted their own life experiences. We knew that there were examples of women's imitating male autobiographical models. But we also noted, from our own work and from the papers at hand, that many women, far from being so restricted, seem to have relied on a variety of models, and even texts, in reflecting on and narrating their own lives. In some cases, the models women drew on contradicted the normative messages and opportunities understood to be available to them. Nellie McKay, in her essay, "Nineteenth-Century Black Women's Spiritual Autobiographies: Religious Faith and Self-Empowerment," suggests that in nineteenth-century black women's reports of Christian faith, spiritual gifts, and accounts of preaching, the narrators achieved a sense of autonomy that was otherwise impossible. While we knew that understanding context alone could not adequately account for how a life was interpreted, we also agreed that we needed to deepen our appreciation for narrative form in order to understand how women shape the stories of their lives. Deeply embedded notions and expectations about the "normal" course of a life, as well as unconscious rules about what constitutes a good story, shape a personal narrative as much as the "brute facts" of existence do.

We created the section on *narrator-interpreter relations* to address the "Arthur Munby problem": the power relationships surrounding the production of personal narratives. At stake were the issues of the production, control, and use of women's narratives. Our consideration of such issues introduced ethical as well as factual questions with respect to all varieties of women's personal narratives. Particular narratives, however, especially those life stories prompted by and told to a specific person, magnified the fundamental issues that had to be addressed. Narrators of life histories, we knew, inevitably respond to the recorder, even when the latter's questions are intentionally vague and noncoercive. Several conference participants, including Marjorie Shostak, Daphne Patai, and Marjorie Mbilinyi, had emphasized the importance of acknowledging and addressing the realities and conditions of inequality affecting and necessarily framing much contemporary life-history work. The most obvious of these include literacy/ illiteracy, poverty/economic security, Third World/First World, lived experience/experience as the subject of research. When an interpreter emphasizes only the interests and purposes she shares with a narrator of a life history, she obscures complex ethical, practical, and political issues. Marjorie Mbilinyi confronts this problem in her essay, "'I'd Have Been a Man': Politics and the Labor Process in the Production of Personal Narrative." She establishes useful new terms for the participants and the process, details important elements in the various stages of work, and insists that the products and outcomes of life-history research must be multiple to ensure that the interests of the narrator and her community are advanced.

Each of these interpretive frameworks—context, narrative form, narrator-interpreter relations—provided a different lens through which to view a life story. Each lens refracted the life from a different angle of vision. As we viewed the complexity of images arising from these multiple perspectives, we questioned what it was we were seeing. The answer came to us in that striking way in which the obvious reasserts itself into conscious thought, and with the answer came our final section title: "Truths." We had all been drawn to women's personal narratives in our research, and to working together on questions of interpretation and analysis, because we knew that fundamental truths were embedded and reflected in women's experiences as revealed in their life stories. We were not talking about *a* truth or *the* truth. We had developed a healthy disdain for reductionist approaches that would have us determine the "truth" of a woman's words solely in terms of their exact factual accuracy, the representativeness of her social circumstances, or the reliability of her memory when it was tested against "objective" sources. We were talking about *truths,* a decidedly plural concept meant to encompass the multiplicity of ways in which a woman's life story reveals and reflects important features of her conscious experience and social landscape, creating from both her essential reality. As feminists we wanted to hear these truths and to understand them. We wanted them to inform our own realities, and to learn what we could from the experiences of other women. These truths were necessary to our work, and to our lives.

At times, these four categories, so vital to our comprehension of the nature of what we were attempting and of the links between the essays we have chosen to publish, seemed like a great madras cloth. Like our initial themes, these too bleed into one another in significant ways. Nevertheless, they reflect our conclusions about what enlightens us in the interpretation of women's personal narratives, even while we remain conscious of the fact that any analytical categories always exist in relationship, if not in tension, with one another. Each essay that follows centers on women's personal narratives seen from each writer's own angle of vision. Taken collectively, they suggest different ways of seeing, thinking, being.

Notes

1. Elizabeth Minnich, "A Devastating Conceptual Error: How Can We Not Be Feminist Scholars?" *Change* (April 1982): 7–9; Gerda Lerner, *The Creation of Patriarchy* (New York: Oxford University Press, 1986), p. 13.
2. Few works have addressed the masculine as constructed. One example is Russell Baker's *Growing Up* (New York: New American Library, 1983), which deals with the role of gender in the construction of Baker's life story.
3. For a helpful review of some of the major areas of discussion in the feminist

psychoanalytic literature, see Jacqueline Rose, "Femininity and Its Discontents," *Feminist Review* 14 (1983): 5–21.

4. Barbara Taylor, *Eve and the New Jerusalem: Socialism and Feminism in the Nineteenth Century* (New York: Pantheon, 1983).

5. For a critical reflection upon the concept of hegemony as developed by Antonio Gramsci and used in recent scholarship, see T. J. Jackson Lears, "The Concept of Cultural Hegemony: Problems and Possibilities," *American Historical Review* 90 (1985): 567–93.

6. Ida Pruitt, *Daughter of Han: The Autobiography of a Chinese Working Woman* (Stanford: Stanford University Press, 1967).

7. Catherine Marshall, *To Live Again* (New York: McGraw-Hill, 1957), pp. 94, 96.

8. For specific examples of the research and writing being done in the area of women's personal narratives, see the list of contributors at the end of this book.

PART TWO

Context

"CONDITIONS NOT OF HER OWN MAKING"

Personal Narratives Group

Feminist thinking has expanded its initial theoretical stance that emphasized the commonality of all women by reason of gender to incorporate a
greater recognition and appreciation of differences among women. If
women share a common need to negotiate their way through varieties of
patriarchy, the particular conditions that prevail in any society—the contexts that both constrain and give meaning to women's lives—vary enor-
mously. Neglecting the context from which a life is narrated invites the risk
of misunderstanding and misinterpretation. Acknowledging the centrality
and complexity of context reveals the range of experiences and expectations within which women live, and provides a vital perspective from which
to interpret women's ways of navigating the weave of relationships and
structures which constitute their worlds.

The word *context* literally means to weave together, to twine, to connect.
This interrelatedness creates the webs of meaning within which humans
act. The individual is joined to the world through social groups, structural
relations, and identities. However, these are not inflexible categories to
which individuals can be reduced. The more we considered context, the
more we realized that while the general constructs of race, class, and
gender are essential, they are not rigidly determinant. Context is not a
script. Rather, it is a dynamic process through which the individual simultaneously shapes and is shaped by her environment. Similarly, an analysis of
context, which emphasizes these dynamic processes, is an interpretive strategy which is both diachronic and synchronic.

Obviously, the richest contextualization would seek to understand all the
relevant parameters of a life. But the very act of interpretation requires us
to choose among the multiple identities and associations shaping a life.
Furthermore, addressing context involves understanding the meaning of a
life in its narrator's frame of reference, and making sense of that life from
the different and necessarily comparative frame of reference of the interpreter. The essays in this section demonstrate both uses of contextualization in interpreting women's personal narratives.

All of the essays in this book are embedded in specific contexts. However,
four essays have been included in this section because each makes a specific
contribution to our understanding of context. Julia Swindells points out the

danger of ignoring context in her essay, "Liberating the Subject? Autobiography and 'Women's History': A Reading of *The Diaries of Hannah
Cullwick*." She focuses on the relationship between Hannah Cullwick and
Arthur Munby as one intricate example of a life which we cannot liberate
from its own context. In Karen Sacks's essay, "What's a Life Story Got to Do
with It?" context, as it emerges in her work on women activists who participated in a union drive at Duke Medical Center in the 1970s, is both central
to her analysis of the "centerwomen" whose life histories she collects, and
critical to her own self-positioning as a scholar/activist. Faye Ginsburg's
essay, "Dissonance and Harmony: The Symbolic Function of Abortion in
Activists' Life Stories," is an analysis of abortion activists in a midwestern
community. Although initially both pro-choice and pro-life activists appeared to share very similar contexts, as Ginsburg elicited life stories from
these women, she found an important set of differences revolving around
generation, and she argues that activism is linked to the intersection of
specific life transitions and a particular cultural and historical context.
Shula Marks, in "The Context of Personal Narrative: Reflections on *"Not
Either an Experimental Doll"—The Separate Worlds of Three South African
Women,"* interprets the dynamics behind the intersecting destinies of three
South African women's lives and shows the necessity of a search into the
sociocultural contexts from which each woman came into the relationship.
Taken together, these essays suggest that context can be viewed in several
ways.

First, the interpersonal context revealed in women's personal narratives
suggests how women's lives are shaped through and evolve within relationships with others. Feminists have long noted the special reliance of
women upon the resources of networks of family and kin, and the important role women play in nurturing and maintaining such networks. Indeed,
this reliance may well be a function of women's relative powerlessness, their
lack of access to more formal and institutional routes to influence, and as
such a survival strategy shared with other relatively powerless groups.
While it must be acknowledged—and all of the authors are careful in this
regard—that the relationships which contextualize the lives of the women
in question are forged, negotiated, and experienced within the framework
of larger social-structural forces and factors, the significance of such relationships is seldom revealed in the analysis of social structure per se, nor
can they be explained through a focus at that level. It is in looking directly
at women's lives that relationships come to assume contextual importance
and interpretive power.

In some instances, the need to understand a relationship as the context
for interpreting a woman's life and life story is readily apparent. As Julia
Swindells points out, Hannah Cullwick's relationship with Arthur Munby is
absolutely central to Cullwick's life, to why she writes about herself, and to
what and when she reports to Munby through her diary. Cullwick can no
more be "liberated" from the unequal class/gender realities of this rela-

tionship than she can be from the limitations placed on her as a maidservant in Victorian England. But it is equally necessary to recognize that this relationship also affected the ways in which Cullwick experienced her life within the generalized status and category of "Victorian maidservant."

Understanding a relationship between unequals as a context for interpreting women's personal narratives is also central to Shula Marks's reconstruction of the intersecting biographies of three South African women in the mid-twentieth century—Lily Moya, a young African schoolgirl; Mabel Palmer, an elderly white social reformer; and Violet Makhanya, the first African female in the country to receive overseas training as a social worker. As Marks interprets the dynamics behind the intersecting destinies of Lily, Mabel, and Violet, it becomes clear that each individual held a set of meanings and expectations shaped by her socioeconomic context. These influenced the attitudes and experiences that each brought to the relationship, and its ultimate breakdown, like Lily's retreat into madness, can be seen as prefigured in, though not necessarily determined by, the particular social distortions of South African society.

Interpersonal relations also emerge as context in the lives of pro- and anti-abortion activists studied by Faye Ginsburg, most notably in women's recollections of family and of childhood friendships (particularly memories of either fitting in or not fitting in), and in their sense of themselves as mothers and the importance they attach to the mother-child relationship. In Fargo, North Dakota, the site of Ginsburg's research, the personal narratives of pro- and anti-abortion activists reveal a struggle to come to terms with an "other"—indeed an enemy—who is not rhetorical but known, yet against whom one's own identity is in an important sense being formed. The context of interpersonal relations, then, is shown to be an extremely complex one in Ginsburg's work, as in that of Swindells and Marks.

The intersection of an individual life course and a specific historical moment is another recurring aspect of context in these essays. It is precisely this intersection that provides insight into the ways that particular lives take the shape they do and how each woman makes sense of her world.

In Ginsburg's study of abortion activists, the context for both pro-choice and pro-life activists is, in a superficial sense, the same: they are educated, white, middle-class women living in the same midwestern community. Moreover, argues Ginsburg, the ideological context in which the two conflicting arguments are constructed is shared by both groups at many points. As Ginsburg elicited the life stories of these activists, however, she discovered that the choices that individual women made regarding abortion depended upon where they were in their own life course at the moment in time when the women's movement and the struggle over reproductive rights emerged. The puzzle of the stances vis-à-vis abortion then becomes, in Ginsburg's interpretation, at least in part a question of the intersection of particular women's individual lives with broader political and ideological context.

For Shula Marks, the reconstruction of the intersecting biographies of three South African women in the early twentieth century entails both an appreciation of the multiplicity of contexts in which individual women live and an awareness of the point in each life course at which they meet. Lily, Mabel, and Violet each held a set of meanings and expectations shaped by her particular place in the colonial setting and its class, racial, and gender systems. Each, moreover, had different needs related to age differences—the particular moment in each life course when their interactions occurred. Lily's place in the relationship is contextualized both by her vulnerability as a young girl coping with sexual maturation and by her blackness. Her madness is simultaneously personal response and a product of a complex social context.

As we considered the ways that context functioned in our interpretation of women's personal narratives, we also became aware of the way that one context frequently emerged from or interacted with another. Karen Sacks's essay illustrates the relationship between the interpersonal context and the intersection of an individual life course within a particular historical moment. The hospital workers she interviewed developed a sense of themselves as responsible adults within their family networks. At work, they also established networks of women who shared a sense of themselves as adults deserving respect. When they were confronted with workplace expectations which undermined this sense of adulthood and autonomy, these networks spearheaded union mobilization.

Women's personal narratives also reveal the frameworks of meaning through which individuals locate themselves in the world and make sense of their lives. For Ginsburg, the issue of abortion itself provided a contextual framework within which both pro-choice and pro-life activists found direction and focus for their lives at a particular moment. The issue became a catalyst in the lives of these women. "The signification attached to abortion provides each side with different but interrelated paradigms for reconstituting and claiming a possible vision of being female that meshes with their historical and biographical experiences." Although their activism emerged in two opposing strategies, it was the shared immersion in the symbolic issue of abortion which provided the context within which these personal narratives make sense.

In Marks's work, Lily, as an African woman, daily confronted not only the concrete limitations of her life but also the less tangible tensions of two cultural systems, two frameworks of meaning, in conflict. Lily's life story raises questions about psychosocial development, about the cultural meaning of sickness, and about how we deal with the concept of "victim" in our interpretation of women's personal narratives.

Finally, the expectations and understandings that the interpreter herself brings to the life story are themselves an essential element in the contextualization of personal narratives. Julia Swindells's essay provides a notable example of why it is important to recognize this explicitly. In questioning Liz Stanley's treatment of Hannah Cullwick's diaries, Swindells notes her eagerness to "liberate" the voices of lower-class working women in Victorian England. Stanley derives a meaning from Cullwick's diaries that in fact reflects the influence of a contemporary feminist agenda and perspective. Thus, Swindells cautions feminist scholars to be aware of both the implications and limitations of one's own intellectual interest when working with women's personal narratives.

Karen Sacks candidly describes the obstacles her own intellectual context created in her attempt to uncover that element in family life that "facilitated women's militance and participation in protest groups." She relates that her own intellectual grounding produced feminist, Freudian, and Marxist explanations for the phenomenon she was investigating. And yet she soon discovered that even though these were the only available conceptualizations of family questions, they prevented her from asking questions that linked family life to social rebellion in a positive way. In her frustration, Sacks finally realized that she would be able to make sense out of this connection only when she put aside her own framework and allowed the connections to emerge from the context in which the women saw their own lives.

These essays illustrate the ways in which context plays an essential role in grounding and validating the interpretation of women's personal narratives. They show the importance of the interpersonal relationships within which the life story emerges; they illuminate the significance of the intersection of individual life and historical moment; they address the importance of the frameworks of meaning through which women orient themselves in the world; and they allow us to explore the ways in which the interpreter's own context shapes both the formation and the interpretation of a personal narrative.

LIBERATING THE SUBJECT? AUTOBIOGRAPHY AND "WOMEN'S HISTORY"
A Reading of *The Diaries of Hannah Cullwick*

Julia Swindells

I see our study of the life stories of women as part of a project to liberate ourselves as women subjects. I show, however, that this cannot be done simply by liberating our sisters from history—either by finding "authentic" voices where these cannot exist, or by deciding, in our eagerness to liberate their texts from silence, that these sisters led liberated lives.

My argument revolves around nineteenth-century autobiography in general and the diaries of Hannah Cullwick, Victorian maidservant, in particular. Hannah Cullwick's diaries are a stark example of autobiographical writing which can tell us much about the class and gender restrictions of writing in the nineteenth century. But in men's histories, autobiography has been taken to be a text of low status, hardly deemed appropriate to the history of "real historians" and unable to tell us very much at all. "Women's history," as well as publishing and republishing silenced texts, must begin to produce a critique of the history which has perpetuated that silence and ignored "personal" histories as inadequate evidence or the product of those who are "not quite" historians. In order to do this, we must look at and challenge what the "real historians" are doing and what they are failing to do with autobiography: and what they are failing to do with his story, and more particularly, with hers.

Our contemporary feminism is in the process of representing and building subjectivities which give meaning to women's identities. In doing so, we are arguing with some historical constructions of subjectivity and identifying with others. We have discovered that, as for our comrades on the Left, liberal humanism may be too partial in its liberality (and from our perspective, in its gendering as well as its classing): but we have also discovered that we may have to reject certain figures who have given the illusion of being fathers. Recent attempts to marry Marx and Freud for the sake of feminism (or, at least, socialist feminism) may be misleading in that sense. It is tempting to join in this grooming for a marriage, but the temptation arises from a powerful illusion—that Freud and Marx can be added together for a feminist honeymoon, that one can make good the other's lack, that all that prevents a unity is Marx's sex and Freud's lack of class. The sense in which this is pure romance, though, is that two staunch patriarchs cannot be added together to provide the critique of patriarchy. They may be helpful to us in critiques of aspects of the system, but they cannot provide us with a unified theory, or, in that sense, a set of subjectivities, because they are in different ways implicated in that system: Marx in his sex, Freud in his lack of class.

But even this inference—that Marx and Freud are a couple in patriarchy—is misleading: for any materialist analysis will lean toward Marxian processes and away from Freud.[1] It is partly these processes that I have in mind when I look at Hannah Cullwick as a subject in her text. I look at her as a woman, but I try to avoid conflating sexuality with textuality. (The sexual/textual punning which frequently occurs in recent deconstructive criticism sometimes gives the illusion that our understanding of "the sexual" can be extracted from the internal mechanisms of the text quite apart from any understanding of history. For a wonderfully clear exposition of this problem, see a recent paper of Lisa Jardine's, "Reading Shakespeare Historically: *Hamlet* and Unlawful Marriage," for the MLA conference, 1987.) I look at her as working-class, but in such a way that that category does not constitute an entire explanation of the material conditions in which her text is produced.

AUTOBIOGRAPHY AND MEN'S HISTORY (AND "WOMEN'S HISTORY")

As a genre, autobiography occupies an interesting position in relation to the expression or articulation of the subject. In the loci of subject disciplines, it is not quite fantasy or Art (in English); neither is it quite evidence (in History). It is this "not quite" status which can frequently be seen in autobiographers' self-justifications drawn from conventions of naturalism in English and History: this is "the true story," this is the tale of "a real life."[2]

In History, it is the "I" of autobiography which has recently attracted an entire debate about "Who speaks for history?", about the subjects and objects of History: a debate which tends to be framed in some problematic language about the relationship between the personal and the social. A volume in the History Workshop series sketches the map of that debate.[3] In one of its contributions, "Beyond Autobiography," Jerry White argues that there are specific and important limitations to the autobiographical mode. Autobiography, he writes, lacks objectivity, is too parochial, and, most seriously, lacks a critical consciousness of capitalism. The autobiographical mode, in his language, "distorts reality." Stephen Yeo, in "The Politics of

Community Publications," takes up the position of antagonist in that exchange. He defends the autobiographical mode as that which "history in general" needs. And then in a syntactic move which is in danger of conflating "autobiographical mode" with "working-class autobiography," he argues that "worker writing and community publishing has a lot to teach historians." We, the historians, can learn from the workers.

At one position, then, is White, finding the autobiographers lacking. He, the subject, the historian, finds the autobiographers "not quite" historians. They are not objective enough, and they are also parochial. If they are not historians, subjects—we assume from White—they must therefore be objects for the historian's use, evidence for the historian's text. We, the historians, can use autobiography if we are aware of its limitations. It can be *read* for History. It just should not be *written* as History. Within this scenario of written and read, historian and evidence, subject and object, the human subject and author of the autobiography is thus conjured away and replaced by the subject historian, the subject History: and this trick—the historian's text displacing the autobiographer's—is performed in the name of "the personal and the social." The autobiographer, in being "personal," is found inadequate in the teeth of the bigger and better "social." White concludes by asking for a "new synthesis" in which an intervention occurs: people need consciousness raising (I am beginning to feel nostalgia for that concept myself) to understand the nature of their own oppressions. That's what autobiographers need before they can begin to be historians. Autobiographers—the people—return, in this way, to be told by us (the real historians) that they are subjects in need of consciousness raising, or rather will be subjects after consciousness raising; consciousness raising, that is, by whom else, whom other than us, the real historians?

Yeo disclaims this reading. He is at pains to allow autobiographers status as subjects, authors of history: they can be human beings who are also historians. But the matter of their being human beings is conflated with assumptions about class. Only working-class autobiographers—the real people from whom we can "learn" (in a previous draft of this script, I mistyped *learn* as *earn*)—are allowed to speak for the social via or in the personal. The argument is attractive in looking for authentic voices of a politicized kind, but it is tautological. Working-class autobiographers can speak as subjects because they speak socialist consciousness. They speak socialist consciousness because they are working-class. It still does not further the case about autobiography. Socialist consciousness and a particular class position are, in this argument, placed as if they are in a direct line, conflated, unmediated. This time, the genre or mode of autobiography, the medium, is conjured away, spurious. And there remains the problem of the real historian. For where does Stephen Yeo, historian, stand, except outside of this process, to the side of this line, learning from the workers about socialist consciousness? Unwittingly, he writes himself in as the real subject, historian, speaking the real subject, History: he, the author, creating the real text, albeit learning the language of that text from others, auto-biographers, the little, "not quite" historians.

More recently, there have been sophistications and disclaimers of these positions. David Vincent, in his study of working-class autobiography, sug-gests that autobiographies are "units of literature."[4] The Birmingham Pop-ular Memory Group also emphasizes autobiography as a mode or form with properties of genre which have to be dealt with: neither an expression of pure consciousness nor vacant of historical consciousness until the latter has been raised. Yet again, though, "the personal and the social" names the ritualistic diminishing of the autobiographers as subjects:

> Oral history and popular autobiography are forms which systematically individualize; yet an historically-informed political knowledge requires a much broader sense of social context.[5]

The delusion in both History and English seems to derive from the pronounced "I" of autobiography.[6] For the historian, it evokes a failure of objectivity, a lack of broad canvas, something personal which fails to incor-porate or be something social. What a feminist reader might see here, though, is rather some problems with *those* subjects—those disciplines of History and English—than with the autobiographer as subject.

For a feminist reader, the male argument about autobiography (versions of which we are seeing here in White, Yeo, Vincent, Johnson) reveals—or masks—a more important argument about texts in History and texts as History. Autobiography, because of its emphatic "I," which is a trans-parency, a vulnerability, becomes the historian's scapegoat for problems with "material" and with other historians. Instead of History being the issue—the relationship between the personal and the social being a prob-lem of all texts, all material, of History—autobiography becomes the issue, leaving our real historian free to patronize autobiographers, and perhaps more seriously, to maintain an unquestioned hierarchy of texts, of evi-dence, operating in the names of the lowly personal and the superior social.

The problem is not necessarily that this hierarchy exists but that it appears as given, naturalized, inevitable, and that, in appearing so, it perpetuates an unexamined place of authority and privilege for the histo-rian who thinks himself real, as well as a good deal of confusion about the subjects and objects of history. My account is not about pursuing, with religious zeal, and for its own sake, the redemption of autobiography—saving the genre. It is rather that, in perceiving the position in which autobiography is placed—its status as text—there is no way of avoiding seeing how other texts are placed and how that places subjects. The low or unplaced status of autobiography in History, which for so long has reflected on the autobiographer, should now begin to reflect rather on the "real historian" and the ways in which liberal humanism and even male socialism arrange their objects and subjects. To see where autobiography is placed is to begin to see, indeed, who speaks for History.

"WOMEN'S HISTORY"

It might be thought that "women's history" has a particular investment in autobiography. Feminist historians and activists frequently talk in terms of recovering woman's voice, women's voices. The search for the auto-biographical "I" of woman in the past is one obvious direction for this interest in the voice to take. The argument has its inflection from English studies. Juliet Mitchell argues recently that the history of the novel is importantly premised in seventeenth-century autobiographies written by women, and that these autobiographies established what she describes as "the subject in process."[7]

It is a difficulty, though, for feminist politics that "women's history" and autobiography can reference each other so easily in this way. Unlike some other historians, feminists know that History is partial, is a partial subject, has a partial subject. These arguments—about how History has systematically silenced, absented, missed, failed to observe, failed to credit the female voice and the female existence—are familiar to feminists. As is so often the case, though, their considerable force has been redirected. They have not been seen, on the whole, as a critique of History but have been read as an interesting feature of feminism, a definition of a new category called "women's history." (And that which defines itself as "social history" is not necessarily exempt from this self-protecting strategy of seeing "women's history" as a solipsism outside of its immediate interests.)

Sometimes, the advances that feminism has made in demystifying relations between that named the personal and that named the social, far from being thought a help by our real historians in sorting out their own difficulties with those terms, have been misdirected into further diminution of both autobiography and "women's history." The low-status scenario reads: the solipsistic feminist historian writing about autobiography (low-status text) in the pursuit of woman's voice (solipsistic activity), claiming the personal (inferior and limited) as the social (superior and broad), which really belongs—don't we all know?—to the real historian.[8]

The point is to produce a reading of autobiography which cannot easily either be relegated to the solipsism "women's history" or be thought a mere holy hearing of voices.

The point is . . .

The point is to produce a reading of autobiography (and particular autobiographies) which uncovers in the vulnerable "I" which our real historians assume is the signal of a low-status text, a particularly explicit and revealing set of textual relations which is also a set of power relations called capitalist patriarchy (. . . and this will also be a set of power relations called History, and the challenge to it will be constituting a material feminism).

The point is to uncover what the relativities of objects and subjects mean in capitalist patriarchy and how these relativities produce and are produced in texts: and this includes uncovering what the male subject does with the female object, whether a female subject can survive, whether, where there are females, a male object is a contradiction in terms, whether, where there are males, a female subject is a contradiction in terms. And the point of that is to produce a gender and class critique which may be a feminist herstory, but, more particularly, will be a set of critiques of particular histories, and of History.

CULLWICK AND MUNBY—WHOSE VOICE? WHOSE STORY?

Hannah Cullwick (1833–1909) worked all her life as a maid-servant, scullion and pot-girl. In 1854 she met Arthur Munby, "a man of two worlds," upper-class author and poet, with a life-long obsession for lower-class women.

The blurb on the back of the recently published Virago paperback *The Diaries of Hannah Cullwick, Victorian Maidservant* begins with these two sentences.[9] A variety of narrative contents suggest themselves. This is to be a romance—boy meets girl. It is an incipient fairytale of a Cinderella and her prince—a common gender and class formation in fantasy. But there are also suggestions of the slightly dubious—that typically Victorian dualism "man of two worlds," Jekyll and Hyde, upper intent on lower.

This, though, is no simple fantasy where the resolving enactment dissolves class differences in a meeting of genders as the clock strikes twelve. Nor is it, I think, a special comment on Victorian low life or sexual perversion, even though a number of reviewers focus on the book's passages of soft porn or kinkiness. This is, rather, the story of a gender and class fantasy enacted and sustained primarily, one might say, in print, and also in life, for a period of over fifty years.

Feminist researchers and historians of gender have already begun to look at the texts of Hannah Cullwick and Arthur Munby for their symbolic properties in revealing or representing the gender and class formations of Victorian society.[10] I take that work to be very useful to this account. What I want to avoid, too, is a simple historical or literary naturalism which sees the central figures—Cullwick and Munby—of this "real-life" drama miming or reflecting the given of Victorian social relations and takes representation to be mimetic. I want, rather, to look at how representations are arranged in texts, at how the autobiographical mode—in the diaries and auto-biographical fragments—places the subjects and objects of its text (produced in conditions of nineteenth-century capitalist patriarchy), and to see whose voices, whose story, whose history emerges.

> *Sunday 31 May* Clean'd 3 pairs o' boots & lit the fires. Did my hair & wash'd in the scullery. Laid the cloth & took the breakfast up. Clean'd away & wash'd up after. Clean'd the knives & made the kitchen fire up. Put the meat to roast. When dinner was over & I'd put the supper ready & clean'd the hearth & all that I got ready & went to Massa. Reach'd him earlyish & we had a nice evening. We petted a bit & then I put my jacket on, & Massa thought I was jolly & fat & he told me to see if I could lift *him* & I laugh'd & said, "Of course I can." I lifted him easy & carried him, & then he lifted me & said I was *heavy*—I am 11 stone & Massa's 13 lbs heavier than me. I got his dinner & clean'd away after & wash'd up. Made cigarettes & then petted & I told Massa things what had happened at Brighton & so he told me not to forget to put them things down what I'd bin telling him. So what I can remember I will, as there's room in this sheet & it's end o' the month.

> Massa met me at the top of Chancery Lane today—walk'd down on the other side & sign'd to me to go in at the other gate. But the gentleman wouldn't let me through 'cause I wouldn't say who I was going to see, so I told him he could leave it alone, 'cause he made me cross, speaking like that. I am thirty years old this month—must be quite a woman now, though I don't feel any different than I ever did except in feeling lower in heart I think, for I've bin a servant now 20 years or more. Always the lowest kind, but I think different about it now a good deal than I did ten years ago 'fore I knew Massa. He has taught me, though it's been difficult to learn thoroughly, the beauty in being nothing but a common drudge & to bear being despised by others what don't have to work the same way. I have hardly ever met wi' a *servant* yet who wasn't ashamed o' dirty work & who wouldn't be glad to get out of it for some thing they think is *better,* but *I* wouldn't get out of it if I could, nor change from being Massa's slave for anything else I know of. I've bin a slave now 9 years & worn the chains & padlocks 6 years—I don't hide 'em now from Mary for she saw 'em every night at Brighton this time.[11]

These two extracts are from a day in the 1863 diary of Hannah Cullwick, one of seventeen diaries written by her for Arthur Munby. Much of the detail which opens the day is like that of many other days of the diary. Despite this being a Sunday, a day of rest, the catalogue of chores denotes a day undistinguished, except perhaps in the character of its "time-off," for a working woman. We learn, though, that the writing (out) of this particular day of the diary does distinguish it, in that Arthur Munby has made a particular point of getting a full account out of Hannah Cullwick: "he told me not to forget to put them things down what I'd bin telling him."

In her introduction to the Virago edition of the diaries, Liz Stanley describes them in the following terms: They "bring home to us with a quite unique freshness and immediacy what it meant to live and work as a lower-class woman 'in service' in early and middle Victorian England." This may be right—that the diaries do produce those meanings, of living and working, of the experience of the lower-class woman. I am not sure, though, that these meanings are produced in the realm of the "freshness" and "immediacy" of which Liz Stanley speaks (even if we could accept those terms as meaningful judgments of texts, and then agree that they are appropriate judgments to make about the diaries); but are rather to do with the ways in which the text is an arrangement of the class and gender relations of experience. In other words, it is not the obviousness of the list of chores (for example) which speaks to the life and work of the lower-class woman in Victorian England, but the ideology produced in implied and explicit textual relations.

Hannah Cullwick, who is already writing the diaries for Arthur Munby, is additionally writing in detail this day—Sunday, May 31, 1863—because he has requested her "to put them things down." He has asked her "not to forget," and she tells us that she is trying to "remember." Those moments in the text are among a number which begin to reveal, fairly explicitly, the position of Arthur Munby in relation to the diaries: their reader, and their editor/author. It is for him, privileged reader, that the events in Brighton are being recalled, and it is in terms of her relationship to him (asking her to remember the events as she had told them to him—"he told me not to forget") that memory is being reconstructed, with Munby in position of control.

Hannah Cullwick is thus requested to experience *for* Arthur Munby: to tell him (and to have something to tell), and to tell him again in print, remembering and recording according to his controls (with the slight implication that it will be naughty to "forget").[12]

If these are some of the arrangements of this "day" of the text—female autobiographer experiencing for male, rendering up that experience to male reconstruction (telling him), telling him again, telling us that she is telling him again (has "told" him)—then where does that put the "freshness" and "immediacy" of the experience of the lower-class woman? What is Liz Stanley seeing, and what can we see of "what it meant to live and work as a lower-class woman 'in service' in early and middle Victorian England"?

Return to that same day of the diary. . . .

On Sunday, May 31, 1863—a rest day—Hannah Cullwick does an extensive round of household chores, including cooking the dinner. She does these chores in the house where she is "in service," as her paid work. She then repeats a version of them—"I got his dinner"—in her "time-off," in the house of the man who is not her employer but is named her master (Massa). On this same Sunday, having worked for her master and her Massa, she does further work in recording (chiefly her work) for Arthur Munby, recording her work done for the master, for her Massa. Paid work is reconstructed as pleasure (to service Massa), and then recorded (more work) as a means of servicing his pleasure, which consists of witnessing and creating her "pleasure" in paid work. On this particular day—a rest day—

the maidservant records, explicitly, and for Arthur Munby's pleasure, what the "slave" has learned from her Massa about work: "He taught me, though it's been difficult to learn thoroughly, the beauty in being nothing but a common drudge." She admits to being "lower in heart" these days, after being the "lowest kind" of servant for so long, and not knowing any other servants who like being low, but she "wouldn't get out of it," "nor change." The experience of life and work for the lower-class woman in Victorian England in this becomes a very material thing (drudgery indeed), expressed in a relativity of objects and subjects: worker to employer, pupil to teacher, drudge to master, slave to Massa: culminating in text to author as woman to man, aesthetic—the beauty of work—to artist, Hannah Cullwick to Arthur Munby.

If the subject has anything to do with power and the power of defining and prescribing the object, then the subject here is the man and the male fantasy; and the fantasy is primarily of labor as sexual aesthetic—and there's nothing very Freudian about that; indeed, it's very material—the woman's work for the man's pleasure. Hannah Cullwick writes: "I am thirty years old this month—must be quite a woman now." She "don't feel any different"—except a bit more depressed than she used to feel—but she must be "quite a woman." This is what Massa wants—"quite a woman." And as well as the woman, he wants the worker whom he can value as "not a woman," celebrating her supposedly masculine traits, her heavy weight, her muscles. The man gets it both ways. He loves her gender for its subjugation and her class for its labor. The combination is an unbeatable sexual aesthetic—"a woman" and "not a woman" for his pleasure. She climbs his chimneys and licks his feet clean, prepared to call it pleasure for the sake of his definition, for the sake of being the object of his pleasure, chief subject in his class and gender fantasy, chief subject of the literary gentleman's narrative.

LIBERATING WOMAN'S VOICE?

But this reading must be very prejudiced. How otherwise can I find Hannah Cullwick so cheated of autonomy, when others—and feminists—find her voice and even her liberation in the diaries? For a Victorian working woman to have written seventeen diaries, to have acquired literacy, to have acquired a "patron" who foresaw that she would have a twentieth-century readership: these factors are of interest to historians and literateurs looking for new evidence, new voices from the past. Isn't the retrieval of this kind of text, indeed, the very restoration of the voice, the very act of liberation—a working woman's voice liberated from the silences of History?

There is some muddle, though, in what we begin to require of this "liberation." In seeking to liberate ourselves—as I mention at the beginning

Hannah Cullwick photographed by Arthur Munby as a maidservant and as a lady.

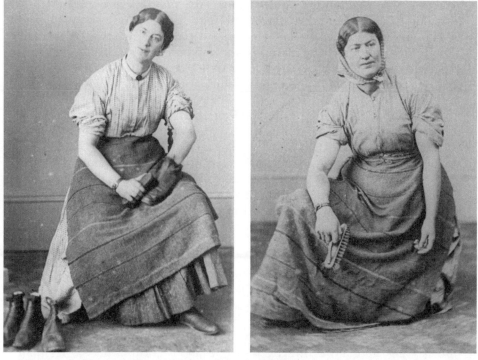

Hannah Cullwick photographed as a "drudge" by Arthur Munby. The photographs were taken in the same setting several years apart.

of this piece—perhaps, out of good intentions, we attempt to liberate our sisters. I do not believe, though, that this can be done in history. There is no "authentic" voice of woman in history, no unity of that sort, transcending history. Neither should we muddle up the business of enabling voices to be heard with finding our sisters in history suddenly "liberated" in their lives as well as in the sounds of their texts. Rather, we should be asking questions about specific histories, specific texts. Whose story do the diaries of Hannah Cullwick tell? Whose subject is being inscribed? And if we listen carefully to the voices, and look at the relative places of the subjects and objects in this business, we begin to hear and see, surely, the liberation, not of Hannah Cullwick but of Arthur J. Munby, finding a voice in text, already a relatively free(d) man in life.

Liz Stanley is one of those who, with the best of intentions toward Hannah Cullwick, wants to liberate her in life in order to present her text as liberated. "The paradox that exists here is that the drudgery that was everyday life for the maid-of-all-work also in a sense liberated her." The source of liberation is seen in the work, the class position of Hannah Cullwick. By virtue of her position as a drudge, argues Liz Stanley, Hannah Cullwick was able to be "not a woman" in a process which can be seen as a type of liberation from Victorian expectations of and constructions of femininity. This, the argument continues, gave her a "freedom" not available to her contemporary women among the middle classes. Even while pursuing this argument, Liz Stanley also sees that the drudgery performed by Hannah Cullwick and other Victorian working women was "crushing." This is described as "the paradox of freedom within drudgery." This supposed paradox seems to me to exist only out of contemporary woman's desire to free "Hannah": and it is a curious freedom which liberates from a preferable set of oppressions into a worse set. (Would we, by the same token, say that the black person in South Africa, or, for that matter, in contemporary Britain, manifests the paradox of freedom in not having to "suffer" the position of the white person?)

The argument, surely, is not that constructions of femininity liberated Victorian working women, but that they were sources of visible oppression of middle-class women—and, if we look closer, of all women. (We have seen, for instance, how it was in Arthur Munby's interest to find Hannah Cullwick "not a woman" on occasions.) It is almost as if those who are seduced by the "paradox" argument are themselves constructing a paradox—that matters of "femininity" are ideological, and matters of drudgery are material—in which ideological oppression can be separated from and found more significant than material oppression. It is right, of course, to show up differences between the classes—but not, surely, in order to create this type of paradox.

When dealing with textuality and with voices, the argument about liberation is translated more directly into one about "ordinariness." Hannah Cullwick's voice is, it seems, authentic, a voice claiming liberation from

History, because it is "the ordinary" speaking for "the ordinary." "Who speaks for history?" goes the question. "The ordinary," comes the answer. If it is not "the unique," "the special," "the famous," "the great," "the professional," it must be "the ordinary." And, again, the suspicion is aroused that who is speaking for history is our "real historian," defining and claiming "the ordinary."

> And out of this has come my realisation the Hannah was not the extraordinary member of her class that Munby, and through him Hudson [Derek Hudson, biographer of Munby], presents her as being.
>
> For both men Hannah is out of the ordinary because she was intelligent, had a great capacity to learn, was distinctive-looking and perceptive.
>
> What I mean is that Hannah's combination of activities and traits was by no means as exceptional or extraordinary as Munby seems to suggest.[13]

Ironically enough, Liz Stanley here goes into battle with Arthur Munby in ways which are likely to find her emptying Hannah Cullwick of distinction, evacuating her subjectivity. He at least found her extraordinary. The man did that for her. She was not merely substitutable—working woman. In the pressure to find the authentic woman's voice—and with other good intentions, such as to liberate the class, working women, by liberating the representative individual—Liz Stanley equates the personal ("Hannah"— first-name terms) with the ordinary.

No doubt, the defense of Hannah Cullwick takes on this aspect partly because of the seeming perverse (perverted)—indeed, extra-ordinary— practices which Hannah Cullwick was prepared to perform for Arthur Munby. It seems no solution, however, to normalize such practices as climbing naked up chimneys by naming them "ordinary." They may well be an extension of the logic of certain Victorian gender and class ideologies, but that very extension into an enactment of the male fantasy surely makes for crucial distinctions, and, indeed, is the raison d'être of the diaries. What is interesting about the diaries is not the "ordinary" life (however fresh and immediate its presentation) of a woman "in service" in early and middle Victorian England, but how fully Hannah Cullwick is prepared to enter into the male fantasy, to internalize it, and to become the subject as the subject of Arthur Munby's narrative.

It is worth noting, too, that it was Arthur Munby who foresaw that someone in the twentieth century would find in the diaries of Hannah Cullwick a voice worth liberating. What he foresaw, though, was that by the 1980s, society's attitudes toward the kinkiness of the diaries would be more "liberal." What he foresaw, then, was that by the 1980s, a particular type of representation of male fantasy via a pseudo-female gaze would be more acceptable—and that a female climbing naked up a chimney would not be a matter for censorship. (These are ironies which may ultimately operate at the expense of the feminist researcher.)

In life, Arthur Munby seems to have got from Hannah Cullwick his pleasure and her work. Reading and writing are his pleasures as a gentleman. He reads and writes Hannah Cullwick. Her work is his threefold pleasure—he enjoys the spectacle of her performing dirty work (this is his "obsession"), he enjoys the servicing work she does for him, and he enjoys her writing of the diaries—her recording (more work) of the spectacle and the performance of work. This threefold process becomes her subjectivity—for his pleasure. As for why Hannah Cullwick ends up loving dirt and drudgery, we cannot be sure. Even with a theory of hegemony or masochism, it is difficult to know why she goes so "far." Even Arthur Munby is ultimately baffled by her apparently complete assimilation of his early teachings.[14]

In these ways, it begins to seem that the diaries leave us knowing little about Hannah Cullwick. It begins to seem, rather, that if we are still talking about liberating subjects, that it is Arthur Munby who is being given a helping hand in this work of restoring the diaries. The most meticulous of social historians cannot avoid offering him further liberation through and in text.

> Despite his, to us, repellent fascinations with certain symbolic themes: the equation of dirt and degradation with female strength and love; the comparison of women to brute beasts, of both to black slaves; and the identification of all these inferior breeds as agents of a threatening but compelling Nature, Munby did recognize, if only dimly, a fundamental contradiction of Victorian society. The sheltered lives that middle-class ladies were ideally supposed to lead depended directly on the labor of working-class girls and women, who through their services created the material conditions necessary to maintain a middle-class life-style for men and women alike.[15]

This is a lot of "despite." It shows, in the context of an excellent article with much revealing study of Hannah Cullwick, some of the difficulty there is in avoiding privileging the man, excusing him, giving him a helping hand, justifying him, whatever his despite. We should not have to be tricked into thinking that we have to follow Hannah Cullwick in loving Arthur Munby. That is her right and her problem. (This raises questions again about the relations between social histories and feminist herstories: about how we can discriminate in favor of women in history without necessarily having to find voices which echo our own, or with whose inflections we agree.) The justification of Arthur Munby made in the text referenced above continues with the apologia that he "wanted to see working women remain independent." That also needs further scrutiny. What do the diaries reveal about the form of that wanting? And what was the price to be for that independence?

Leonore Davidoff is right, though, to conclude that "a detailed study of such a source as the Munby collection brings alive the connection between social structure and personality."[16] I have argued elsewhere that the literary production process, including the commentaries of editors (for the most part, male) and researchers, is crucial (in its gender relations) not only to the ways in which we read texts, but also to the make-up, subjectivities, personalities of authors.[17] Victorian working women have, on more than one occasion, been destined to play in autobiography the Cinderella to the literary prince, the heroine to the editorial hero. These relations are further transparent in *The Diaries of Hannah Cullwick,* where the textual relations are so clearly and revealingly informed by the lived relationship of Hannah Cullwick and Arthur Munby.

The Cullwick diaries (or the Munby diaries?) are strikingly useful in giving examples of some of the problems involved in discovering woman's voice in history: problems acutely realized in a reading of the illusory and elusive autobiographical subject.

Arthur Munby's part in the creation and prescription of that subject was modeled and recreated in the history of the text, the diaries, until recently. Before Virago (etc.) set out to discover the Cullwick voice, the volumes were available for reading only in the Wren Library at Trinity College, Cambridge, where they are kept in discreet boxes, filed, appropriately enough, under "Munby." Needless to say, women readers did not have the equipment to penetrate that sanctuary until recently, and then were obliged to give thanks to the Master (of the college) for any use of the texts. It seems like the old story, then—woman, in pursuit of her own story, having to go by the men, having to please the master.

Notes

1. See Christine Delphy, *Close to Home* (London: Hutchinson, 1984), for a materialist analysis of women's oppression. I cite this to substantiate my own position, which is a leaning toward Marx and away from Freud—a necessity, it seems to me, in any materialist analysis. But I also share with Delphy a resistance to substituting Marx as guru for Marxian analysis. Her argument about this is very powerful as well as witty!

2. I tend to dwell on the case in History rather than English. I capitalize *History* when I am referring to the academic discipline.

In English, it is autobiography or certain autobiographical conventions which draw from critics and commentators the most sexual of textual criticism. The narrative "I" appears to legitimate a thorough probe by said commentator into the authorial deep psyche—into the unconscious privacies of repressed desire. For ways in which the Freudian novel and the male author exploit the "feminine" first person, see Susanne Kappeler, "The White Brothel: The Literary Exoneration of the Pornographic," in *Feminist Review* 16 (Summer 1984).

3. Raphael Samuel, ed., *People's History and Socialist Theory* (London: History Workshop Series, Routledge and Kegan Paul, 1981).

4. David Vincent, *Bread, Knowledge, and Freedom: A Study of Nineteenth-Century Working Class Autobiography* (London: Europa, 1981).

5. Popular Memory Group, "Popular Memory: Theory, Politics, Method," in *Making Histories,* ed. Richard Johnson, Gregor McLennan, Bill Schwarz, and David Sutton, Centre for Contemporary Cultural Studies (London: Hutchinson, 1982), p. 231.

6. With the mention, though, of units of literature and of forms and genres, it might be tempting to glance again at English studies, if it were not for the suspicion that "the personal and the social" is a dimension too much for the literary critic. He (occasionally she) is, rather, busy being a voyeur, getting too busy with the personal, getting personal. Why have recourse to "the social" when you can privatize your author—take your autobiographer to the confessional, or out for the talking cure? For the literary commentator, it is as if the autobiographical "I" reminds too much of the sexed (sexy?) deep psyche.

7. Juliet Mitchell, *Women: The Longest Revolution: Essays in Feminism, Literature and Psychoanalysis* (London: Virago, 1984), p. 288.

8. My book *Victorian Writing and Working Women* raises questions about status in relation to autobiographers and other authors (Cambridge and Minneapolis: Polity Press and University of Minnesota Press, 1985).

9. Liz Stanley, ed., *The Diaries of Hannah Cullwick, Victorian Maidservant* (London: Virago, 1984; New Brunswick, N.J.: Rutgers University Press, 1984).

10. Leonore Davidoff, "Class and Gender in Victorian England: The Diaries of Arthur J. Munby and Hannah Cullwick," in *Feminist Studies* 5 (Spring 1979), reprinted in *Sex and Class in Women's History,* ed. J. L. Newton, M. P. Ryan, and J. R. Walkowitz (London and Boston: Routledge and Kegan Paul, 1983). Also Liz Stanley's introduction to *The Diaries of Hannah Cullwick.*

11. *Diaries,* pp. 124 and 125.

12. For another reading of "naughtiness," see Liz Stanley's introduction, p. 18.

13. Stanley, pp. 10 and 11.

14. When he eventually wanted to marry her, he professed not to understand why she wanted to continue her "dirty work."

15. Davidoff, *Feminist Studies,* p. 130.

16. Ibid., p. 130.

17. Final chapter of my book *Victorian Writing and Working Women.*

THE CONTEXT OF PERSONAL NARRATIVE
Reflections on *"Not Either an Experimental Doll"—The Separate Worlds of Three South African Women*

Shula Marks

It is now almost half a dozen years since I first discovered the letters between the seventy-four-year-old white Fabian socialist Mabel Palmer, the fifteen-year-old Xhosa schoolgirl Lily Patience Moya, and the first Zulu woman to train as a social worker in the United States of America, Violet Sibusisiwe Makhanya.[1] At the time I had little intention of writing biography, or indeed specifically about women. I was intent on finding material in Mabel Palmer's voluminous works in the Killie Campbell Library, Durban, on social and economic conditions in twentieth-century Natal, and anxious to discover the links I assumed she had with African political and trade union figures—mainly male—for a project concerned with African political organization and consciousness in that province.[2] Quite by chance I ran across a file labeled "Lily Moya," and somewhat idly flipped through. Thus began a six-year project and my current concern with women's history and with life stories as a way of getting beyond the somewhat rigid structuralism which characterized much of South African historiography in the 1970s.

Over a hundred letters written between 1949 and the middle of 1951 provided a glimpse into a painful yet not uncommon relationship at a particular moment in time. They also reveal the separate worlds which we all inhabit, but which are made more frightening and more separate by the divisions of age, ethnicity, and race. The correspondence between Mabel Palmer, Lily Moya, and Sibusisiwe Makhanya helps to move us beyond the aridity of an unpeopled political economy, to the ambiguities of everyday life. Through it we see the overarching constraints of social structure on human agency, and the complex relationship of individual psychology to a culture-bounded social order. If what is precious in the letters is the personal and the idiosyncratic, it is nonetheless possible through them to show that "the private lives, even [the] obsessions of . . . individuals, far from being simply psychological quirks or even aberrations, flowed directly from the social situation of these . . . individuals."[3]

In discussing the relationship of history and fiction, the illustrious South African writer Nadine Gordimer has argued that the novelist is able to deal in a way that historians usually cannot with the way in which historical process is registered as the subjective experience of individuals in society; fiction is able to give us "history from the inside."[4] Yet as Stephen Clingman points out in an illuminating discussion of Gordimer's historical consciousness, novelists not only may be fallible in their understanding of history, they are also themselves historical subjects, influenced by "the needs and assumptions of [their] time, not to mention any ideological framework or preoccupation that may have modified [their] vision."[5] The life story and autobiography through which historical actors present themselves share in the strengths and weaknesses of "history from the inside," which "is not only privileged but also confined by its 'inside' position," for the primary material that a novel, like an autobiography or life story, presents is "not so much an historical world, but a certain consciousness of the world."[6]

Historians do not necessarily escape the dilemma of the "insider": like the novelist, we may well be structured and caught up in the very processes we are trying to analyze. This is particularly the case when we record the stories of living subjects, in whose lives we inevitably become a part. If the dilemma is inescapable, the endeavor is nonetheless worthwhile, for it is through the presentation of the life story that we can try to capture both the internality of experience and the externality of structure. By intervening between subject and reader in the presentation of self, we grapple with the central problem of human agency, "the problem of finding a way of accounting for human experience which recognizes simultaneously and in equal measure that history and society are made by constant and more or less purposeful individual action *and* that individual action, however purposeful, is made by society and history."[7]

Through the contextualization of the letters and lives of Mabel Palmer, Lily Moya, and Violet Sibusisiwe Makhanya, something of the differentiated meaning of the complex South African social order can be seen, a tapestry where the specificities of race, gender, and class are densely interwoven. Unraveling these threads through the relationship of Mabel, Lily, and Violet inevitably undermines any simple-minded feminist assumption of the power of "sisterhood" in which the fractures of class, age, and ethnicity are of no account. As Jill Mathews has recently observed:

> There can be no unified history of women, only a multitude of histories of women as members of specific social groupings. . . . [Moreover,] beyond acknowledgement of diversity among the groups of women, there is the need to acknowledge the diversity of each individual woman. . . . Each woman in any society is not simply a member of one definite social

category, but is a unique and female focus of a multitude of coexisting and competing social groups and relationships. . . .[8]

Equally, however, they share in a "woman's world," shaped, it is true, by different forms of male domination, but in which men rather than women recede into the middle distance. The letters provide an entry into a more intimate and personal world where women's voices, articulating very different concerns with obligation and duty, philanthropy and welfare, sexuality and social control, are heard. It is, however, only an entry point. The letters do not stand on their own: to contextualize them I had to find their authors, whether in the historical records they left, as in the cases of Mabel and Violet, or through actually tracing Lily herself. At this point the simple record of the correspondence intersected with the complexities of the life story, and not only its historical context but my own.

The story told by the correspondence can be briefly recounted. At the beginning of 1949, Lily wrote to Mabel Palmer, then the organizer of what was known as the "Non-European Section" of Natal University, from the home of foster parents in Umtata in the Transkei:

> I do not moralise when I tell you that I'm a helpless orphan. I have obtained this educational status through my being a day student, only due to my financial embarassment [sic].[9]

She appealed to Mabel to grant her a place in what she conceived of as "her" (i.e., Mabel's) high school. Taken by the liveliness evidenced in the letters and a certain amount of identification with the young Lily, the aging and arthritic Mabel responded with generosity. As she wrote to the native commissioner (NC) in Umtata:

> The letters are very well expressed giving me the impression of a young thing straining at the leash with desire for some training to fit her to take part in the life outside a native location.[10] When I remember the many people who helped me in years gone by to get the education which has enabled me to lead what has on the whole been a happy and successful life, I feel that I cannot shut my ears to her appeal.[11]

On discovering that her correspondent was still only fifteen, and following the advice of the NC in Umtata as well as of some of her black friends, Mabel suggested that Lily come to Natal in the following year. In the meantime, with characteristic energy and perseverance, she explored the possibility of getting Lily into a mission high school in Natal,[12] and of finding funds from her more affluent friends in order to do so. By the middle of 1950, Lily had been accepted at Adams High School, one of the most famous schools for Africans in Natal originally founded by, and still heavily imbued with the spirit of, the Congregationalist American Board of Missions. Before the relevant documentation could be sent to Lily in Umtata enabling her to cross the provincial boundaries—in South Africa, women could travel only with the written permission of their guardians, or with certificates from an employer or school—Lily ran away and made her own way to Adams. In a somewhat patronizing but not unsympathetic account, Mabel described the flight:

> She certainly is, in spite of her very quiet and shy exterior, a young woman of extraordinary resource. I do not know if you have heard of her adventures. She was told at Kokstad that she could not have a ticket for Pietermaritzburg unless she could produce a permit or Concession form, so the resourceful little thing took a ticket for the station in the boundary between Natal and the Cape and then took another ticket for Pietermaritzburg from there . . .[13]

The reasons for Lily's urgent appeals to Mabel for assistance and the precipitate flight were more complex than Mabel had anticipated, however. In a letter to Mabel shortly after her arrival at Adams, Lily explained:

> The climax if not reached, was about to be reached. Besides all the other reasons I once gave you before, all along our long correspondence, I had never told you this and now I feel compelled to tell you that I could, or in fact [would] try to endure every other difficulty patiently and humbly, but not to see myself getting married in an awkward manner to a man I hated so much. That is one of the things I so much hate being married. I don't even dream about it. That awful bondage. That is what my uncle did to me. . . .[14]

Initially, Lily did relatively well in her classwork at her new school. Ominously, however, within a couple of weeks, she was writing to Mabel:

> I can just say I am happy here, I'm alright. I cann't [sic] help those who are very good at laughing at others. Perhaps they are not used to such individuals who have striven nearly all their lives under unsympathetic individuals and who have been brought up in poverty. They will soon get used to me. . . .[15]

By the end of the year, Lily was decidedly unhappy with her new school; she found herself teased and perhaps sexually harassed by the male students and teachers, and was appalled by the low academic standards of the school.[16] In fact, the Adams she had come to was in turmoil. By an unfortunate coincidence, the very week of her arrival, the principal had suspended 175 of the male students, the result of a series of incidents which arose out of his refusal to allow a dance in honor of Shaka Day (a Zulu cultural festival) on the grounds that it would arouse "inter-tribal conflict."[17] In a tense situation, Lily, of alien background in both religion and ethnic identity, found herself the object of much suspicion, which was reinforced by her own dependence on her white patron. In January 1951, she appealed to Mabel to allow her to finish her schooling in Durban, where she would "be in touch with your school, your people and with many other civilized branches which would be of better use in my future."[18]

Mabel's response was swift and devastating. Clearly unaware of the significance of the ethnic tensions at Adams, and of the difficulties which Lily experienced as a vulnerable outsider, and fearful of accepting the burden of responsibility which Lily's dependence undoubtedly threw upon her, she replied in typically blunt fashion. After listing Lily's various misdemeanors at school, she continued:

> You say that among your reasons for wishing to be in Durban is that you want to see more of me, but have you ever asked yourself whether I wish to see more of you? As a matter of fact I do not. Your romantic and self-centered imagination has built up for you a picture in which you are to be my devoted and intimate friend. Now you must forgive me for saying that this is all nonsense. Even if you were a European girl of your age it would still be nonsense. What basis of companionship could there be between a quarter educated girl of eighteen and an experienced old lady like myself? And of course the racial situation in Durban makes all these things more difficult. . . .[19]

This letter was to mark a turning point in Lily's life. Despite a duly submissive response, from this point her work began to deteriorate, and she began to complain of a variety of physical ills. Yet despite her emotional rejection of Lily's appeals, Mabel tried to help her "little protegée." Even before this particular exchange, she had written to an African friend, the Zulu social worker Violet Sibusisiwe Makhanya, who ran a social center near Adams. Now she wrote again, hoping that Sibusisiwe could help, for "poor little Lily is completely cut off from her own people and rather in need of some contact with Bantu friends outside Adams College." Despite Sibusisiwe's attempts, however, Lily remained unhappy and isolated. In May she asked permission to visit her family, newly discovered in Sophiatown, an African township near Johannesburg. When permission was refused by the school, for fear that her visit would enable her guardian to reclaim her, Lily's behavior deteriorated even further. In a furious attack on Adams, she accused the school of indiscipline, a lack of morality, and "education which is barbarism under a camouflage." She continued bitterly:

> A parent or a guardian who wishes or wants to reap a good crop, who really wants her daughter or adopted child [to have] fruitful results [from] his or her struggle in educating her, should place her under good influence.[20]

For Mabel this sentence went beyond the nature of the relationship she was willing to establish:

> In your letter you use the phrase "adopted daughter." I don't know if you were thinking of me and yourself when you used those words, but I feel I must make it plain that I do not and will not regard you in any such light and that I have never said anything to justify you in believing so. I was interested in your letters and sympathetic towards a girl struggling for better education, and I felt it was up to me to give you some help. That help I will give. . . . But what I want is that you should as soon as possible be in a position to stand on your own feet. Also as a rather forlorn little protegée I will from time to time see you for a talk and arrange for you small treats. . . . But beyond that I will not go and every time you press on me a desire for a more intimate relation you really force me back into reserve and guardedness in dealing with you. . . . but any close or intimate friendship between us is really not possible and you will only spoil things if you grasp at it. But this doesn't mean that I am not interested in you or do not want to be kind to you; *I do* within due limits.
>
> You talk a good deal of your prayers. Do you ever pray to be made more humble and less self-righteous, more adaptable and more sensible?[21]

For Lily, this final rejection seems to have been the last straw. She responded with what can only be read as a paranoid attack on one of the teachers, and by the end of June she had left Adams under a cloud to spend the vacation with Sibusisiwe. She was clearly in an unhappy and truculent mood, still anxious to go to visit her "relatives" in Johannesburg. After further "bad behavior" at Umbumbulu, she once more sought resolution in flight in the middle of July. Ostensibly on her way to visit Mabel, she ran away to Sophiatown. From Sophiatown she wrote to Mabel:

> For congenial reasons I had to leave Adams, due to the fact that I was never meant to be a stone but a human being with feelings not either an experimental doll. . . .
>
> About Adams, I think in December 1950 . . . I told you I didn't want staying. I had to work and I had clerical vacation [vacancy?] to fill. You refused. I really ignored going back and I stayed there in Adams . . . not according to my will. I didn't want staying there, You arranged that at my back. You badly handled [*sic*; handed?] me back.[22]

This was to be her last letter. Sibusisiwe's response was instructive:

> I shall not be sorry Dr. Palmer, if you part with Lily. You gave her a splendid chance, and she has abused it. I shall not be at all surprised if the girl is pregnant. All the accusations she has made . . . were intended to cover up the problem. I began to suspect this when she pressed so hard to go to Johannesburg and her general behaviour went to point to one suffering from early pregnancy. . . .[23]

In another note, Sibusisiwe further consoled Mabel, "Well, Dr. Palmer you did all you could for that girl but it seems it is difficult to find out what she really wants. . . ."[24]

These letters in themselves do not, of course, constitute either biography or life history. Nevertheless, they capture a historical moment in the lives of the three women when their experiences intersected. By bringing them together, certain common themes in the lives of women, drawn from different generations and cultures, if not classes,[25] became clearer. Clearly the letters could not stand alone, however. From the letters, I was drawn ineluctably into considering both the lives and the times of the three women who had created them.

This was easier to do in the case of Mabel and Sibusisiwe: both were public figures, and both had left a body of private papers. In Sibusisiwe's case this was rather disappointing in personal terms, but I was fortunate to find a biography—albeit a somewhat uncritical one—based on substantial interviews before her death.[26] I was, in addition, able to follow in Sibusisiwe Makhanya's footsteps in the United States, through the records of the American Board of Missions in Boston, her admission records at Tuskegee, and the papers about her unhappy relationship with the Phelps Stokes Fund in New York.[27] Both Sibusisiwe Makhanya and Mabel Palmer were well-known figures in Natal, and were remembered. As early as the 1900s, Mabel had made her mark on her contemporaries, and she is recorded as Mabel Atkinson in the papers of the Fabian Society and the Fabian Women's Group. Margaret Cole describes Mabel in her history of Fabian socialism as "something of a stormy element in Edwardian Fabianism, a very truculent member of the Fabian Women's Group and a supporter of the Fabian Reform Committee."[28] Mabel's papers and my discussions with her biographer and some of her contemporaries filled out the picture of this formidable and doughty fighter for women's and black rights.[29] Inspiring both love and hate in equal measure, she was old and tired by the time Lily encountered her. Her immense strengths and weaknesses are revealed in the correspondence.

It was Lily, however, who was at the center of these letters. I had to get behind their anguished appeal. It was not only that I wanted to know what had happened to her. The letters belonged to her, and if she was alive I wanted to have her permission to publish them and to ensure that she would have the benefit of any royalties. Apart from the letters, revealing as they were, there was little I could find out about her, however. Although she was clearly a product of mission endeavors in the Eastern Cape, I knew little of her immediate family and background, or about what had become of her. In part because the number of African girls who reached the final school-leaving examinations or matriculation in the midcentury was so minute—in the whole of South Africa only 201 reached the final two years of senior school in 1949,[30] the year in which Lily first failed her matriculation examination—and because the Christian intelligentsia is relatively tightly knit, I assumed that I would be able to find Lily if she was still alive. Nevertheless, the obstacles were formidable: her last address was in Sophiatown, which no longer existed. It was one of the freehold African townships destroyed by the South African nationalist government in the mid-1950s when Soweto was created. It was unclear how much of her family was left in the Eastern Cape or whether they would welcome inquiries. Despite the efforts of a variety of friends and colleagues who were drawn into the search and gave unstintingly of their time, I had little success.[31] The only response to a prominent article in a major daily newspaper was an intriguing but disturbing letter which led me to reexamine my own role in trying to find Lily. Signed "Lily (deflowered)," it read:

> Dear Sir,
>   It is surprising that you should claim "a special place in history" for a promiscuous drop out. Such persons (of all races) are not infrequently pushed upstairs as it were, by misguided do-gooders, who eventually come to realize that they are simply wasting time and money. An old story not worth the telling. . . . The crowning fatuity of your article comes when you express a desire to talk to [Lily]. . . . By what right? And why assume she wishes to talk to you?
>   In conclusion, forget about it. Sales will be small and you would be well advised to mind your own business.[32]

Almost fortuitously, within days of receiving this letter, with its uncanny echoes of the correspondence which had been cited in the newspaper article, I learned that one of Lily's aunts was still teaching at a mission school in the Eastern Cape mentioned in the text. And from her I discovered that Lily was living with her mother and sister in Soweto. After a good deal of hesitation—was I perhaps simply another Mabel Palmer, another "do-gooder" about to interfere in Lily's life once more?—I decided to make contact with her through the good offices of the Oral History Project at the African Studies Institute at the University of Witwatersrand.

The encounter transformed the nature of the exercise. My role as historian changed as I had to come to terms with dealing with the lives of real people. Moreover, Lily's subsequent story raised major issues both about women's experience in general and about the black women's experience in South Africa in particular.

By the time she arrived in Johannesburg in the middle of 1951, it is clear that Lily was in a disturbed state. By the end of the month she had written in her last letter to Mabel, "I am very ill."[33] And although she did not specify the precise nature of her illness, it was clearly of a psychiatric character. She was withdrawn and depressed, and talked to herself incessantly. The only phrase her sister recalls as intelligible at this time was "Mabel Palmer." Lily spent the next twenty-five years in two mental hospitals on the Witwatersrand, Sterkfontein and Randfontein.[34] Labeled a "chronic schizophrenic,"[35] by the time I met her she was a shadow of her former self, her English all but forgotten. She looked, as she was, drugged, somehow absent. Although she was able to answer quite detailed factual questions about the past—remembering, for example, the names of the headmaster at St. John's in 1949—there was no recollection of affect in the past, and no expression of affect in the present. Mabel Palmer had been transformed into an idealized benefactress. Most of my subsequent interviews were, perforce, with her remarkably articulate and vivacious younger sister, a fully trained nurse, who had finally managed to bring Lily home in 1976.

Lily's tragedy raises in acute form some of the central questions for the social scientist: not simply how to interpret personal narrative, but how to relate individual psychology and psychopathology to social structure and the gendered realities of any particular social order, and how to understand the subject as "victim." The accidental nature of my discovery, moreover, drew me into considering themes which the social historian often avoids in his or her choice of subject: in general we are more comfortable in dealing with the lives even of "ordinary" people if they were "successful," and even if their achievements can be measured only by future generations. Through their lives we can draw inspiration for the future. It is far more difficult to encounter those who have been destroyed in the very process of their adaptation and resistance to the structures of domination. It is disturbing to have to confront the enormous price tag of history.

The nature of Lily's "breakdown" especially poses many problems for the historian, problems which are untackled, let alone resolved, in the conventional psychiatric literature, on the one hand, or in most historical literature, on the other. In Western medicine in general and psychiatry in particular, despite a certain lip service to the significance of "social factors," there is a certain reluctance to accept the social etiology of disease, or the specific cultural forms it may present. This is in profound contrast to African cosmologies of healing, which see most affliction as intrinsically social and cultural. As John Janzen shows in relation to the Lower Zaire— and his remarks are widely applicable in southern and central Africa:

> A feature of therapy management in Kongo society is the collective orientation of medicine. The whole diagnostic apparatus is sensitive to the social cause of physiological affliction. African traditional medicine has been criticized by Western missionaries and colonials as superstition that victimizes individuals ostensibly to benefit the social group. But it could be equally well argued that Western medicine focuses on the individual patient and leaves the social context of his illness in pathological chaos. Kongo therapeutic attitudes, like those in many other African societies are composed to discern the social and psychosomatic causes of illness.[36]

Contemporary Western psychiatry tends to stress the biological and genetic etiology of disease, rather than the social; it is so much easier to measure and to treat illness on an individual basis and so much less threatening to the status quo. Feminist literature, more alert to the socially constructed, ethnocentric, and gender-biased categories of most psychiatric theories, is more helpful, although it is more usually concerned with the plight of First World women. Western feminists have shown the male bias of the profession, and the way in which many psychoanalytical theories are shaped around a male definition of appropriate female behavior. In South Africa, even in the mental hospital Lily would have seen a white male psychiatrist at very infrequent intervals, although in the final analysis it would have been his views that prevailed.[37] Yet this does not fully address the question which Lily's subsequent life story raises, and in some sense also answers. Murray Last has termed this the first and most important question to be asked by medical anthropology, "Who gets sick?"[38] Confronted with the evidence of these letters and their social context, the historian, at least, can make sense of the personal and the idiosyncratic only through an analysis of social process and social structure, both of which are gender-differentiated.

At one level, Lily's background in the Eastern Cape, and the way she imbibed the lessons of the mission education to which she was exposed, lend credence to Fanonesque notions of alienation and psychological colonization.[39] In a very general sense, her letters indicate an identification with the values and culture of white mission Christianity which could lead only to a personal identity crisis when she found herself—almost inevitably— rebuffed. Yet concepts of deracination and psychological alienation are in general too simple to cope with the complexities of colonial psychology and psychopathology. As Margaret Field has shown, for example, so-called culture conflict is frequently in the mind of the Western beholder rather than in that of the African.[40] The same Christian heritage can, under only slightly different circumstances, constitute a source of inner strength and fortitude rather than vulnerability: this is very clear from the contrasting life stories of Sibusisiwe Makhanya and Lily Moya. We have to be open, too, to the possibility that Lily was deliberately overplaying her identification with the values of school and mission in the hopes of enlisting Mabel's support and sympathy. It would be foolish to read all her protestations at face value, despite the undeniable authenticity of her alienation.

Nevertheless, it is difficult to overstress the significance of Lily's background in the Anglican schools of the Eastern Cape. Both her maternal grandparents and her paternal grandfather were converts to Christianity in the last decade of the nineteenth century. Prosperous small farmers and local headmen in the Tsolo district, as well as teachers and lay readers in the St. Cuthbert's mission established there in the 1880s, her grandparents were all members of the Christian elite of the Eastern Cape. The close identification of her maternal grandparents with the mission church can be seen from the fact that Lily's mother was named after the wife of Bransby Key, the first missionary and later bishop in the area, while an uncle was both the godson of Key's successor as missionary bishop and named after Key's son. All four of her mother's sisters became teachers, a vocation essentially tied to the mission, which provided the only schooling available to Africans at that time. Lily's manifest ability and the family premium on education took her to half a dozen different schools before she arrived at Adams, the changes dictated by the limited number of classes available at each school.

Crucial to the self-definition of the Eastern Cape Christian elite was their ideology of respectability, with the value it placed on education and its tightly puritanical sexual code.[41] Much of this was common to mission converts in general, a reflection of the middle-class evangelism which had attempted to change working-class morality in Britain, transposed to Africa. And among the "labor aristocracy" in Britain, as well as among the African petty bourgeoisie, the pursuit of respectability was "an assertion of social superiority, a self conscious cultural exclusion of less favoured groups."[42] The construction of an alternative sexual code was of particular importance, perhaps, to the Anglicans of Tsolo district. From the very beginning, the missionaries at St. Cuthbert's had been concerned with "the question of purity." Bransby Key, the first missionary, later to become bishop, had considered it a "burning question" in 1883, and planned "to start a guild for the promotion of purity among the girls."[43]

This was perhaps no more than the stock Victorian missionary response to African nudity, female initiation rites, and openness about sex. Nevertheless, the fact that St. Cuthbert's Mission was placed in the hands of the celibate brotherhood of the Society of St. John the Evangelist may have reinforced this preoccupation with African sexuality in church teaching in the Tsolo district. By the beginning of the twentieth century, a sisterhood had been formed at St. Cuthbert's, and the first black nun had been confirmed. "A spinning wheel and the knowledge of how to use it" were seen as most useful in filling the "somewhat dangerous time between the completion of a girl's schooling and her marriage."[44]

Concern with the virginity of young African girls remained a recurrent theme among missionaries, administrators, and Christian Africans in twentieth-century South Africa. It lay behind the repeated fears expressed by African men and colonial administrators of the temptations in the way of young girls in towns,[45] the formation of mothers' prayer unions or *manyanos* by African women in the mission churches as early as 1912, the establishment of hostels for unmarried women in Johannesburg and Durban by missionaries of the American Board, and the organization of the Bantu Purity League in 1919 by Sibusisiwe Makhanya[46]—hence, perhaps, her conclusion that Lily was pregnant in the middle of 1951, a suspicion which seems to have been unwarranted.

For Lily, the particularities of Christian Xhosa patriarchy and the construction of sexuality in the Anglican milieu of the Eastern Cape were inescapable; anxiety about "purity," and perhaps her own adolescent sexuality, permeates her correspondence. This we have already seen in the letter she wrote Mabel after she ran away from home in September 1950, even before she had received the necessary documentation from the school.

Even before this, in response to a request from Mabel that she write a short paper on "The Life of a Native Girl in a Native Reserve," which she "might try to have printed somewhere," Lily had written:

> I'm very sorry for not producing you a good draft to the "Life of an African Girl." I have not been a good traveller or very observant to such a subject, you will see little of my experience only based to what our people say of our girls and what we ought to do, to be preserved divinely devoted and single-minded, expecting ourselves to be the future mothers, the examples to be admired and to be selfrespective of ourselves.
>
> We are frequently mislead [*sic*] by minor misdeeds. We never use our intelligence. We are flying for only outside admiration, our actions are rot, revealing our internal impurity.
>
> We have a thrilling audacity to do evil. We forget the meaning of the word "girl," that a girl should be preserved. We make people believe that civilization came with evil. Yes, we are people surrounded by stumbling blocks, things which look inviting. . . . We live only for the present but not for the future. . . . We are only advised to marry and as we grow we think only of marry. . . .[47]

Mission records of the nineteenth and early twentieth centuries are replete with stories of women fleeing to the stations to escape an unwelcome marriage. In Lily's case—and perhaps, too, in that of Sibusisiwe Makhanya, who quite deliberately decided against marriage, in contravention of her people's norms—there may have been additional elements: the desire of the ambitious and clever woman to distance herself from the "frivolity" of peer-group preoccupations with courting and marriage, and the desire for independence from the patriarchal demands of African marriage. Nor should effects of the teachings of the church on a serious-minded adolescent be forgotten. The contradictions between Lily's notions of the "good woman" imbibed from the Anglican mission and the African emphasis on marriage and motherhood were acute. They were to explode when confronted further by the conflicting ideals of femininity held by Mabel Palmer and Sibusisiwe Makhanya. As Jill Matthews argues, the existence of a "maelstrom of changing and contradicting ideals" of femininity means that a woman's

> pursuit of any, let alone a unified, ideal of femininity . . . must inevitably lead to failure at some point or another. She will inevitably transgress some norms of femininity no matter how diligently she tries to conform to a true pattern. Indeed, such transgression is structured into the very pursuit

itself, since the individual desires an internally consistent femininity, whereas the ideal is socially structured as inconsistent.[48]

Although Matthews is writing of the very different situation of Australian women, these contradictory norms were very much part of Lily's world. Harassment from the opposite sex continued to plague Lily even at Adams, and seems to be among the reasons for her increasing unhappiness at the school. Thus, in her bitter attack on Adams, she not only called its coeducation "abominable," but added for good measure:

> P.S. and I have never come across such raw school-boys as Adams students who have no respect who force and say anything they like to girls. . . . I can be very glad if I can go to a school with no boys what-so-ever.[49]

We cannot know precisely what lay behind Lily's outspoken antipathy toward the "raw school-boys" at Adams in June 1951. The pressures can only be guessed at from her fleeting remarks. Some further idea, however, of the extent of the problem can be gauged if we put it in the context of the records of the American Board of Missions in Natal. In 1940, for example, the famous girls' school at Inanda, the sister school to Adams, experienced the "loss" in one week of two unmarried teachers and two students as a result of pregnancy; in the following year seven girl students, four of them new and including one aged fifteen who subsequently died, presumably in childbirth, were sent down as a result of "moral failure."[50] The problem was not confined to students. In 1946, an African teacher was dismissed from Adams "because of serious indiscretions in his conduct with one of the girl students," and anecdotal evidence suggests that this was more widespread.[51] It is difficult to find statistics of sexual "misdemeanors" for Adams for the year that Lily was there, but the problems for an inexperienced, new teenage girl at a coeducational school, at which boys considerably outnumbered girls, were likely to have been intense. Given her fear of being married off for the bridewealth, which precipitated her flight to Natal and hints at a very real threat of coercion, her antipathy to males is more than explicable. In the light of the nature of sexual relations at this time, there is certainly some evidence for thinking that Lily may have been subjected to fairly violent sexual advances, which she could not handle.[52]

If there can be little doubt that Lily's alienation and lack of support were socially structured, in part a result of her socialization through mission education, her breakdown goes beyond generalities about the impact of colonialism and psychological colonization. Not only do these fail to look at the effects of class, gender, or age differentiation on the incidence of disease, they also ignore the variety of individual experience and the different ways individuals reflect on and refract the same experience. Despite the undoubtedly pathogenic nature of her environment—a frightening amalgam of the cruelties structured by colonialism and individual circumstance—to environment must be added the unknown quantity of her personal frailty and the way this was shaped by her childhood.

It is impossible to write with certainty of Lily's early childhood experiences. Apart from a few illuminating but elusive comments, she was largely silent in the interviews with her family. The drugs on top of twenty-five years in a mental hospital had destroyed the liveliness and intelligence so evident in the letters. Yet her early years are suggestive: the death of her father when she was only five or six, her mother's remorseless struggle for a livelihood, and her own frequent moves from school to school were surely traumatic. Her father died in 1939, having spent most of Lily's childhood away from home. Like the majority of young men in the Transkei in the 1930s, he was forced to seek work as a migrant laborer in the gold mines of the Witwatersrand.[53]

After her husband's death, Lily's mother had been forced to leave the Transkei to seek work in Johannesburg just as the adolescent entered her final years at school at St. John's in Umtata. This was her fifth school in less than ten years, the moves dictated by the limited classes available in the local schools. Not surprisingly, she said she had little opportunity to make friends. At St. John's she was the only girl and the only day student in a class of young men. She was eight years younger than the next-youngest pupil.[54] Lily's description of herself as "a helpless orphan" in her letters to Mabel was, under the circumstances, an apt account of her sense of desolation and loneliness.

That she should have been found "difficult" by her teachers at St. John's is also hardly surprising. The term was to dog her through her stormy career at Adams. It is useful to recall how frequently this word has been applied to intelligent and ambitious women who have refused to accept society's definition of their station in life. Indeed, a number of psychologists have observed that female schizophrenics are more dominant and aggressive than female or male "normals" or male schizophrenics, and in one study, at least, "were perceived by both their parents as the 'least conforming' of all the groups. Their parents remembered them as unusually 'active' [for girls?] during childhood. . . ."[55] These observations have led Phyllis Chesler to remark, in her pioneering study of *Women and Madness,*

> Perhaps it was this rather specific rejection of one aspect of the female role that caused family conflict, and ultimately led to psychiatric labelling and incarceration. . . . *What we consider "madness," whether it appears in women or in men, is either the acting out of the devalued female role* [which she argues is the case in the women labeled "neurotic" or "psychotic"] *or the total or partial rejection of one's sex-role stereotype.*[56]

It would be wholly rash to jump to the conclusion that it was her family's inability to cope with Lily's rejection of her "sex-role stereotype" which led to her being labeled "schizophrenic" and to her committal to a mental hospital; however, there can be little doubt that she was severely disturbed by the time she arrived in Sophiatown. As Lily herself put it, she was "very ill." The behavior her mother and sister report is consonant with that most frequently described for schizophrenic patients: unintelligible babbling, restlessness, hearing voices, bad temper.[57] Their response was to seek the advice of traditional healers. They, in turn, diagnosed her as suffering from spirit possession, which they would probably have distinguished quite carefully from "madness," although in many ways it can be argued that this too involved the rejection of one's "sex-role stereotype."[58] It was only after Lily rejected the ministrations of the traditional healers and reported the second of them to the police that she was taken to a mental hospital. Ironically, it was a sign of her relative "privilege" that she had access to Western medicine at all.

Yet both Mabel and Sibusisiwe Makhanya were known in their day as "difficult women"[59] and rejected their "sex-role stereotype"—and of course they were also both regarded as highly successful as well. Sibusisiwe was described by the missionaries of the American Board in the 1920s as "the most outstanding Zulu woman of her generation," "the answer to the question, 'Why missions?' "[60] Mabel achieved a position of some eminence in Natal society, although she was regarded with an affection tinged with hostility by many of her peers. Lily, however, for all her innate ability, was in a far more vulnerable psychosocial position. She had to face the insecurities and anxieties of puberty on her own, unsupported by either peers or kin, and the deck was stacked against her. The extent to which her subsequent problems revolved around her inability to cope at this time with her own adolescent sexuality is perhaps intimated by a clue she herself provided in the course of our interviews in Soweto in 1983.

During my first visit, in a discussion with her sister about her visit to the traditional healers, Lily interjected, apparently at random, "Witchdoctor is menstruation." On my second visit, when I inquired how she was, she replied, "I am suffering from menstruation," an unlikely remark contradicted by her sister. The repetition was at least symbolically appropriate, perhaps pinpointing the moment of Lily's greatest distress. For a mother-bereft adolescent trying to come to terms with her own sexuality in a class full of young men, menstruation, the most manifest symptom of puberty and incipient adulthood, may well have constituted a major crisis. In "traditional" society, menstruation was a time of danger and taboo, during which women were not supposed to even speak to men. It is perhaps not wholly fanciful to suggest that Lily's repetition of the syllable *men*—in *mental* and *menstruation*—was not entirely random, in view of her problematic relationship with members of the opposite sex.

This is not to say that her breakdown was simply an adolescent crisis over sexuality. There were additional sources of strain. With her close family gone and with few friends, Lily staked her all on her scholastic achievements. She was intensely ambitious, finding self-identification through her

intellectual ability, so one can only imagine that her failure in the matriculation examinations in 1948 and again in 1949 must have come as a severe
blow. Desperately she tried to find in Mabel the mother figure she lacked.
And Mabel's undisputed generosity partly drew her on. Yet Mabel was
fitted by neither temperament nor experience to fulfil a maternal, or
indeed even a supportive, role. Perhaps sensing the danger of Lily's dependence on a sickly old woman, she reacted with her typical acerbity, and
explicitly dissociated herself emotionally from her charge. There is
no indication in her letters to Lily that she had even an inkling of the suffering experienced by her "poor little protegée," and in many ways it would
be unrealistic to have expected more. A single woman who had made
her way in a male-dominated world, she too had grown up in a hard school
and had become accustomed to hiding her emotions. In an intensely racist
colonial society, she had gone as far as she personally could in extend-
ing the hand of benefaction to the hapless Lily. And as she herself put
it, generational divisions made it all the more difficult. Given liberal
notions of philanthropy in South Africa, it is unlikely that an impoverished "white" Afrikaner schoolgirl would have fared as well. Indeed,
Mabel would probably not have extended herself on her behalf in the
first place.

Given the ethnic divisions at Adams at the time of her arrival, however,
and the intense suspicions students had of "outsiders," Lily's isolation was
now complete. As her last lifeline was cut by Mabel's rejection, Lily became
depressed and finally suffered a psychotic breakdown, her last way, perhaps, of seeking "the support, sympathy and attention that depressed
people often long for."[61]

Whatever the relationship between individual psychology and social
structure, and whatever the precise diagnosis of Lily's disturbed behavior,
whether it was the intense depression manifested in spirit possession diagnosed by the traditional healer or the schizophrenic illness she was treated
for by the mental hospitals—and the two are by no means mutually ex-
clusive—her incarceration for twenty-five years in mental institutions was
unlikely to improve her condition. Quite apart from the specific repres-
sions of mental institutions for blacks in South Africa, the evidence is
overwhelming that prolonged confinement in the "total" institution of the
asylum tends to exacerbate rather than heal mental illness. Social depriva-
tion, uncertainty, and coercion are the hallmarks of mental hospitals in
many parts of the world; in the absence of a supportive therapeutic community, confinement alone was likely only to increase her anxiety, withdrawal, and suffering.[62] To the frequent depersonalization and
humiliation experienced by the mentally ill in the "total institution" of the
mental hospital was added the discrimination experienced by Africans in
South Africa's psychiatric institutions.

Yet for Lily, being an "inmate" was perhaps no new experience. In her
interviews, she makes an explicit link between the boarding schools and the

mental hospitals she has experienced. Commenting on her inability to form enduring friendships, she explained, "My life was a transfer. I was transferred from St. Cuthbert's to Shawbury, from Shawbury to St. Matthew's, from St. Matthew's to St. John's, from St. John's to Adams, from Adams to Sterkfontein, from Sterkfontein to Randfontein and from Randfontein to Soweto." It has all become a seamless web. In another interview, she maintained, "Mrs Palmer gave me scholarship to Sterkfontein."[63] The perceptions are symbolically piquant.

Notes

1. The names in this story have a peculiar charm. In fact, "Lily Patience" is a pseudonym, adopted in response to the request of the family to protect their anonymity. Mabel Palmer and Sibusisiwe ("the Blessed One") Makhanya (who was usually known as Violet in the mission records of the 1920s and 1930s, but who seems to have returned to her African name in the course of the 1930s in response to the cultural nationalism of the time) needed no such protection. I have tried hard to capture the essence of Lily's original names.

2. This work came to revolve around the lives of three men, since published as *The Ambiguities of Dependence in South Africa: Class, Nationalism, and State in Twentieth-Century South Africa* (Baltimore: Johns Hopkins Press, and Johannesburg: Ravan Press, 1986). The difference in focus is instructive.

3. L. Davidoff, "Class and Gender in Victorian England," in J. L. Newton, M. P. Ryan, and J. R. Walkowitz, *Sex and Class in Women's History* (London: Routledge and Kegan Paul, 1983), pp. 17–71, esp. p. 30.

4. S. Clingman, *The Novels of Nadine Gordimer: History from the Inside* (Johannesburg: Ravan Press, 1987), p. 1.

5. Ibid., p. 4.

6. Ibid., p. 2.

7. P. Abrams, *Historical Sociology* (Somerset: Open Books, 1982), p. xii.

8. Jill Julius Matthews, *Good and Mad Women* (North Sydney, Australia, and Hemel Hempstead, Herts.: Allen and Unwin, 1984), p. 17.

9. Lily Patience Moya to Mabel Palmer (henceforth LPM and MP), 4 January 1949. Here and elsewhere the correspondence cited has been published in *"Not Either an Experimental Doll."*

10. I.e., an area set aside for sole African occupation under South Africa's segregationist land and residential laws. Although the term applied more usually to segregated urban areas for Africans, in this case Mabel was referring to the rural "reserve" of the Transkei.

11. MP to Native Commissioner (NC), Umtata, 14 April 1949.

12. Virtually all African education at this time was still in the hands of mission schools of various denominations. The Bantu Education Act of 1953 brought most of them under direct state control for the first time.

13. MP to NC, Umtata, 14 April 1949.

14. LPM to MP, 12 September 1950.

15. LPM to MP, 18 September 1950.

16. See below, p. 73.

17. G. C. Grant to "Parent and Guardian," 18 September 1950. For the further implications of this episode, see *"Not Either an Experimental Doll,"* Introduction, and my "Patriotism, Patriarchy, and Purity: The Politics of Zulu Cultural Ethnicity, 1936–1948," in L. Vail, *The Creation of Tribalism in Southern Africa* (London: James Currey, forthcoming, 1988).

18. LPM to MP, 2 January 1951.

19. MP to LPM, 12 January 1951.

20. LPM to MP, 3 June 1951.

21. MP to LPM, 7 June 1951.

22. LPM to MP, 26 July 1951.

23. Sibusisiwe Makhanya (SM) to MP, 14 August 1951.

24. SM to MP, 31 July 1951.

25. The class differences between these three women are difficult to define. In objective terms, both Mabel Palmer and Sibusisiwe Makhanya were educators and in some sense members of the petty bourgeoisie. (Lily was undoubtedly a daughter of the African petty bourgeoisie.) While, however, the letters between Mabel and Sibusisiwe bespeak a certain equality, Mabel's letters to Lily seem to be written to someone belonging to a lower order, and in their tone are reminiscent of that adopted by middle-class Fabians to the working class in Britain. In his account of Mabel Palmer's activities in establishing evening classes for black (African and Indian) teachers, Edgar Brookes revealingly remarks that her "background [was] admirably suited to an experiment in workers' education" (*A History of the University of Natal* [Pietermaritzburg: Natal University Press, 1966], p. 45).

26. M. Trowbridge, "Sibusisiwe," unpubl. TSS, Killie Campbell Library, Durban.

27. Sibusisiwe was given a scholarship by the Phelps Stokes Fund, but very rapidly rejected the paternalist and inferior education she felt she was being offered under their auspices. She broke her ties with the fund and financed her own way first through the Theological Seminary at Cleveland, and then at Columbia Training College, New York. For this episode, see R. Hunt Davies, Jr., "Producing the 'Good African': South Carolina's Penn School as a Guide for African Education in South Africa," in A. T. Mogomba and M. Nyaggah, *Independence without Freedom: The Political Economy of Colonial Education in Southern Africa* (Santa Barbara: ABC-Clio, 1980), pp. 83–112, and the Introduction to *"Not Either an Experimental Doll."*

28. *The Story of Fabian Socialism* (London: Heinemann, 1961), p. 349.

29. Dr. Sylvia Vietzen is currently writing a biography of Mabel Palmer. I am most grateful to her for her pioneering work.

30. Union of South Africa, UG 53–1951, *Report on Native Education in South Africa* (Pretoria: Government Printers, 1951), pars. 689–93.

31. This project has relied even more than usual on the generosity of friends, ex-students, and colleagues. Four should perhaps be singled out here, though there were many others who gave help along the way: Dr. Debbie Gaitskell, who put me in touch with the mission schools in the Eastern Cape; Rosalie Finlayson, who conducted field research for me in the Transkei; Professor Charles van Onselen of the African Studies Institute, who organized members of his Oral History Project to conduct interviews on my behalf and who has unfailingly given of his time and energy in assisting me; and Moses Molepo, one of the African Studies Institute's oral researchers, ex-student, and friend, who was tragically killed in Soweto in August 1985. *"Not Either an Experimental Doll"* is dedicated to Lily and to his memory.

32. I have not given the precise dates of the newspaper correspondence because it would breach the confidentiality of "Lily" to do so.

33. LPM to MP, 16 July 1951.

34. For an account of mental hospitals in South Africa at this time, see the Report of the American Psychiatric Association delegation to South Africa, 1979, *American Journal of Psychiatry* 136 (1979): 1498–1506.

35. The vast majority of black mental patients in South Africa are diagnosed as suffering from "schizophrenia," although according to the World Health Organization (WHO), it "may be wrongly diagnosed in at least 25 per cent of the Blacks so classified." Only a very small proportion of the mentally ill, however, receive psychiatric attention of any kind. See WHO, *Apartheid and Health* (Geneva: WHO, 1983), pp. 242, 234–40.

36. *The Quest for Therapy in Lower Zaire* (Berkeley and London: University of California Press, 1978), p. 9.

37. Sterkfontein, the first mental hospital that Lily experienced, was state-run; the second, Randfontein, was run privately by the Smith-Mitchell Company on behalf of the state. In the late 1970s, in state-run hospitals, each full-time psychiatrist was responsible for over six hundred patients. At Randfontein with thirty-two hundred patients, there were two part-time psychiatrists. At that time there was no African psychiatrist in the whole of South Africa. *Apartheid and Health,* pp. 240, 247.

38. "The Presentation of Sickness in a Community of Non-Muslim Hausa," in J. B. Loudon, ed., *Social Anthropology and Medicine* (London: Academic Press, 1976).

39. For an illuminating exposition of Fanon's psychiatric and political writings, see J. McCulloch, *Black Soul, White Artifact: Fanon's Clinical Psychology and Social Theory* (Cambridge: Cambridge University Press, 1983).

40. *Search for Security: An Ethno-psychiatric Study of Rural Ghana* (London: Faber and Faber, 1960).

41. Not for nothing are the African Christians known to the non-Christian community as the *AmaRespectables.*

42. The quotation is from R. Q. Gray, *The Labour Aristocracy in Victorian Edinburgh* (Oxford, 1976), p. 142, cited in J. Weeks, *Sex, Politics, and Society: The Regulation of Sexuality since 1800* (London and New York: Longmans, 1981), p. 74. This section draws heavily on Weeks.

43. Society for the Propagation of the Gospel (SPG) Archives (London), vol. D 65, 1883: Report of Rev. Bishop Bransby Key for the year ending 31 December 1883.

44. *Occasional News of St. Cuthbert's,* 1905, p. 7. Letter from Fr. Puller, 3 November 1905.

45. See, for example, the letter between MP and the Native Commissioner, Umtata, 14 April 1949.

46. In an interview (22 August 1979), Bertha Mkhize described the object of the Bantu Purity League as "to keep the girls pure in the right way." Killie Campbell Library, Durban, Oral Archive, KCAV 180.

47. LM to MP, 12 October 1949.

48. Matthews, pp. 17–18.

49. LPM to MP, 3 June 1951.

50. American Board Archives, Harvard, AB 15 April 1954, vol. 4, p. 17, Lavinia Scott (Inanda) to R. Emerson (secretary, ABM, Boston), 27 November 1940; and ibid., 14 November 1941.

51. Killie Campbell Library, MS ADA 1.07 Minutes of General Purposes Committee, Adams, 10 May 1946, p. 4. The seduction of African schoolgirls by their schoolmasters was common gossip in South African high schools in the 1940s and 1950s. Personal Communication, Professor John Blacking, Belfast, May 1985, and see the title story in Njabula Ndebele's *Fools and Other Stories* (Johannesburg: Ravan Press, 1984). Significantly, it is also among the list of grievances presented by the youth boycotting South Africa's schools at the present time (1985–87).

52. The extent of violence against African women is a relatively unremarked aspect of the South African social system. Apartheid breeds antisocial and criminal behavior, which manifests as drunkenness, robbery, assault, rape, and murder. All these forms of violence impinge directly on the lives of women. In 1983, over

15,000 rapes against African women were reported—the actual incidence was probably far higher. (In "Western" society it is estimated that only 2 percent of cases of rape are reported.)

53. W. Beinart and C. Bundy, "State Intervention and Rural Resistance: The Transkei, 1900–1965," in Martin A. Klein, ed., *Peasants in Africa* (London and Beverly Hills: Sage, 1980), pp. 271–315, discuss the nature of migrant labor from the Transkei at this time.

54. I am grateful to Rosalie Kingwill for finding the matriculation reports at St. John's College, Umtata, which show this statistic.

55. F. Cheek, "A Serendipitous Finding: Sex Role and Schizophrenia," *Journal of Abnormal and Social Psychology* 69, no. 4 (1964), cited in Phyllis Chesler, *Women and Madness* (New York: Avon Books, 1972), p. 52.

56. Chesler, pp. 52, 56. Italics in the original.

57. Ibid., pp. 51–52.

58. For a discussion of Lily's visits to the traditional doctors and the implications of their diagnosis, see the Epilogue to *"Not Either an Experimental Doll."*

59. As David Plante's recent account of Germaine Greer, Sonja Orwell, and Jean Rhys, entitled *Difficult Women: A Memoir of Three* (New York: Atheneum, 1983), suggests, it is a term that has been applied to many creative and intelligent women who assert themselves against their allotted "feminine" role.

60. The phrases are from the American Board Archives, Boston, AB 15.4 vol. 41, p. 656, M. Walbridge to M. Emerson, 20 June 1927, and "Miss Makanya in Boston," *Missionary Herald,* November 1927, p. 411.

61. H. Ngubane, *Body and Mind in Zulu Medicine* (London and New York: Academic Press, 1977), p. 149.

62. Ibid.

63. John Blacking suggested in conversation (Belfast, May 1985) that Lily may in fact have seen Sterkfontein as part of her "medical training" to be a diviner, in the same way as the schools were a means to the same end.

DISSONANCE AND HARMONY
The Symbolic Function of Abortion in Activists' Life Stories

Faye Ginsburg

I began to explore the idea for this research on female grassroots abortion activists in 1980, the year that Ronald Reagan was elected president. What role, I wondered, were women playing in the nation's rightward swing? Since women were most prominent as players in the right-to-life movement, I decided to focus on activists involved in the abortion issue.[1] In the 1980s, the abortion controversy has been most engaged and effective at the local level. For this reason, my work was designed to illuminate the lives of grassroots activists rather than leadership, both pro-choice and pro-life. I viewed local activists as cultural agents mediating between a social situation they inhabit in the present and a desired alternative future, a world they are envisioning and attempting to bring about through their abortion activism. I wanted to see how abortion is used as a symbol in the ways that committed activists interpret their behavior and beliefs to themselves and others as part of an ongoing narrative of their lives. My goal was to understand how this grassroots conflict shaped and was shaped by people's experiences of self, gender, family, community, and culture in a specific setting.

In order to understand the abortion controversy from "the actor's point of view," in the context of everyday life, my field research was set in one locale, Fargo, North Dakota, where the issue was of current interest at the time of my fieldwork from 1981 to 1983. I chose subjects who were most prominent in local activity at the time and who reflected, in my estimation, the range of diversity encompassed in the active memberships of both pro-life and pro-choice groups in terms of age, socioeconomic status, religious affiliation, household and marriage arrangements, style of activism, and the like. Altogether I collected twenty-one life stories from right-to-life activists and fourteen from pro-choice activists. While most of these people are still active, each side continues to undergo rapid permutations both locally and nationally. Thus, as is the case in all anthropological work, the benefits of in-depth, long-term participant-observation research must be balanced against the debits of a small sample bound by the conditions of a particular time and setting.

However, when working in a complex society on a well-researched topic, one can contextualize a small sample by placing it in more general frame-work. According to surveys, the people I worked with in Fargo are, so-ciologically, similar to grassroots abortion activists around the country. Both pro-life and pro-choice activists are primarily white, middle-class, and female; they do not divide neatly along ethnic, economic, occupational, or religious lines (Granberg 1981; Luker 1984). Ideologically, much of the agenda of either side could be interpreted, more generally, as part of an effort to reform the more dehumanizing aspects of contemporary Amer-ican culture. Despite their differences, most abortion activists share a cri-tique of what they see as increasing materialism and narcissism displacing nurturant ties of kin and community.

In the life stories of activists on both sides, activism is linked to the intersection of specific life transitions with particular cultural and historical moments, marked narratively as pivotal points that changed or reinforced the course of an assumed life trajectory. In using the term *life stories*, as opposed to *life histories*, I am stressing the narrative devices used by activists to frame their lives, not actual experience or behavior (if one can ever know that, especially regarding the past). In fact, what is striking about the narratives, even in this small and relatively homogeneous sample, is the diversity of these women's life courses. Despite this variety, the strategies used to create a coherent life story out of past experience are relatively consistent for each group. And for *all* the activists, confronting the abortion issue seems to figure both as a moment of coming to consciousness in relation to broader historical and cultural contexts, and as a framework that gives symbolic order to life transitions that had been experienced as disor-derly. In the life stories, the narrator shows how these events take on new meaning as the self is realigned in relation to some larger collective body and ideology, in this case one of the social movements involved in the abortion issue. Thus, members of each group lay claim to a particular view of American culture and the place of men and women in it, in a way that creates harmonious narrative out of the dissonant experiences of history, both personal and generational.

On the basis of my analysis of this particular case, I would suggest a more general model for exploring the dynamics between social action and self-constitution for women in American culture. When cultural definitions of the female life course are in dispute, activism is a critical mode women use to resolve felt dissonance between cultural codes and subjective experience. Narratives about individual transformations, cast as conversions in life stories, serve as models for envisioned changes in the social and cultural order that accommodate female activists' self-understandings.[2]

THE SETTING

Fargo, North Dakota,[3] is a small metropolitan center and crossroads providing commercial and service industries for the surrounding rural area. The residents of Fargo, numbering about 61,000, pride themselves on their clean air, their regular church attendance, their rich topsoil, and their actual and metaphorical distance from places like New York City. The orderly pace of Fargo's daily life was disrupted in the fall of 1981 when the Fargo Women's Health Center—the first free-standing facility in the state to publicly offer abortions—opened for business. A local pro-life coalition against the clinic formed immediately. Soon after, a pro-choice group emerged to respond to the antiabortion activities. By 1984, each group had stabilized at about one thousand supporters and a hard core of ten to twenty activists.

For the local pro-life movement, the availability of abortion in their own community represented the intrusion of secularism, narcissism, materialism and anomie. Pro-choice activists reacted to right-to-life protesters as the forces of narrow-minded intolerance who would deny women access to a choice that is seen as fundamental to women's freedom and ability to overcome sexual discrimination. Each asked for support by presenting itself as under attack, yet simultaneously claimed to represent the "true" interests of the community. An attachment to and pride in local sensibilities is voiced by women on both sides. The "community" has become a locus of interpretive struggle, expressed organizationally in the independence each group maintains from national and local affiliations.

In a setting such as Fargo, where there is a dense overlapping of social networks, the opposition cannot be encountered simply as the rhetorical "other." Opponents are well known to each other; their humanity cannot be denied but must be incorporated and transcended. This accounts in part for the paradoxical appearance of shared elements along with the expected differences between activists on both sides. By constructing an identity around an issue defined dialectically, the "other" is a critical counterpoint on whom one's own identity depends. I should point out here that it is the pro-choice activist and not the abortion-clinic client who constitutes the "other" for pro-lifers. In general, women getting abortions are seen as weak, ignorant, or victimized, and therefore potential converts. While neither position can exist without its real or imagined opposition, each is engaged, nonetheless, in a positive, culture-reconstructing agenda on its own terms.

In a situated contest such as that which occurred in Fargo, one can see more generally how abortion comes to signify conflicting social and personal identifications capable of mobilizing and polarizing people, realigning the distribution of power, resources, and sexual meanings. The local conflict thus illuminates larger cultural processes that set the context for the intense struggle over the interpretation of gender in contemporary American culture that is being played out in the abortion controversy.

LIFE STORIES: REPRODUCTION, GENERATION, AND THE FEMALE LIFE COURSE

To better understand this process, I asked activists in Fargo to work with me in clarifying the connections they saw between their sense of personal identity and their abortion activism. I worked with people whom I already knew well, in tape-recorded sessions lasting four to five hours. The result was a set of what I call life stories,[4] four segments of oral autobiographical narratives which focus on the symbolic aspects of social life and the meanings particular forms—in this case, abortion—assume for an individual. In the ways that the rhetoric and action of abortion activism are incorporated into life stories, one can see how cultural definitions of the female life course, and the social consequences implied, are selected, rejected, reordered, and reproduced in new form.

More generally, the narratives show how activism operates to mediate the construction of self with social, political, and cultural processes. Difficult reproductive events, shifts in household composition and kin arrangements, and tensions between the work of wage labor and mothering are prominent in the texts as sources of critical conflict at both the individual and collective levels. These transitions constitute life crises for these women at this moment in American history, I would argue, because of the dissonance between their experience of discontinuous changes in their own biographies and the available cultural models for marking them, both cognitively and socially. As increasing numbers of women are entering the wage-labor market and traditional marriage and familial arrangements seem to be in disarray, it is hardly surprising that the relationship of women to reproduction, and mothering in particular, is the object of tremendous logistical and interpretive struggle. Clearly, the contention over the proper shape of the female life course has a range of causes and effects, experienced differentially by women of different class, racial, ethnic, and sexual identities. For women reaching adulthood in the face of such cultural discord regarding women's lives in relation to the larger social order, at least some use activism on the abortion issue to lend order and meaning to their personal and historical experience.

THE "PROBLEM OF GENERATIONS"

Of the life stories I collected from abortion activists in Fargo, in almost all cases, pro-choice and pro-life alike, women described a coming to consciousness regarding abortion in relation to some critical realignment of personal and social identity, usually related to reproduction. Initially, this recognition seemed only to confound the problem of trying to explain the differences between the women on opposite sides of the issue. From accounts of their early histories, up to the age of eighteen or so, it would be hard to predict whether women would end up pro-choice or pro-life in their views. Working-class Catholics became ardent pro-choice activists; middle-class college-educated Protestants became staunch pro-lifers. As I puzzled over the seeming convergences in catalyzing experiences, social backgrounds, and even sentiments—most see themselves as working to-ward the reform of society as a whole—I began to consider a generational distinction.

The pro-choice activists cluster in a cohort born between 1945 and 1950. For the most part, these women had reached adulthood—which usually meant marriage and children—in the late 1960s and early 1970s. It was a moment when many began to question full-time motherhood as their assigned role; it was also a time when feminism and reproductive-rights activity were culturally ascendant. When these women sought new cognitive resources with which to understand and frame their experiences, feminism provided an analysis, a community of others, and a means for engaging in social change that legitimated their own dissonant experiences. Their life stories indicate that the social protests of the 1960s, including the second wave of feminism, were a central experience. Almost all describe their encounter with these movements as a kind of awakening or passage from a world defined by motherhood into one seen as filled with broader pos-sibilities.

The right-to-life women, on the other hand, cluster in two cohorts. Those born in the 1920s were most active in pro-life work in the early 1970s. A second cohort, the one currently most active, was born in the 1950s. Almost all the younger women had infants and/or children at home, had worked prior to having children, and left wage labor when they became mothers. For most, this transition occurred in the late 1970s or even more recently, a period when feminism was on the wane as an active social movement and pro-life and anti-ERA activity were on the rise. Many members of this latter group claim to have been or even to be feminist in many respects (on issues not directly related to sexuality, such as compara-ble worth). Many describe their commitment to the right-to-life movement as a kind of conversion; it occurs most frequently around the birth of a first or second child, when many women of this group decided to move out of the paid work force to stay home and raise children.

While the positions of women from each group differ on abortion and the connections drawn to it, they are all struggling to come to terms with problematic historical and life-cycle transitions.

In his classic essay "The Problem of Generations," Karl Mannheim un-derscores the importance of this nexus between the individual life cycle and rapidly changing historical conditions in understanding generational shifts in the formation of political consciousness and social movements (1952, p. 381). His model suggests that one must consider the intersection of two unfolding processes in order to understand what attracts women to oppos-ing movements in the abortion controversy. One is the trajectory of a woman's sexual and reproductive experiences over her life course and her interpretation of those events. The second is the historical moment shaping the culture when these key transitional points occur, what Mannheim calls "fresh contact." Thus, each generation has "a changed relationship" and a "novel approach" to the culture that ensures its continual reorganization. Such "fresh contact" is manifest in the self-definition and social actions of women engaged in the abortion controversy, some of whose life stories are analyzed below. The embracing of a pro-life or pro-choice position emerges narratively out of a confluence of reproductive and generational experiences. In the negotiation of critical moments in the female life course with an ever-shifting social environment, the contours of biographies and the larger cultural and historical landscape are measured, reformulated, and given new meaning.

NARRATIVE STRATEGIES: PROCREATION STORIES AS COUNTER-DISCOURSE

The point of the stories and my analysis of them is not to show that specific experiences *determine* whether or not an individual will become an activist. Rather, my interest is in the formal strategies activists use to structure and give meaning to the recounting of life stories that distinguish the women of each group. If these indeed reflect the efforts of social actors to constitute order and cultural transformations at "disjunctive" historical moments, then this activity must be apparent in concrete forms of symbolic action.

In their narratives, activists use the stories of their lives to construct a plot in which the social consequences of different definitions of the female life course in contemporary America are selected, rejected, reordered, and reproduced in new form. This plot/story distinction is based loosely on the framework developed by the Russian Formalist Viktor Shklovsky for analyzing narrative. He distinguished between the story *(fabula)*, i.e., the "raw" temporal-causal sequence of narrated events, and the plot *(szujet)*, i.e., the way in which these "raw materials" are formally manipulated in unconventional ways that make the audience reconsider the usual ordering of events. So, for example, for activists, the "story" is the expected arrangement of a woman's biography according to Western narrative and social conventions (birth, childhood, marriage, motherhood, etc.); the plot emerges from the unexpected twists in the narrative that draw attention to differences from the conventional story, thus "defamiliarizing" the taken-for-granted assumptions, for example, of a "typical" biography. Activists are aware of the tension between their own plot and the expected story and indicate that awareness by a variety of devices, often as simple as a prefatory comment such as "I guess I'm different because . . ." preceding an unconventional anecdote.

I found consistent patterns to the plot twists in the life stories of each group. A summary of the "plot line" that, in general, distinguishes the pro-choice and pro-life narratives should clarify the point. For pro-choice women, these are, typically, a differentiation of self from family in early life; a questioning of the confines of motherhood, usually after first birth; a "conversion" brought about by contact with feminism and other social movements of the 1960s and 1970s; and a subsequent reframing of understandings of self, women's interests, and ideals of nurturance in terms of the broader domain we call "the public" through their activism on the abortion issue.

For the younger pro-life activists who were the key players at the time I was in the field, the plot takes shape as an "awakening" to pro-life activism from what they would consider a feminist position, usually after having left the work force to have a baby. Unlike the pro-choice women, these activists came of age in a world reframed by the second wave of feminism, the existence of legal abortion, and at least a surface acceptance of women's working. The key twist lies in the construction of nurturance as an *achievement*. Their stories of pregnancy, birth, and mothering are told not as a matter of course but as dramas of overcoming hardship and doubt. This plot exists in complex tension with changing understandings of the "proper" female biography in America. On the one hand, it subverts the conventional story of reproduction as "natural" to women's lives. On the other hand, it reasserts the primacy of reproduction and mothering for women's identity and authority, but it does so on the grounds that female nurturance offers an alternative model and powerful critique of increasingly materialistic and individualistic trends in American culture.

In analyzing activists' life stories, one sees how narrators' verbal and self-conscious understanding of their society develops out of their own historical experiences as social actors and also inflects the way they communicate this knowledge—what Giddens would call the "discursive penetration" of "practical consciousness" (1979, p. 5). However, the narratives are more than simply discursive knowledge. In them, activists reframe experiences they originally felt were dissonant with social expectations by constituting them as new cultural possibilities. Their plots articulate a kind of "counter-discourse"[5] which has "the capacity to *situate:* to relativize the authority and stability of a dominant system" (Terdiman 1985, p. 16), in this case, presumed models of the female life course in America. The tension between plot and story in the narratives shows how their knowledge of the culture is embedded in critiques of it that are drawn from the practices and problems of everyday life (Marcus 1986).[6]

For almost all of the activists, reproduction is central to these critiques at a number of levels. In their constructions, reproduction is a key turning point, not as a biological occurrence but as a class of life-cycle events that forced an encounter with the inequalities of a gendered social world. These encounters, as told in the stories, led the women to reconsider their relationship to and understanding of their assigned place in society. Once these women were catalyzed, their activism took discursive shape as a concern not only with the place of procreation in women's lives but with the reproduction of the culture as a whole. Whether pro-life or pro-choice, activists express their motivation for social action as a desire to alter the meaning and circumstances of procreation in order to make conditions better for the next generation. In other words, they are concerned, as female activists, with their role in reproducing the culture, but in terms different from the present. Because procreation in American culture is so deeply connected to asymmetrical understandings of male and female, any question raised about it is, necessarily, also one about gender identity and cultural reproduction.

In their stories, then, speakers from each side use the abortion issue as a plot element connecting different but interrelated understandings of gender, sexuality, and reproduction. Abortion activism consistently provides a central narrative turning point in the life course of activists, confirming or changing their subjective relationship to their own past and future. In this narrative refiguring, activists create alternative "life scripts" to what they consider to be a conventional form for a female life trajectory. The disjunctive transitions accommodated in their plots illuminate sources of dissonance between cultural codes, social process, and individual transformation. As a counter-discourse, they take on particular power now, a historical moment when there is no clear hegemonic model for the shape of the female life course in America.

When the definitions of a particular life event—such as pregnancy or abortion—become the object of a contentious political struggle, it reveals a larger disruption occurring in the social order as well. In the narratives I collected, *every* plot rests on some sense of tension between domesticity and the workplace. Responsibilities of women in relationship to nurturance are the salient issue and contradiction for women on both sides of the debate.

As is the case for *all* the activists, a tension between their participation in domestic and public domains is prominent. The pro-choice women, however, stress the latter domain. While nurturance, caring, and communal concern are presented as natural to women, emerging from female domestic activities, they are seen as values to be carried *outside* that domestic domain and into a more broadly defined social arena. In this way, the separation between motherhood and the workplace and their culturally assigned attributes is blurred or violated. The narratives suggest that it is this question of the moral authority of nurturance attributed to domesticity, and its relationship to both female identity and action, that is critical to understanding the nature and larger significance of the contemporary abortion controversy for American history and culture.

THE PRO-CHOICE NARRATIVES

The majority of women activists who organized the pro-choice efforts to defend the Fargo abortion clinic represent a range of backgrounds in terms of their natal families. While their current household, conjugal, and work arrangements differ, for almost all, the strong commitment to pro-choice activism in particular was connected to specific life-cycle events, generally having to do with experiences and choices around sexuality, pregnancy, and childbearing, including the choice not to have children. In the pro-choice narratives, certain themes emerged consistently in the plots. In almost every case, the speaker's recounting of her birth or childhood stressed her difference and independence from others in her family or her social milieu early in life. Similarly, the speaker's encounter with the protest movements of the late 1960s and early 1970s is told as a key transformative event, a second moment of differentiation from either natal family or local community. In all the pro-choice plots, contact with the feminist movement is central, an event that turned each one toward activism, a new social identity, and a particular understanding of the culture and her place in it. In most cases, that encounter is tied into what one might loosely call a transition to adult female identity—often a story of an abortion, pregnancy, or birth. This not only is apparent to the analyst but also is clearly framed as a transformative element by the pro-choice narrators.

The central figure of the current controversy in Fargo is Kay Bellevue, the woman who opened the abortion clinic in 1981. Kay grew up in the Midwest, the oldest of seven children. Her father was a Baptist minister; her mother was a homemaker and part-time worker in the public school system. As is the case for many of the pro-choice activists, Kay began her narrative with the biographical "reasons" that, in her view, made her different. The plot begins with this early sense of differentiation, the source of identification with a key family member who served as a model for what she sees as her later oppositional stance toward the culture:

> I always perceived myself as different from other kids. As a preacher's kid, whether it was true or not, I always felt people expected me to be perfect and to behave in a ladylike manner. . . . My dad was always interested in what was going on politically and took a keen interest in the antiwar movement and rights for blacks. I was the apple of his eye, and he's always been proud of the things I've done. My dad's a real independent person, and I see a lot of that in me.

In her senior year of college, Kay got pregnant and married, and soon after she moved to Denver, where her husband was pursuing graduate studies in English. Like almost *all* of the women activists, regardless of their position on abortion, Kay's transition to motherhood was an event surrounded by ambivalence. Although her behavior was not in fact that different from that of many right-to-life women—i.e., as a young mother she worked part-time and became involved in community associations—Kay's *interpretation* of her actions stresses the limitations of motherhood. Her plot turns on her unexpected reaction to her assigned and chosen role as mother.

> I enjoyed being home, but I could never stay home all the time. I have never done that in my life. After being home one year and taking care of a kid, I felt my mind was a wasteland. And we were so poor we could almost never go out together.

By contrast, pro-life women faced with the same dilemma emphasize the drawbacks of the workplace. Not surprisingly, for both groups of women, voluntary work for a "cause" was an acceptable and satisfying way of managing to balance the pleasures and duties of motherhood with the structural isolation of that work as it is organized in America. For example, La Leche League, an international organization promoting breastfeeding and natural childbirth, is a group where one stands an equal chance of running into a pro-life or pro-choice woman. In her early twenties, Kay became active in a local chapter of La Leche League. In Kay's case, she met a woman who introduced her to feminism, a critical twist in the plot that sets it in tension with the "story." She marks this as a key event.

> I met someone who said, "You should come to a La Leche League meeting with me because one of their sessions is on prepared childbirth, and after your experience, you might appreciate hearing what they're talking about." My first child had not been a pleasant birth experience, so I went and I was really intrigued. There were people talking about this childbirth experience like it was the most fantastic thing you'd ever been through. I certainly didn't feel that way. I had a very long labor. I screamed, I moaned. . . . My husband thought I was dying. So anyway, this group introduced me to a whole different conception of childbirth, and my second experience was so different I couldn't believe it.

Kay's growing sense of consciousness concerning the way women's reproductive needs were mishandled by the medical profession crystallized during her third pregnancy.

> The way I came to feminism was that through all of this, I became acutely aware of how little physicians who were supposed to be doctors for women actually knew about women's bodies. So I became a real advocate for women to stand up for their rights, starting with breastfeeding.

The concerns she gives voice to are not so different from those articulated by her neighbors and fellow citizens who so vehemently oppose her work. In 1972, Kay moved to Fargo because of her husband's job. She joined and continued as a leader in La Leche and got pregnant again. Kay marks this period as one of crisis. Her parents were divorcing, and one of her children was having problems.

> Then I ended up having an abortion myself. My youngest was eighteen months old, and I accidentally got pregnant. We had four small kids at the time, and we decided if we were going to make it a family unit, we had all the stress we could tolerate if we were going to survive.

In her more public role, as in the case of her personal decisions regarding abortion, Kay always linked her activism to a strong commitment to ethical principles and strong family ties.

> I have always acted on what to me are Judeo-Christian principles. The Ten Commandments plus "Love thy neighbor." I was raised by my family to have a very, very strong sense of ethics, and it's still with me.

> I think it's easy for them to stereotype us as having values very different than theirs, and that's not the case at all. Many of the people who get abortions have values very similar to the antiabortion people. The right-to-life people don't know how deeply I care for my own family and how involved I am, since I have four children and spent the early years of my life working for a breastfeeding organization.

Most of Kay's fellow activists shared her resentment of right-to-lifers, labeling them as "anti-family." This sensitivity may account for the fact that Fargo's pro-choice women stressed repeatedly the connections they saw between abortion rights and a larger defense of the cultural values associated with nurturance which, in their view, women represent.

> It's important that we remember our place, that we remember we are the caregivers, that we remember that nurturing is important, that we maintain the value system that has been given to us and that has resided in us, and that we bring it with us into that new structure. . . . It's important that we bring to that world the recognition that eighty-hour weeks aren't healthy for anyone—that children suffer if they miss relationships with their fathers and that fathers suffer from missing relationships with their children. . . . This society has got to begin recognizing its responsibility for caring for its children.

These words are those of Janice Sundstrom, a peer of Kay. Janice grew up in a Catholic family of seven children that struggled in the shadow of poverty when they lost their farm through foreclosure in the early 1950s. Like many of the activists both for and against abortion, Janice traces the roots of her current commitment to early biographical moments. The pro-choice narratives, however, are distinguished by the way the speakers emphasize their differentiation from rather than integration with their childhood milieu. Like Kay's, Janice's plot begins with her unusual role in her family, to which she attributes her iconoclasm in later life.

> In 1945, shortly after I was born, my mom and dad moved here and brought me along and left all the other children with them with relations back in Illinois. I think I'm different from the rest of them because I had the experience of being the only child at a time when they had far too many children to deal with. . . .

The transformations Janice eventually experienced are cast, in her plot, as almost predictable. However, they hardly seem the inevitable outcome of her youth and adolescence: twelve years in parochial school and marriage to her high-school sweetheart a year after graduation, followed immediately by two pregnancies.

> We were both nineteen then, and I didn't want to have another child. We were both in school and working, and there we were with this kid. But I didn't have any choice. There was no option for me about birth control because I was still strongly committed to the church's teaching. And then, three months later, I was pregnant again. After Jodie was born I started taking pills, and that's what ended the church for me.

For Janice, her encounters with reproduction and contraception that made her question her church are key events in her plot. They are central, pivotal moments in her life, which turned her toward alternative cultural models. In this way, her interpretation of her experiences resembles the way that pregnancy, a conversion or return to organized religion, and pro-life activism are linked in right-to-life narratives.

Janice considers her contact with the social movements of the late 1960s as catalytic. With her sister's encouragement, Janice became involved in politics, worked on McCarthy's presidential campaign, and was on the state delegation to the Democratic Convention in Chicago in 1968. She began working as a teacher and continued her political work as well, and was introduced to feminism by friends who by 1970 were identifying with the woman's movement "and opened it to me and me to it, as the case may be. I learned real fast, and basically it seemed the lesson was that through law I could help effect change for women, so I decided to go to law school and worked to save for that."

> Up to that time, I felt very strongly about abortion, as my church had taught me to think, and somehow between 1968 and 1971—those years were crucial to the political development of a lot of people in my genera- tion—I came to have different feelings about abortion. My feeling toward abortion grew out of my personal experiences with friends who had abortions and a sensitivity to the place of women in this society. It was a recognition that this basic medical service called for by women by the tens

of thousands was not available for them and that restriction worked its most severe burden on poor women.

For Janice, her abortion activism frames a transformation in self-understanding as she came to identify her own situation with the collective needs and interests of women as she understands them. Janice is now a mother of two grown children, married to a white-collar professional, herself a lawyer and political activist, and her dreams for her college-age daughters are prominent for her at this point in her life. She hopes that, unlike her, they will postpone marriage and prepare themselves for fulfilling work before they have family obligations. These concerns are linked to her pro-choice activities.

> It seems to me it's restrictions on abortion coupled with a failure of sex education and a general social milieu that points to sexual activity as some means of personal fulfillment, whatever else it is supposed to mean to children, that leads to the increased rate of unwed parenthood among young women.

Several pro-choice women referred to this constellation of concerns as "midwestern feminism." When I asked what they meant by the term, one woman described it in the following way:

> It's a sense of connectedness, a valuing of life, kindness, and gentleness and all the qualities that I think are important in human beings.

Another was more concrete:

> Well, it's why I don't really even read *Ms.* magazine anymore. It just doesn't talk about my life or other women in Fargo. You know, we still have potlucks here. We're worried about our community, raising decent kids, our marriages, getting old with or without a man. These are basic priorities that we all have to work together on.

What is striking in the connections these pro-choice activists make between their position and female gender identity is the similarity of their concerns to those of their opponents. Like many pro-life women, they are disturbed by cultural currents that promote, in their view, narcissistic attitudes toward sexuality and personal fulfillment in which the individual denies any responsibility to kin, community, and the larger social order.

SUMMARY: PRO-CHOICE NARRATIVES

In the plots of their life stories, pro-choice activists stress their work and activities outside the home over motherhood, but always in terms of the values of caretaking that are identified with motherhood and domesticity. Thus, their defense of abortion rights is linked to a larger goal of (re)producing on a larger social scale what they would call female cultural values and what I am calling nurturance. This is apparent in the way their life stories uphold nurturance as a valued quality that is considered natural to women as well as the basis of their cultural authority; they reject it as an attribute that might confine them to childbearing, caretaking, and domesticity.

For the Fargo pro-choice activists, their marking of their own ideology as "midwestern feminism" specifies both the regional and temporal location of these women, yet also gives a particular utopian subtext to their stories. It emerges narratively in the repeated insistence that their activism is not for personal gain or individual indulgence but serves the interests of women and social justice. In this way, nurturance takes on a broad definition: though it is viewed as rooted in particular female experience, it is seen as a guide to action and a goal for social change in general. In other words, nurturance is understood as an oppositional stance to a world that is viewed as materialistic, male-defined, and lacking in compassion.

This negotiation of a pro-choice position that establishes activists' connections to family and community, as they understand them, is prominent for pro-choice women both in their narratives and in the public performance of their activism. It is emblematic of a broader agenda for improving the conditions of women's lives in a less than perfect world. However, for most, the enactment of these goals was dispersed over a range of other activities. This distinguishes them from pro-lifers and may be due, in part, to the fact that the pro-choice position is, at least legally, the status quo. In both their self-definition and social action, then, these women are attempting to transform the cultural meaning and social organization of human reproduction and dependency, so that they are not confined to arenas defined as female but are viewed as conditions to be met collectively.

Their narratives and action stress a stated and actual preference for nonhierarchical relationships and group organization; they insist that their activism is not for personal glory, financial gain, or individual indulgence but is in the interests of women and social justice. The utopian subtext of their stance is rooted in their historical encounter with feminism. It is expressed as a desire to create a world more hospitable to the qualities and tasks they, as feminists, identify as female: the reproduction of nurturant, compassionate, or at least tolerant relationships between friends, family, members of the community, people in the workplace, and even the nation as a whole.

THE PRO-LIFE NARRATIVES

Like the pro-choice life stories, the pro-life narratives reveal how these activists are continually reworking ideologies[7] about the place of women in

American culture so that they are contextualized in their historically specific experiences of everyday life. However, for many pro-life activists who came of age in the 1970s and left the work force to have children, this encounter with feminism is worked into the plot as a misguided identity they have transcended. This sort of generational shift in interpretations of female experience is a reminder of Mannheim's idea of "fresh contact," which stresses the temporal elements—both life cycle and historical—which affect political consciousness. This shift also shows how the controversy develops as a dialectic in time; the plots of pro-life procreation stories address and attempt to incorporate historically prior pro-choice positions.

Sally Nordsen is part of a cohort of women born between 1952 and 1958 who formed the majority and were the most dedicated right-to-life activists mobilized around the initial opening of the clinic. Like most of the other pro-life women of this group, Sally went to college, married soon after her graduation, then worked for seven years as a social worker. In her late twenties, she got pregnant and decided to leave her job as a social worker in order to raise her children. The birth of her first child is narrated as a radical life revision from wage labor to motherhood. This is a critical element in her plot, a difficult passage. While she regards the choice as a positive one, it was nonetheless marked by ambivalence.

> I had two days left of work before my resignation was official, but Dick was born earlier than expected. So I left the work on my desk and never went back to it. There were so many things that were abrupt. When I went into the hospital it was raining, and when I came out it was snowing. A change of seasons, a change of work habits, a new baby in my life. It was hard. I was so anxious to get home and show this baby off. And when I walked in the door, it was like the weight of the world, and I thought, "What am I going to do with him now?" Well, these fears faded.
>
> So it was a change. When Ken would come home, I would practically meet him at the door with my coat and purse 'cause I wanted to get out of there. I couldn't stand it, you know. And that's still the case sometimes. But the joys outweigh the desire to go back to work.

Sally explained how she became "converted" to the right-to-life cause shortly after the birth of her first child. A reevaluation of the meaning of her continuing belief in "women's rights" and "freedom" is critical to this twist of her plot.

> When the abortion chamber came to town, it just hit me that I was responsible for this. I was walking in front of the clinic, and all of a sudden, many things just came crashing down, you might say, about my attitudes and values and things. . . . And some of these things I equated with being a free woman were not necessarily good and did not necessarily have to do with freedom. Women's rights were important to me. But sometimes I acted as if I was downtrodden. I have a husband who respects me com-

pletely, who shares in the work around the house. I have no reason to complain. I didn't live in a home where I was belittled for being female.

I go around acting like I had to be the champion for women's rights. But I honestly have a hard time with some of the screaming that goes on because some of those women also feel that abortion is one of those rights, and they call it reproductive freedom. To me, yes, it is your freedom to choose to reproduce or not to reproduce. But once that's done, you've already made that choice. So when those things get lumped together with women's rights, like equal pay, I get really upset. There are some things, such as abortion, that can actually be destructive to other people. If we are so right, let's not repeat the same mistakes that other people have made. Let's not repeat the mistakes that men have been making.

For Sally and the other pro-life activists her age, the move from wage labor to motherhood occurred in the late 1970s or more recently. This critical moment in their life histories intersected a paradoxical moment for American feminism. Much of what the prior cohort of feminist activists of the 1960s and 1970s had struggled for appeared to have been achieved. Fargo, for example, by 1979 had an excellent rape-and-abuse center, a women's studies curriculum at the university, two daycare centers for low-income women, several gay and lesbian groups, and a women's health hotline, and by 1981 had an abortion clinic. For many of the younger women, the institutions that feminists had struggled to establish over the last decade were now taken for granted. Feminism was identified, more often than not, with its distorted reconstruction in the popular media, in the image of the young, single, upwardly mobile corporate woman. Women like Sally, who have decided to leave the work force for a "reproductive phase" of their life cycle, are keenly aware of the disjunction of their choice with the images that surround them.

Sally's colleague Roberta makes the case succinctly. Married to an auto mechanic, Roberta worked as a college teacher and a graphic designer before she gave birth to her first child. She is now a full-time homemaker, raising her two girls, and is active in the pro-life movement as well as democratic politics.

> They paint the job world as so glamorous, as if women are all in executive positions. But really, what is the average woman doing? Mostly office work, secretarial stuff. Even teaching gets routine after a while. When you watch TV, there aren't women being pictured working at grocery store check-outs.
>
> I just don't see homemaking as any worse than eight to five. I really like homemaking. It's something I've chosen. I can, I bake, I garden, I sew; I see it as an art. I don't say everyone should do it that way. And my husband likes to do it, too. People should be able to do what they like to do. That's the part of the women's movement I've really been in favor of.

This is not simply a defense of homemaking as a choice of vocation. It is a recognition of the social and economic consequences of having made a decision that she senses is an unpopular one. The choices Roberta has made represent a critique of what she considers to be the dominant culture. It is important to remember that the pro-choice women only ten years Roberta's senior felt that their decision to do the opposite, leave motherhood for the work force, was similarly controversial. What this indicates is how rapidly the definition of "normal female behavior" has changed. For example, Roberta sees in the lack of recognition for domestic work an extension of a more pervasive condition, the increasing commercialization of human relations, especially those involving dependents.

> You know, the picture painted these days is how much kids cost. These are the reasons given for most abortions. How much work kids are, how much they can change your lifestyle, how they interrupt the timing of your goals. What is ten years out of a seventy-year life span? You know, I've done a lot of volunteer work in nursing homes, and it's just a lonely world to see women who don't have families. . . . If you don't have your family, if you don't have your values, then what's money, you know?

In her view, legal abortion represents the loss of a locus of unconditional nurturance in the social order; in concrete terms, the threat is constituted in the public endorsement of sexuality disengaged from motherhood. In the right-to-life perspective, this situation serves to weaken social pressure on men to take responsibility for the reproductive consequences of intercourse.

A similar theme emerges in Sally's narrative. Sally's developing plot indicates the hidden toll of feminism's rapid successes. In her narrative, she progressively differentiates herself from feminist rhetoric that was so powerful ten years earlier yet, did not reflect her experience in the late 1970s.

> I think men can get away with certain things that women can't, like infidelity, and I don't want to count that in my package of rights. To me sexual freedom is a loving relationship with one person. It came to me at that prayer vigil that all these things follow in a chain. There are consequences we're not ready for, and that plays a big part in legalized abortion. And really, the other way I was living, I was really bored. I just wanted more and more and more.

These pro-life activists' plots stress the negative consequences for women of the dismantling of a system which links male sexuality to childrearing and marriage. Sally draws on her experiences as a social worker as evidence that abortion undercuts women's ability to gain the support of a man.

> In my work, I saw a lot of people who were part of the middle class, and then because of a divorce or having a child out of wedlock, they became

part of the welfare system. I saw how really necessary, how many reasons there were to really maintain that relationship. There's a very real world out there. I feel sorry for men that they can't have the same feelings I do about pregnancy. But in the situation of a woman, where all of a sudden after twenty years of a marriage she has nothing, and he at least has a business or a job or whatever . . . women just have a different kind of investment in the marriage situation.

Right-to-life women such as Sally and Roberta are well aware of the fragility of traditional marriage arrangements and recognize as well the lack of other social forms that might ensure the emotional and material support of women with children or other dependents. Nonetheless, the movement continues to be stereotyped as wholly reactionary, an eddy flowing from the cultural backwaters. Almost all of the Fargo pro-life activists were aware of these stereotypes and addressed them in a dialectical fashion, using them to confirm their own position. Roberta, for example, expressed it in the following way:

If you take the pro-life stand, you're labeled as being against anything else that women stand for. And ironically, it's mostly women in our movement. The pro-choice people say about us, "Well, they must have feelings, but they're so put down they can't make up their own minds, you know." And they think we're just saying what we do because that's what men have taught us. Well, if the men have taught us, why aren't the men helping us?

The women I have been talking to are strong and independent, hardly weak women, homemakers by choice because they value that. They support equal pay for equal work. I know about that because I sued the company I worked for and won. . . . No, we aren't quiet. You know, we couldn't have a movement if we were all the way we're stereotyped.

There a lot of pro-life people who choose to stay at home with their children like me. A secondary income is not that important to us. My income would be pretty darn good if I took off for the work force again. My husband alone can support us, but we have to pinch and budget, and so we don't go to the fundraisers. And now that my husband and I have become evangelicals, we don't really believe in drinking for the sake of drinking. So we're severely criticized for that. Anyway, to completely exclude us for that one reason, being pro-life, just blows my mind.

Roberta's growing religious commitment reflected a similar process, and one that was typical of at least some of her cohort as well. Seen in the diachronic perspective of a life history, the relationship between religiosity and right-to-life activism is not a simple case of cause and effect, with religious faith a prior condition for pro-life belief, as Roberta's case makes clear. She had not been particularly interested in religion most of her life and had been attending a mainstream Lutheran church in Fargo, more for social reasons than out of spiritual conviction. Like Sally, her "conversion" to born-again Christianity and the right-to-life cause emerged more or less simultaneously.

In choosing to leave the work force, Roberta knew she would be greatly reducing the disposable income for her household. The economic consequences of her ideological choice, then, have restricted the activities in which she and her husband can participate. In moving to an evangelical Lutheran congregation, they have found a setting and a group of people whose values are consistent with those they have been gradually formulating over the last few years.

For the most recent wave of right-to-life activists in particular, the pro-life movement speaks to their concerns. Through it, their own dilemmas are framed as a noble struggle to reform the culture in the interests of women. The right-to-life cause legitimates their dissonant experiences as women, as mothers, and as political activists. As Roberta explained to me while I cleared my tape recorder from her kitchen table to make room for freshly baked bread:

> The image that's presented of us as having a lot of kids hanging around, and that's all you do at home and you don't get anything else done, that's really untrue. In fact, when we do mailings here, my little one stands between my legs, and I use her tongue as a sponge. She loves it, and that's the heart of grassroots involvement. That's the bottom. That's the stuff and the substance that makes it all worth it. Kids are what it boils down to. My husband and I really prize them; they are our future, and that is what we feel is the root of the whole pro-life thing.

SUMMARY: THE PRO-LIFE NARRATIVES

The collective portrait that emerges from these stories, then, is much more complex than the stereotypes that portray right-to-life women as housewives and mothers passed by in the sweep of social change. They are astute, alert to social and political developments, and on many issues not antifeminist. They approve of and endorse women's seeking political power. Most held or had held jobs, some had careers, and a few, such as Roberta, had even brought comparable-worth suits against former employers. The marriage relationships I observed were generally equitable; husbands helped out regularly in domestic duties and were pragmatically and emotionally supportive of their wives' political work.

What is striking in the narratives is how most of these women had assimilated some version of feminist thought and woven it into their life choices. The plot of almost every story hinges on how the narrator either repudiated or reorganized these ideas into a right-to-life framework. Sally's narrative of how her ideas have changed as she became active in the pro-life movement is illustrative.

You're looking at somebody who used to think the opposite. I used to think that sex outside of marriage was fine. Now I see I don't believe that anymore. I believe when you practice sex outside of marriage you are taking all kinds of chances, including walking out on each other and not having to accept the responsibility of children or whatever. And to me, once you engage in the act of sex, it's a big emotional commitment. If my boyfriend walked out on me I would be devastated. I think the world preaches you can have it all . . . doing lots of things without getting caught, and I guess over the last few years, I've really changed my mind about a lot of things.

And when I see the abortion clinic, there's proof positive to me that my values are right and an innocent human being is paying the price for all this.

I think there was part of me that never fully agreed. It wasn't a complete turnaround. It was kind of like inside you know it's not right, but you make yourself think it's OK.

It is this negotiation of feminism into their life stories that distinguishes these younger right-to-life women in particular. Rather than simply defining themselves in opposition to what they understand feminist ideology and practice to be, many claim to have held that position, and to have transcended it. What they consider feminism to be is another issue. The point here is that *they* assert the prior alliance. Sally, for example, describes her former "liberated" ideas about sexuality as a repression of her true self. Her "conversion" to the pro-life position often follows a first birth or pregnancy; this becomes the basis, in the plot, for a reexamination of the previously held position. Thus, they narratively subsume their opponent's ideology into their own and thereby claim authority over it. The essence of this stance is captured in political rhetoric as well. For example, the title of a pro-life lecture popular in Fargo in 1984 was "I Was a Pro-choice Feminist, but Now I'm Pro-life."

It is not that they discovered an ideology that "fit" what they had always been. Their sense of identification evolves in the very process of voicing their views against abortion. In the regular performance of their activism, they are, simultaneously, transforming themselves and their community, projecting their vision of the culture into the future, both pragmatically and symbolically. Much the same way that pro-choice women embraced feminism, this younger cohort of right-to-life women find in their movement a particular symbolic frame that integrates their experience of work, reproduction, and marriage with shifting ideas of gender and politics that they encounter around them.

CONCLUSION

Through the prism of these activists' life stories, one can see in the abortion controversy of the 1980s the most recent manifestation of an ongoing cultural process in which struggles over the material, political, and symbolic definitions of gender are intertwined, dramatized, coded, and continually transformed. The signification attached to abortion provides each side with different but interrelated paradigms for reconstituting and claiming a possible vision of being female that meshes with their historical and biographical experiences. Activists, as narrators of their life stories, create symbolic control over discontinuous transitions in the female life cycle that, for larger reasons, are particularly problematic for specific cohorts in ways that mark them as "generations" in Mannheim's sense. Their current activism serves as a link that allows them to not only reframe their past lives but also project into the future a potential vision of the place of their own and other women's lives in the social order.

In their narratives, abortion activism not only provides plot elements that make sense out of "disorderly" life transitions and extends a newly articulated sense of self in both space and time. It is significant that they also provide narrators a means of symbolically controlling their opposition. The narratives show how activists, in constructing an identity around an issue defined dialectically, require the "other" in order to exist. Moreover, to ignore their enemies' humanity violates a central value of concern for others, both sides claim. This is what gives these stories their dialectical quality; in them the two sides are, by definition, addressing the other, and in so doing, incorporating them into their own identity. Thus, in these stories, a level of dialogue which underscores the *common* elements between opponents can be heard.[8]

While their solutions differ, both sides share the goal of transforming a society that no longer values or rewards those who care for dependents. The plots constructed by women on each side suggest different interpretations of the place of procreation in women's lives, and the place of women in reproducing the culture. Grassroots pro-life and pro-choice women alike envision their work as an effort to enhance rather than diminish women's position in a cultural system in which motherhood and wage labor are continually placed in competition. All American women are faced with this contradiction. However, in the abortion debate, two interpretations of this situation are cast in opposition, masking their common roots in and circumventing effective resistance to the problematic conditions engendered by this central conflict for women in America. In this sense, there is a tragic dimension to the polarization around the abortion issue.

At the practical level of daily life—the place where an ethnographer's project must begin and return—the dilemmas shared by pro-life and pro-choice activists are apparent, on occasion, to the actors themselves. However, the differences are what get played out politically. Despite shared concerns, as the abortion debate increasingly is embedded in conflicting narrative models of the female life course, the possibility of mutual recognition seems to decrease. The assertions of both pro-life and pro-choice advocates that they represent the *real* interests of all women give the overt public controversy over abortion, such as that played out over the Fargo clinic, the quality of irreconcilable conflict. Each version of the truth—spun from the uneven threads of everyday life and woven into life stories that give shape to the experiences of different generations—is both compelling and conclusive, yet intolerant of other possibilities.

Notes

Another version of this paper was written for the conference on Autobiographies, Biographies, and Life Histories of Women: Interdisciplinary Perspectives, University of Minnesota, May 23, 1986. I am grateful to the Personal Narratives editors for their helpful editorial comments on this work. I also want to thank Fred Myers, Susan Harding, Rayna Rapp, and Connie Sutton for their insights and encouragement. A similar version of this paper, "Procreation Stories: Reproduction, Nurturance, and Generation Life Stories of Abortion Activists," was published in *American Ethnologist* 14, no. 4 (November 1987).

I carried out research in Fargo during 1981–82 as a producer for WCCO-TV Minneapolis, for a documentary on the clinic conflict, "Prairie Storm," broadcast in 1982. I would like to thank Joan Arnow, the George Gund Foundation, Michael Meyer, and the Money for Women Fund for their financial assistance; and Jan Olsen, Greg Pratt, and Mike Sullivan, with whom I worked on that project. I returned for another eight months of participant-observation fieldwork in 1983. For their support of research and write-up, I am grateful to the American Association of University Women, the Charlotte Newcombe Dissertation Fellowship for Studies in Ethics and Values, Sigma Xi, and the David Spitz Distinguished Dissertation Award of City University of New York.

1. As I initially read the journalistic and scholarly works coming out on the New Right, I became even more curious. With the exception of a few (Fitzgerald 1981; Gordon and Hunter 1977–78; Harding 1981), most who wrote on the topic, it seemed, were either intent on uncovering a conspiracy, or focused exclusively on the political organization and leadership of a few well-known groups and leaders—Phyllis Schlafly and the Stop ERA movement, Jerry Falwell and the Moral Majority, Richard Viguerie and the National Conservative Political Action Committee (NCPAC). Generally, local-level activists are assumed in these writings to be rather ignorant people, at the mercy of the "forces of modernity," pawns of organized religion and conservative politicians (e.g., Crawford 1980; Merton 1981). Since then, several studies more oriented toward the grassroots viewpoint have come out, such as Connie Paige's *The Right-to-Lifers* (1983), Kristin Luker's *The Politics of Motherhood* (1984), and more recently, Rebecca Klatch's book *Women and the New Right* (1987).

Because the right-to-life movement seemed to challenge simplistic explanations, it became the initial and enduring focus for my research. I discovered that contrary to popular stereotypes, pro-life activists are generally well informed, alert to and involved in much of what is considered to be mainstream culture and politics. Many are educated professionals who have the resources and privileges that come with such positions. The organization of the movement deemphasizes hierarchy; it is extremely and purposefully decentralized. The largest and most representative umbrella group, the National Right to Life Committee (NRLC), claims over ten million members in three thousand chapters across the country. In addition, there are innumerable local groups such as the one I studied that form in response to specific community developments.

The movement should be distinguished from the New Right in other respects as well. The mainstream right-to-life movement has, for the most part, resisted efforts of New Right leaders to claim the abortion issue as their own and to coopt existing groups. Such alliances are seen as potentially dangerous to the single-issue organizing style and philosophy that characterize the pro-life movement. In addition, the political conservatism and laissez faire capitalism that constitute the New Right program are not central to, and often are at odds with, the mainstream right-to-life agenda. This movement, like many other single-issue groups, encompasses people holding a broad range of ideological positions, from radical pacifism—Pro-lifers for Survival, an antinuke group, for example—to liberal Catholics and Protestants, to fundamentalist Christians.

2. Anthropologist David Mandelbaum's analysis of the life history of the paradigmatic social activist of this century, Mahatma Gandhi, is a model of such an approach. He uses Gandhi's life course to understand

> the effective interplay and real relations in the course of which actors may alter the roles, change the nature of the choices, and shift the cultural definitions. So the cultural expectations for a life course may be revised in the midcourse of actual lives . . . in acts of personal choice and the common ways of working out the recurrent conflicts of life. Some of these regularities are recognized by the participants, others are not. (Mandelbaum 1973, p. 180)

This orientation, similar to that used by Sidney Mintz in *Worker in the Cane,* or Vincent Crapanzano in *Tuhami,* in which the agency of the actor is prominent, provides the framework I use in interpreting the narratives of abortion activists in relation to the social movement which engages them.

3. Like Muncie, Indiana, described in the classic *Middletown* studies (Lynd and Lynd), Fargo is small enough to provide a coherent social universe, yet sufficiently large and diverse to encompass farmers and professionals, a working class, and a university community; Catholics, Lutherans, Evangelicals, a small Jewish population, and some Native Americans. While many people in Fargo view themselves as politically conservative, they also value a tradition of populism and defense of individual rights. The recent discovery of oil in the area, the use of the state as a nuclear missile base, and the legalization of gambling have all brought new wealth to Fargo; yet for long-time residents, they also engender a nervousness that undesirable and irreversible social change is being imposed on them from without.

4. In a 1984 review article on life histories in the *Annual Review of Sociology,* Daniel Bertaux and Martin Kohli use the term *life story* in this way. I find it a useful way to distinguish such narratives from more comprehensive, fully developed narrative texts that would more properly be called life histories, such as Vincent Crapanzano's *Tuhami* (Chicago: University of Chicago Press, 1980), Sidney Mintz's *Worker in the Cane* (New York: Norton, 1974), or Marjorie Shostak's *Nisa* (New York: Vintage, 1983). See Daniel Bertaux and Martin Kohli, "The Life Story Approach: A Continental View," *Annual Review of Sociology* 10 (1984): 215–37.

5. I use this term along the lines established by Terdiman (1985) in his illuminating elaboration of Michel Foucault's (1971) discourse theory. As Terdiman defines the terms,

> Put simply, discourses are the complexes of signs and practices which organize social existence and social reproduction. In their structured, material persistence, discourses are what give differential substance to membership in a social group or class

or formation, which mediate an internal sense of belonging, an outward sense of otherness.

But we need to be careful about *defining* a concept like the discourse. Such a notion must be referred to the problematic from which it emerges, for this determines its operational sense. (p. 54)

Situated as other, counter-discourses have the capacity to *situate:* to relativize the authority and stability of a dominant system of utterances which cannot even countenance their existence. (p. 16)

We might argue that counter-discourses tend, in their relation to the dominant, to homology with the body's reaction to disease: either they seek to surround their antagonist and neutralize or explode it; or they strive to exclude it totally, to expunge it. . . . Between these theoretical extremes, like an unpredictable series of guerilla skirmishes, the multiform violations of the norms of the dominant constitute the realm of functionality of the counter-discourse. (p. 69)

6. In my use of this idea of "counter-discourse" as well as the "plot/story" distinction used below, I am indebted to George Marcus for his insights regarding the use of literary criticism in the analysis of "elicited fieldwork dialogue" that embodies a cultural critique. In a paper prepared for a talk delivered at the "Constructing America Seminar" at the New York Institute for the Humanities in March of 1986, Marcus writes,

I believe the hope of probing for counter-discourses in the field is indeed to find a fellowship between the criticism of everyday life and that of the intellectual. . . . But this hope is most often disappointed. Rather, the originality and depth of the ethnographically derived counter-discourses of subjects are in the form of such discourses. . . .

7. Giddens's working definition for ideology as "any system of belief which proclaims the need for radical change, reactionary or progressive, in the existing order of things" is useful for the purposes of this study (1979, p. 197).

Althusser's definition of ideology as representing "the imaginary relationship of individuals to their real conditions of existence" is also useful, but problematic in its assumption that one can establish with certainty what the "real conditions of existence" are (1971).

8. This has been noted by other scholars of the abortion controversy. In an article addressing this topic, authors Callahan and Callahan note,

Both sides tend to share a distrust of that form of libertarianism that would wholly sunder the individual from the community, setting up the private self as an isolated agent bound by no moral standards other than those perceived or devised by the agent. . . . They want to be able to use the past selectively, preserving what remains valuable and rejecting what has either been harmful or wholly overtaken by time, and in general, they see the past as a resource, requiring constant adjustment and adaptation for life in the present. (1984, pp. 220–21)

References

Althusser, Louis
    1971   "Ideology and the State Ideological Apparatuses." In *Lenin and Philosophy and Other Essays.* London: New Left Books.

Bertaux, Daniel, and Martin Kohli
1984   "The Life Story Approach: A Continental View." *Annual Review of Sociology* 10: 215–37.
Callahan, Daniel, and Sidney Callahan
1984   "Abortion: Understanding Differences." In *Family Planning Perspectives* 16, no. 5: 219–20.
Crapanzano, Vincent
1981   *Tuhami.* Chicago: University of Chicago Press.
Crawford, Alan
1980   *Thunder on the Right: The New Right and the Politics of Resentment.* New York: Pantheon.
Fitzgerald, Frances
1981   "A Reporter at Large: A Disciplined and Charging Army." *New Yorker,* May 18, pp. 53–141.
Foucault, Michel
1971   *L'ordre du Discours.* Paris: Gallimard.
Giddens, Anthony
1979   *Central Problems in Social Theory.* Berkeley: University of California Press.
Ginsburg, Faye
1988   *Contested Lives: The Abortion Debate in an American Community.* Berkeley: University of California Press.
Gordon, Linda, and Allen Hunter
1977–78   "Sex, Family, and the New Right: Anti-feminism as a Political Force." *Radical America,* November 1977–February 1978.
Granberg, Daniel
1981   "The Abortion Activists." *Family Planning Perspectives* 13, no. 4.
Harding, Susan Friend
1981   "Family Reform Movements: Recent Feminism and Its Opposition." *Feminist Studies* 7, no. 1.
Klatch, Rebecca
1987   *Women and the New Right.* Philadelphia: Temple University Press.
Luker, Kristin
1984   *Abortion and the Politics of Motherhood.* Berkeley: University of California Press.
Lynd, Robert, and Helen Merrill Lynd
1929   *Middletown.* New York: Harcourt Brace and Jovanovich.
Mandelbaum, David
1973   "The Study of Life History: Gandhi." *Current Anthropology* 14, no. 3: 177–206.
Mannheim, Karl
1952   "The Problem of Generations." In *Essays on the Sociology of Knowledge,* ed. P. Kecskemeti. New York: Oxford University Press.
Marcus, George
1986   "The Finding and Fashioning of Counter-Discourses in Ethnography." Talk delivered at the New York Institute for the Humanities, March 1986.
Merton, Andrew
1981   *Enemies of Choice.* Boston: Beacon Press.
Mintz, Sidney
1981   *Worker in the Cane.* 2d ed. New York: Norton.
Shklovsky, Victor
1965   "Art as Technique." In *Russian Formalist Criticism: Four Essays,* ed. L. T. Lemon and M. J. Reis. Lincoln: University of Nebraska Press.

Shostak, Marjorie
    1981   *Nisa: The Life and Words of a !Kung Woman.* Cambridge: Harvard
                University Press.
Shuppe, Anson, and David Bromley, eds.
    1984   *New Christian Politics.* Macon, Ga.: Mercer University Press.
Terdiman, Richard
    1985   *Discourse/Counter-Discourse.* Ithaca: Cornell University Press.

WHAT'S A LIFE STORY GOT TO DO WITH IT?

Karen Brodkin Sacks

When I began to participate in a union drive at Duke Medical Center and to interview women activists in 1978, I was certain that there was something in family life that facilitated women's militance and participation in protest movements. I had no words to describe what that something might be, but I hoped to find it in the course of participant-observation research in one such movement. Black service workers at Duke had been attempting to unionize since the mid-1960s. By 1972, after sustained grassroots efforts, they succeeded in organizing Local 77 of the American Federation of State, County and Municipal Employees (AFSCME), a predominantly campus-based union of food, grounds, and cleaning-service workers. This left hospital-based food, transport, and nursing-service workers, as well as a growing number of clerical and technical workers, unorganized. Between 1974 and 1979, these workers continued their efforts to win union repre-sentation. About 80 percent of the potential members of this hospital-based union were women, and they were about half black and half white. Though there were a significant number of black men, there were very few white men in jobs that would be included in the union. It seemed like a good situation for learning about women's activism.

Events proved to be more complicated than I anticipated at the outset. In particular, the union drive in which I was working had lost its steam over a year before I arrived, so there was not much in the way of militance to observe. Nevertheless, learning the life histories of a number of activist women provided valuable clues to some of the family values and skills I sought; and my subsequent historical reconstruction of a successful walk-out allowed me to discover these values in action. I have given a fuller historical and ethnographic analysis of the ways race, gender, and family interacted in work and organizing at Duke in *Caring by the Hour* (Sacks 1988). This paper focuses on the ways that life history helped me see the unities and connections among these somewhat abstract sociological con-cepts.

What was the relationship between family values and organized activism? If the women I knew in 1978 and 1980 could mobilize like that a few years earlier, why were they not doing the same thing in the current union drive? The narrative and analysis of one activist woman, strategically placed in job

85

and history, provided the clues to the links between family values and the internal structure of a movement, and this connection in turn helped explain the rise and fall of organized militance at Duke. This paper is a narrative of how life histories and conversations about them were the stuff of social and historical analysis. In a dialectical way, it contributes to and grows from a broader historical analysis of the union movement at Duke.

This analysis contributed to understanding the *conditions* under which women were likely to politicize—and to depoliticize—their networks. Life histories and participant observation revealed the *processes* by which they did so. By conditions for mobilization I mean larger political and social conditions. In the sixties and early seventies, these were certainly more supportive of grassroots activism than they were in the late seventies and eighties. For much of the sixties there was nationwide support for civil rights and poor people's issues. The economy was strong and the government better able to fund the health, education, and social welfare programs demanded by a robust movement. By the late seventies, the Southeast Asian war and economic decline produced a powerful coalition in business and government that successfully implemented militaristic programs together with cutbacks in social programs and antiunion policies. While national and local political conditions nurtured Duke workers' efforts through the mid-seventies, they became an obstacle in later years. National political conditions affected the patterns of local activism in Durham, as well as that of labor unions. These political and economic conditions certainly influenced Duke workers' willingness to organize and the ways in which they expressed their grievances. But there is another level to understanding the daily life of a movement's existence: how, or the process by which, individuals weld themselves into a group, how they establish the trust which they need in order to risk their bosses' disapproval, and perhaps their very jobs. This level, the *process* of movement building, is an interpersonal one, and hence is best learned by life history and participation.

FAMILY ISSUES AND VALUES

Feminist researchers in the middle and late seventies were up against a paradigm. As soon as one tried to think theoretically about family and family relations, one confronted the nineteenth- and early twentieth-century intellectual grooves and agendas created by Freud or Marx. For example, pondering interpersonal dynamics, learning, or personality, I found myself face to face with Freudian ideas about the unconscious, passions, and destructive impulses locked in battle with the public faces of rationality and sentimentality. Thus, it was the underside of nuclear family life that emerged from theorists as diverse as Shulamith Firestone, Batya Weinbaum, Nancy Chodorow, and Dorothy Dinnerstein.[1] They were at once influenced by and critical of Freudian theories of the unconscious and of the gender- and generationally based power dynamics in ideal-typical white middle-class family life. When I turned to issues of class struggle and social revolution, I confronted Marxist views about political conservatism, short-sighted vision, and retrograde sentiments, usually embodied in women, and continually recreated in their narrow and oppressed sphere of family experience. These were less manifest in the literature than in the daily practice of male-dominated labor unions and leftist groups of the 1970s.[2] Even though I knew these were not what I was after, they stood as the only available conceptualizations on family questions, thereby making it difficult to frame questions that linked family life to social rebellion in a positive way.

The feminist movement added another dimension to understanding women's experience. With the knowledge that "the personal is political," it validated the contradictions between the ideology of romantic egalitarianism and the realities of structured subordination of women by men in housework, reproduction, and sexual relations.[3] Still, there were no texts or testimonies that could be titled anything remotely resembling "How My Mother Taught Me to Be a Revolutionary." Indeed, prior to the late seventies, women militants, troublemakers, revolutionaries, squeaky wheels, and survivors were few and far between in the feminist literature. And searches for their roots did not look to their mothers or their cousins or their sisters or their aunts.

More recently, feminists have begun to explore work relations and class conflict, and have focused on women's resistance and collective efforts in the waged workplace. Some of these studies responded to views prevalent in labor unions and on the left that women were unorganizable, not least because of their family focus. As historians studied women's labor militancy, they began discovering that ties of family and kinship, especially among women (but also between women and men), often acted as facilitators of rather than barriers to mobilization.[4] As the daily realities of women's double shift combined with feminist scholarship to begin eroding stereotypes about women and militance, it became easier to ask whether and how family life might contribute to that process.

All of this was part of the baggage I brought with me to the southern black and white working-class women who were involved in a hospital union-organizing drive at Duke Medical Center. I intended to participate in the union drive, and in the process to learn more about women's daily union, work, and family lives, so that I could describe reasonably precisely *how* families might support union militance and women's leadership. I did not intend to collect life histories, nor did I expect that I would need any detailed historical research. The kind of understanding of resistance that I sought was one which I believed was be found in ongoing everyday life, but that played itself out in organizing.

As it happened, those everyday processes and their significance were invisible to me as long as I looked directly at them in the present. They became visible only when I saw them out of the corner of my eye, as it were—when I saw the mundane in historical perspective. Life histories were the key to making this transition.

Several months of participation and observation of union women's daily life gave me no clues to family-based sources of militance or women's leadership. Part of the problem lay in the fact that I was not sure what forms those things might take. I knew about kin networks and women rebels, but I saw no public rebels, and the kin networks I learned about did not seem to be resisting anything. Still, there was an ongoing union drive in a work force that was about 80 percent women, and I knew from published sources that union activity had been more or less continuous for more than a decade. Something had to have sustained it, and I was not willing to exclude women and families from contributing to it.

In part to learn more about their families, and in part for want of a better thing to do, I interviewed several women on the organizing committee about their family histories. I took full notes on everything that was said and taped wherever possible. Still no clues and no patterns. In the spirit of feminist collectivity, though naively, I put my problem to as many of the women as I knew who were willing to discuss it: I had a strong hunch that women learned the values and skills to resist oppression at work from their families. Did they share that feeling? If so, could they figure out what they learned and how they learned it?

The questions I posed to the women were sociological, and women responded in that mode, giving me answers that linked sociological variables to personal militance. At first there was no definitive pattern: maybe birth order was important, maybe race, or working mothers, marital status, and so on. Their answers were as abstract and uninformative as my own thinking.

Though I interviewed many women, I did not collect many life histories. Indeed, nothing could have been further from my goal, which was an understanding of *general* social processes. Still, the general comes from particular lives, and I was looking for lives that would shed some light on the problem. When that illumination came in the course of an interview, it became an idea I sought to verify in other interviews and conversations. I backed into life history as the beginnings of my answer.

There were a few women whose constructions of their life narratives and analyses became exemplars of how family learning empowered women to rebel, and whose experiences became central for developing that model. This happened when I finally asked them how they learned about work and what it meant to them. That question generated narratives about work— childhood chores, and a progress report about the kinds of tasks and responsibilities each woman had at different ages.

As women began discussing their teenage years, the discussion turned more toward conflicts about boyfriends and hours with their parents, especially their mothers. Their central complaint was that their parents expected them to take full responsibility for their (often large) share of household work, usually in addition to a paid after-school job and school-work, but were not willing to let their daughters determine how late they would stay out, or where and with whom they would spend their recreational time. Actually, women were addressing the same point here that they discussed in their work narratives: delegation of responsibility and the respect it entails. Both responsibility for housework and responsibility for social life were about the centrality of respect and responsibility in the process of learning to be an adult. Central to that process was a sense of competence and self-worth that was the basic idiom for union mobilization.

As I examined these childhood and family chronologies and their embedded messages, I realized that the ideas women held about work were very different from and quite at odds with hospital management's notions of their work and the job descriptions for their hospital work. Where job descriptions—indeed, the implicit premise of an industrial division of labor—separated mental organization from manual labor, women's interviews stressed the unity of the two and the continuity of waged and unwaged work. One medical center housekeeper described it vividly: "I have six kids and I'm thirty-six years old. I'm a mom. I'm a housekeeper . . . I'm everything. I just do the things that's natural for my children. And working is one of them . . . working is a part of my job." Women discussed their hospital and household work, child care, and the part-time jobs they held while still in school in qualitatively similar terms. The women did not describe any of their jobs as lists of particular tasks, although that is the way their job descriptions read. Instead they stressed the unity of planning a day, a week, a life. That was work: some of it was "public work"—that is, it paid a wage; some of it was unwaged. It included a large number of manual tasks, but its real heart and soul was being able to take responsibility and initiative for knowing what needed to be done, and knowing how to do it. A woman had to have manual, mental, and organizational skills to be an adult.

As children, women recalled that success in this regard was rewarded by being given more responsibility and decision-making latitude. Adulthood was gained as part of a process of demonstrating an ability to take responsibility for making and meeting commitments and obligations, for making decisions, and for arranging one's life to do all that one sets out to do.

As I explored mother-daughter conflicts about hours and dating, I began to see that being an adult entailed the right to make decisions for oneself, and to expect respect for those rights. A reciprocal meaning of respect emerged from discussions of these conflicts and their resolution: all adults are expected to give and receive respect, regardless of their social status. Failure on either count is personally demeaning, and in at least one instance was explicitly likened to being yelled at by one's boss. One woman's son said that her yelling at him was "child abuse," and she empathized with him, saying ruefully, "It makes him mad—maybe the same way as being yelled at on the job—it's demeaning."

These understandings of work, adulthood, and respect that women learned in their families clashed with job classifications constructed in such a way as to reserve mental skills and adult competence and the respect they entail for management, and to implicitly deny that workers are able to use their heads, or can behave like responsible adults. Moreover, the process of being given more responsibility as a person demonstrated greater ability to handle it, a process that was part and parcel of coming to adulthood in a family context, had no parallel in the hospital's formal job structure. Most jobs were entry-level, and promotion ladders were token or nonexistent. There was no built-in reward for competence or learning.

Life-history narratives about work indicated that families could give women a sense of the worth of both their waged and unwaged labor and of their right to be treated as competent adults. Women took their family-learned expectations with them to the hospital, only to be confronted with job descriptions that consisted of lists of unintegrated tasks, and with intense supervision usually by people who could not do the work themselves. Here women's family-based interpretations countered management with a sophisticated understanding of the invisible mental planning and coordinating needed to execute their hospital jobs and their household responsibilities alike. Not surprisingly, many workers regarded close supervision and assembly-line pacing as demeaning as well as exploitative, in that it robbed them of adult decision-making prerogatives. Here, too, family-based values challenged bureaucratic ideas about economic rationality, and in that respect operated as a language used by women for creating an oppositional worker consciousness. This seemed to be an important part of the kind of resistance values that women learned in their families.

This contradiction between women's view of themselves and their work and management's view of them was a persistent irritant, and it periodically flared into overt confrontations between workers and management. Indeed, that contradiction was the stuff of most hospital "shop talk," a culture of griping. I heard and saw it on a daily basis, but I did not link it to family learning. I also did not link it to organized activity to press for concrete economic and political demands. How the two might be linked was unclear without an activity that shed light on their relationship.

I had expected that the organizing drive would do that, but I was frustrated because I did not find the kinds of work cultures and networks I had expected, nor did I find much in the way of active mobilization. As I sought to discover instances of activism, what was originally meant to be a synchronic description of women's contemporary work culture and activism turned into a history of Duke workers' organizing efforts. Workers told me about national and local events that had taken place over a decade earlier as if they had happened yesterday. Organizers referred to strikes and big demonstrations at Duke in an indeterminate past. Many of them seemed to know of and to take heart in a golden age of activism when they won real victories and when unity happened almost spontaneously—or as one woman later put it, "We didn't have a bit of trouble; they just had confidence, I guess."

In my search for a time or event that would provide a window on family contributions to militance, I learned of a walkout by ward secretaries, or data terminal operators (DTOs), and tried to reconstruct why they walked out and how they organized themselves to do so. Analysis of that event provided the connection I sought between family values and militance and also showed the informal social networks by which women organized both parties and picket lines.[5]

VALUES AND STRUCTURES OF MILITANCE

Beverly Jones was a DTO who began working at Duke after the walkout, and who became a union activist in the organizing that followed it in 1974. By 1978, when I met her, she was no longer involved in union organizing, though she was still an active participant in a large social network of DTOs, many of whom had been active in the earlier walkout. This informal network, like several others, spanned the period from the walkout through the rise and fall of unionization. It was a visible node of political activism through 1976, but afterward it seemed to mobilize exclusively for social events, and played no visible role in the last stages of the union drive. Beverly's trajectory of activism followed the network's. When I met her in 1979, she was organizing a large Christmas dance for hospital workers.

I use the term *centerwomen* for women who initiate and sustain informal workplace social networks, and who are often keystones of family and kinship networks as well. They tend to initiate activities that maintain group cohesiveness. People expect them to know the events, opinions, and needs of those in the network, and to use that information for their shared well-being. They tend to keep centerwomen well informed about what is happening on personal, family, and work-related issues. As a result, center-women are likely to know everyone's business, not least because people seek them out to discuss it. The role of centerwoman is informal; it is not a named status, and if no one takes it up, it does not exist. Women who were at the centers of informal hospital worker networks were a key part of the leadership of the union movement, not least because of their initiative in translating into political demands the values of an informal work culture which were expressed in a family-based idiom.

Beverly Jones's analysis of her work and family life crystallized the ways that centerwomen link family values to workplace organizing, to social cohesiveness, and to political mobilization. Her comment "I'm usually the one to initiate anything. People say, 'Jones, why don't we do this?'—and they wait for me to do it" was an ironic summary of things other women had said about organizing social and political events. She followed it up with an explanation of how she came to be the central repository for her coworkers' agendas, and how she saw that as part of a political leadership role. Getting to know people was part of Beverly's organizing agenda when she began work at the hospital. But her first activity was to organize a party for a coworker, and keeping people together socially has remained very important for her. She likes it, and others have come to expect it from her. In the DTO walkout and in union mobilization, it was the political mobilization of this and similar *social* networks of black workers that gave the drive its movement vitality.

Beverly's experience became a hypothesis, and I examined it against the interviews and life histories of other activists. In so doing, I was able to identify several centerwomen, and to see this as a role that created and sustained social networks. Likewise, it became clear that in these networks an informal work culture was shared and reinforced. That culture centered on reinforcing family-based values to validate women's view of their work as requiring both mental and organizational skills, and of themselves as responsible and competent adults. This was the unifying set of informal understandings that underlay more than a decade of political mobilizations among hospital workers. Workers mobilized around these consensus values that had been translated into union demands, and centerwomen were key in expressing the consensus.

In life-history interviews, both Beverly and her mother made it clear that they shared the same values about work and adulthood. Beverly also learned from her mother's central role in church activities how to organize, to build a consensus and activate people around it. Both women consciously valued the interpersonal skills required to succeed.

LIFE HISTORY AND SOCIAL HISTORY

Still, I was puzzled at the contradiction between what I learned from interviews about the past and what I saw in the union drive—which had no networks, no centerwomen's leadership, and indeed, no active participation on the part of most of the women who told me they had a long history of activism. I could believe either what I saw or what I was told. Archival research confirmed the general picture of a "golden age" that had been lost only recently, so it became necessary to explain what had caused the decline. It was only by working back and forth from individuals to movements, from family to work, that I was able to answer this question, and in so doing learn more about the nature and roots of women's activism and leadership and their relationship to family life.

Just as centerwomen were key to group formation and political mobilization, they were also key to demobilization. A leftist political faction fight in 1976 among prounion workers destroyed the political consensus of hospital networks. Centerwomen's informal role was to articulate and translate underlying consensus values based on family values of work, worth, respect, and adulthood into union terms: decent pay, nondiscriminatory promotion ladders, freedom from supervisory harassment, impartial grievance procedures, and so forth.

However, the informal social groups in many activist units contained people of both factions, each of whom sought to persuade others of the rightness of their position. The areas of sectarian disagreement about the larger radical meaning of unionization eclipsed the painfully built consensus around the immediate meanings of unity and unionization. Under the circumstances, there was no consensus for centerwomen to express, and thus no way for them to be effective mobilizers. Jones, along with a number of other centerwomen, became so disgusted that she simply ceased to participate in the union drive. Another woman recalled that she felt so pulled apart by people's contradictory demands on her that she stopped planning even social events, and that network temporarily disbanded. For her, there was no area of consensus to be found. Beverly Jones found that there was a consensus, but only around social events, so that her group dropped activism in order to stay together. The union drive lost its steam when the work groups of black women clerical, kitchen, and service workers that had given the drive its high profile and public expressions of militance depoliticized or disintegrated. It was in networks, not as individuals, that people had participated in the union movement, and it was the life histories of four or five centerwomen that made especially visible the ways that family teachings, workplace networks, and grassroots mobilizations were interconnected.

CONCLUSION

This level of understanding amplifies the larger history of organizing at Duke, which grew out of the convergence of the civil rights movement and the industrialization of health-care work. At Duke, that coming together created the spark for black service workers to take a sustained initiative to press for unionization. For most of its history, those efforts took the form of a locally based grassroots movement. Its leaders were black workers, and its sustaining core was black women, with critical participation from several networks of white workers, especially women. These efforts rested on an internal structure of women's work groups and community and family networks. Though it sometimes looked as if workers simply followed articulate and popular leaders, leadership came at least as much from collectivities of women as from articulate speakers. The collective leadership of black women's work-based networks was the organizational strength and sustaining force of the movement. When those networks mobilized, the movement lived and grew; when they depoliticized or demobilized, the movement died, and unionization died with it, as it did in 1979 when workers lost the union election. A historical analysis of unionization efforts focuses on the *conditions* under which women's workplace networks did and did not become active politically; life histories and participant observation revealed the *process* by which they did so. The heartening aspect of the synthesis is that it indicates that the seeds of activism seem to be preserved, even if they stay dormant, in the stuff of daily work culture. And that stuff, at least in women's workplaces, seems to include a family-based idiom of resistance. That is, women used family-derived values about adulthood, work, and respect to assert and legitimate their positive evaluation of their own skill and work in opposition to the hospital's denigration of them. This oppositional culture remains alive and well even in periods of political inactivity. It survives in a culture of griping, in wall hangings, and in the efforts women put into maintaining active social ties and groups among workers in the hospital.

Notes

This paper would not have been born without Carol Lasser's editorial midwifery in the last stages of labor, and the collective encouragement of the Personal Narratives Group at the Center for Advanced Feminist Studies.

1. Shulamith Firestone, *Dialectic of Sex* (New York: Bantam, 1970); Batya Weinbaum, *Pictures of Patriarchy* (Boston: South End Press, 1983); Nancy Chodorow, "Family Structure and Feminine Personality," in *Woman, Culture, and Society,* ed. M. Z. Rosaldo and L. Lamphere (Palo Alto: Stanford University Press, 1974), pp. 43–66; Dorothy Dinnerstein, *The Mermaid and the Minotaur* (New York: Harper and Row, 1977).

2. For a theoretical statement, see Wally Secombe, "The Housewife and Her Labor under Capitalism," *New Left Review* 83 (1974). For recent critiques of union practice, see essays in Ruth Milkman, *Women, Work, and Protest* (Boston: Routledge and Kegan Paul, 1985); Nancy MacLean, *The Culture of Resistance: Female Institution-Building in the Ladies Garment Workers' Union, 1905–1925,* Occasional Papers in Women's Studies, University of Michigan, Ann Arbor, 1982. For analyses of the importance of community and kinship to class resistance, see Mina Davis Caulfield, "Imperialism, Family, and Cultures of Resistance," *Socialist Revolution* 4, no. 2 (1974): 67–85; Martha Acklesberg, "Women's Collaborative Activities and City Life: Politics and Policy," in *Political Women,* ed. J. Flammang (Beverly Hills: Sage, 1984), pp. 242–59.

3. Influential early works include Betty Friedan, *The Feminine Mystique* (New York: Dell, 1963); Juliet Mitchell, *Women's Estate* (New York: Pantheon, 1971); Pat Mainardi, "The Politics of Housework," in *Sisterhood Is Powerful,* ed. Robin Morgan (New York: Random House, 1970), pp. 447–54; Margaret Benston, "The Political Economy of Women's Liberation," *Monthly Review* 21, no. 4 (1969): 13–27; Mariarosa dalla Costa and Selma James, *The Power of Women and the Subversion of the Community* (Montpelier, England: Falling Wall Press, 1972).

4. Ardis Cameron, "Bread and Roses Revisited: Women's Culture and Working Class Activism in the Lawrence Strike of 1912," in *Women, Work, and Protest,* ed. Ruth Milkman (Boston: Routledge and Kegan Paul, 1985), pp. 42–61; Herbert G. Gutman, *The Black Family in Slavery and Freedom, 1750–1925* (New York: Columbia University Press, 1976); Temma Kaplan, "Female Consciousness and Collective Action: The Case of Barcelona, 1910–1918," *Signs* 7, no. 3 (1982): 545–67; Louise Tilly, "Paths of Proletarianization: Organization of Production, Sexual Division of Labor, and Women's Collective Action," *Signs* 7, no. 2 (1981): 400–417.

5. Karen Brodkin Sacks, "Kinship and Class Consciousness: Family Values and Work Experience among Hospital Workers in an American Southern Town," in *Interest and Emotion,* ed. Hans Medick and David Sabean (Cambridge: Cambridge University Press, 1984), pp. 279–99; and "Computers, Ward Secretaries, and a Walkout in a Southern Hospital," in *My Troubles Are Going to Have Trouble with Me,* ed. Karen B. Sacks and Dorothy Remy (New Brunswick, N.J.: Rutgers University Press, 1984), pp. 173–92. For a full discussion, see Karen Brodkin Sacks, *Caring by the Hour: Women, Work, and Organizing at Duke Medical Center* (Urbana: University of Illinois Press, 1988).

PART THREE

Narrative Forms

FORMS THAT TRANSFORM

Personal Narratives Group

We chose the term *narrative forms* rather than *genres* or *models* to describe this section because it best speaks to the complexity and importance of the different shapes assumed by personal narratives. *Genre,* a literary term, carries with it the notion of tidy categories and adherence to rules; *model,* a term derived from the empirical sciences, may imply a structure to be imitated. Both seem restrictive in projects involving interdisciplinary research. *Narrative form,* an inclusive term amenable to cross-disciplinary studies, suggests in its more encompassing nature that a narrative might be viewed as fluid rather than fixed in the variety of shapes that it can assume. Thus it is important to locate and interpret its sources and to pinpoint the particular form that is adapted.

Narrative form essentially refers to the structure of the narrative. Is the life recounted, for example, in linear, chronological fashion? Is it presented, as Elisa von der Recke (discussed in Katherine Goodman's essay "Poetry and Truth: Elisa von der Recke's Sentimental Autobiography") chose to do, in a series of letters? Or does the ordering follow a logic suggested by the emotional resonance in the narrator's memory, as suggested in Luisa Passerini's essay, "Women's Personal Narratives: Myths, Experiences, and Emotions"? The narrative form a writer gives to a life necessarily involves her sense of the purpose for which her or another's story is told and is responsive to her notions of audience. Thus, the emphases and omissions in the story of Christina Sibiya, as told by Rebecca Reyher in *Zulu Woman* (discussed by Marcia Wright in "Personal Narratives, Dynasties, and Women's Campaigns: Two Examples from Africa"), are consistent with the aims of Christina's story as campaign autobiography, marshaled in the interests of her son's political future and ambitions. Narrative form is also necessarily linked to the interpretation or meaning the writer or teller gives to a life. The fact that Elisa von der Recke presents her life in a form resembling the sentimental epistolary novel suggests that she viewed such a form as illustrating the melodramic qualities and the central importance of heroines that such works exhibit. That Christa Wolf creates new forms, as Sandra Frieden suggests in her essay, "Transformative Subjectivity in the Writings of Christa Wolf," aids her in opposing fixed literary forms and emphasizing the importance of the individual in a political state that valorizes the collective idea. Elizabeth Hampsten, in "Considering More than a Single Reader," finds different voices attached to

99

different types of information in diaries. She argues that the material can never be understood apart from the voice in which it is written.

Autobiography, life history, and biography are usually chronologically organized. The life course itself may be experienced, however, around other organizing principles, from major events to important self-discoveries, none of which necessarily corresponds to linear time. Gender may be an important determinant of the organizing features of life experience. The narrator of the life story—whether it is her own or that of another—creates the life as she organizes and tells it. This shaping is a complex process and draws upon an array of sources, including the various forms oral or written storytelling takes in a given time and place. As the following essays demonstrate, the forms available to men and women often differ, and the limits placed on women's lives may also affect what models are available to them for telling their own life stories. The process of self-interpretation, the most salient aspect of the personal narrative, is partially revealed through the choice of narrative form.

The form of the narrative is shaped most importantly by cultural and historical contexts, which make available a striking range of possibilities relative to one's gender and status in society. In the nineteenth-century French and German working-class autobiographies that Mary Jo Maynes describes in her essay, "Gender and Narrative Form in French and German Working-Class Autobiographies," the choices of narrative form were marked by the fact that the autobiographers lived before the rise of popular literacy. Indeed, some of them learned to read and write later in life. Therefore, the narrative forms they chose are more often found in oral forms of narrative, such as storytelling, parables, or street theater, than in the literary models offered by Rousseau and Goethe, the exemplars of life-story narrative for the emergent bourgeoisie in France and Germany. On the other hand, Elisa von der Recke, a member of the aristocracy, used letter writing, a form that was appropriate and familiar to literate women.

In addition, a reading of Maynes's essay demonstrates that the writer's gender is relevant to the choice of narrative form. Despite the fact that the working-class women and men whom Maynes studies emerged from the same social milieu and the impulse to write their autobiographies came from similar sources, the men often depended on the picaresque to tell their stories, whereas the women chose a variety of other forms. Similarly, Luisa Passerini finds that the Italian women she interviewed were much less likely than men to structure their narratives around their work life, and much more likely to employ images of rebelliousness in shaping their life narratives.

Personal narratives are marked by historical context, but they are also shaped by the available cultural models, which are adapted to the writer's own experiences and needs. The spiritual narratives described by Nellie Y. McKay in her essay, "Nineteenth-Century Black Women's Spiritual Autobiographies: Religious Faith and Self-Empowerment," for example, illustrate ways in which the writer's position as both a member of an oppressed group and an individual woman exposed to unique circumstances influences the form her narrative takes. Jarena Lee and Rebecca Cox Jackson, two black women living in the antebellum North, used the journal form and presented their lives within the framework of spiritual conversions. Their choice reflects their place within society, yet the particular configuration of their texts implies that they define the importance of their lives differently. Lee emphasizes her politics as she struggles to minister within a black church dominated by the male hierarchy; Jackson stresses her visions, the gift that sustained her ministry. In addition, the conversion narrative, popular and well known in nineteenth-century America, possessed different significance for a black woman than it did for either a black man or a white person. Use of such a narrative form by a black woman indicated how exceptional she was: she was literate, a public figure, and especially talented. Yet nothing in the historical moment suggested such possibilities. Because the form of spiritual autobiography was available, it allowed Lee and Jackson not only to bear witness to their experiences, but to shape them as well in their narratives.

Finding a form in which to present a life means, in addition to choosing from the available models, adapting those models to suit one's needs and purposes. This process is active rather than passive, and engages the teller's full creative energies. Elizabeth Hampsten's efforts as the interpreter of women's autobiographies written primarily for themselves or their families suggests how difficult this endeavor is, how the realities of a woman's life may resist available forms, and how the interpreter/biographer may well engage herself—may well "nudge a story along"—in the process. Epistolary novels were a part of Elisa von der Recke's library, yet her decision to shape her own autobiography in that fashion required the imaginary leap between the fiction of others and her own life. By blending autobiography, biography, and fiction, Christa Wolf did not simply adapt existing forms, but created something new in a political system often marked by the perils of censorship and ideological rigidity.

By choosing and adapting the form her narrative will take, the narrator interprets and, in a sense, makes or remakes her life. She can define, shape, and interpret her life in ways that may be impossible within the actual, present context. Dominated by a repressive husband, Elisa von der Recke can elevate her suffering to the kind of heroic martyrdom reserved for the heroine of fiction. As a woman caught in the oppressiveness of a bad marriage at a time when women's options for change were few, she seems to have decided to lend a certain fictional meaning to a difficult life, choosing to live it out in punishing fashion rather than looking actively for ways to improve her situation. Through her writing as a woman and as an individual, Christa Wolf finds a freedom of thought and communication that her immediate circumstances might belie. By casting their stories in the framework of conversions, Jarena Lee and Rebecca Cox Jackson lend significance to their lives when the dominant culture in which they exist might well deny such opportunities to them as black women.

All of the following essays can also help us to understand the ways that context shapes a life story and to see the interplay between context and narrative form. Yet their placement in this section is ultimately appropriate, for they emphasize certain features of narrative form and raise questions concerning the ways that it is used by narrators or interpreters. Mary Jo Maynes's essay on nineteenth-century French and German working-class autobiographers looks closely at the context of the writers she examines, yet it also helps us to understand the interplay of form and context. Sandra Frieden's essay on Christa Wolf suggests the ways a writer may use form creatively as an oppositional strategy in the telling of an individual life story within a determinedly collective culture. In her discussion of two ante-bellum black women ministers, Nellie McKay illustrates a way in which writers may use narrative form to circumvent their oppression. Katherine Goodman's examination of Elisa von der Recke enables us to see clearly how narrative form and interpretation are linked, how the narrator's choice of form necessarily indicates how she perceives and values her life. Marcia Wright's analysis of campaign autobiography suggests how form and polemical purpose are connected and raises questions about the way in which we read and interpret life stories. Elizabeth Hampsten's account of stories of women's lives told in diaries and journals shows how disparate and often unformed the story of a life as lived may be, and how the interpreter of such a life will feel obligated to become involved in the shaping of that life story.

Taken as a whole, these essays invite us to examine more carefully the ways in which context affects the choice of form; to consider the extent to which a writer or teller must adapt the form she chooses or create an entirely new form; to see how the choice of form may relate to the purpose for which the life is told as well as to its interpretation and significance. They demonstrate that the choice of a narrative form may well be a political act and a rebellious statement of opposition toward the power structure.

The available forms from which a writer can choose—and which she ultimately must adapt to her own purposes—are the result of social and political relations in which a woman acts within a given historical moment. To interpret the narrative form, then, means attending to cultural models, power relations, and individual imagination. All are brought to bear on the act of self-interpretation articulated in the choice of the narrative form.

GENDER AND NARRATIVE FORM IN FRENCH AND GERMAN WORKING-CLASS AUTOBIOGRAPHIES

Mary Jo Maynes

The urge to write history "from below"—from the perspective of ordinary men and women rather than that of the dominant classes—along with the distinctive feminist agenda focused on making women central to historical interpretation has over the past few decades dramatically altered the study of history. If much social history has in practice centered on the recovery of often quantitative sources that allowed the writing of the collective biography of underclasses, the attention of feminist historians has more often turned to sources permitting glimpses into female perspectives on life in the past. The personal testimony so central to both the women's movement and feminist theory and scholarship was often shunned by those social historians who sought to recreate the "average" experience and who perhaps feared that reliance on such testimony represented a continuation with past practices that had privileged the viewpoint of the educated and powerful creators of most written records. Current reworking of social-historical methods and theory suggests that the cost of this choice is being reassessed. While much of the social history that has been written has provided us with a valuable alternative to earlier histories, it nevertheless has often tended to leave the experiences of individuals by the wayside as it reconstructed the powerful historical processes that contextualized individual lives. The personal documents so critical to feminist history can, it seems to me, help to resolve the social-historical dilemma. This essay will discuss one such set of personal narratives—autobiographies published by men and women of working-class origins who lived in France and Germany in the nineteenth century.[1]

Until recently, literary historians who have discussed the genre of autobiography have generally tended to concentrate their analyses upon canonized texts, "classic" autobiographies that have served to define the form and act as the models against which other examples were judged and interpreted. Feminist literary critics, in their approach to autobiography, as to other genres, have begun to undermine the domination of the canon and the rules and evaluations that proceed from the analysis of a restricted set of texts. In addition, some critics have also begun to place autobiographical criticism in the context of the history of class relations.[2] These efforts have implications for the historian's use of autobiographical sources, which in some sense requires that a writing of a social history of autobiography accompany the social-historical interpretation of autobiographical texts. I will thus first examine the implications for historians of some of the generalizations drawn from the history of "literary" autobiographies and the feminist critique of that history. Then, I'll turn to a discussion of narrative structures employed in the set of French and German working-class autobiographical texts, and examine the particular historical context in which these texts were written. My aim is to contextualize these autobiographies as social-historical sources and to contribute to the rethinking of the history of autobiography.

WHY START WITH ROUSSEAU AND GOETHE? AND WHY STOP THERE?

Those who involve themselves with the history of autobiography in Europe inevitably discover the centrality in literary analyses of J. J. Rousseau (1712–1798) and J. W. Goethe (1749–1832), each of whom was a noted philosopher and "man of letters," and each of whom wrote an autobiography deemed by subsequent generations to be a landmark which was widely imitated. What marked their autobiographical works and made them seem so critical to the history of the genre was the personal note of their revelations. Unlike the generations of memoirists and spiritual autobiographers who had preceded them, both of these men wrote autobiographies that took the development of an individual personality as their major concern. Standard histories of autobiography in France and Germany often suggest that subsequent autobiographies in those two languages were in some way marked by these creative models.[3]

Social-historical accounts of the genre regard the timing of its emergence as critically significant. Rousseau and Goethe are viewed as more than creative individuals; in writing autobiography, each was, in a sense, giving literary form to a new kind of class consciousness. Autobiography, it has been suggested, was the genre par excellence of the emergent bourgeoisie. It was the literary expression of the individualism and the faith in an integrated and coherent personality so central to the bourgeois economic and political philosophy that was groping its way to preeminence even as the two literary giants revealed all that was of consequence to their personal growth. By describing their process of becoming, by deeming this story worth telling, the two philosophers and the genre they helped to reshape became part of the broader historical creation of the bourgeois personality.[4]

Feminist critiques of the history of the autobiographical form have begun to challenge some aspects of our understanding of the genre. How did women's autobiographies fit into this history? Were the historical periods in which autobiographical writing flourished different for men and women, as Estelle Jelinek has suggested?[5] To what extent do men and women auto-biographers construct their life stories following different models? How are we to interpret the systematic similarities and differences between men's and women's autobiographies as genre?

Recent interest in working-class autobiography has led to analogous questions, for autobiographers who have emerged from popular or pro-letarian milieux often defy the rules of the genre just as women auto-biographers do.[6] Autobiography, it has become clear, can emerge from a variety of impulses and follow a variety of models. If we broaden our vision to attempt to incorporate texts other than those by middle-class, educated men, the history of the genre and its meaning begins to shift. For one thing, as Wolfgang Emmerich and others have pointed out, the equation of successful autobiography with the unfolding of individual personality breaks down. Indeed, Emmerich argues that the kind of linear, progressive developmental process so central to the German tradition of literary auto-biography, and to the closely related genre of *Bildungsroman,* holds little meaning for the proletarian. The image of the human life course proceed-ing in an "aufsteigende[n] Linie" ("ascending line," in the often-repeated words of Goethe) could not capture the experience of people struggling to stay afloat, and beset by the chronic insecurity, poverty, illnesses, accidents, and family tragedies so common in working-class existence.[7]

LIFE COURSES AND MODELS FOR STRUCTURING LIFE ACCOUNTS

This last suggestion brings us to the central question of how lives (as lived and as written) are structured. Certainly lives are ultimately structured by the rhythms of biological regimes that predominate—patterns of birth, physiological maturation, reproduction, pathology, and mortality. Never simply "given," however, these biological rhythms are variable both within a society and over time. And these rhythms are shaped by and interpreted through social and cultural institutions.[8] As an interpretive act, the auto-biography is, among other things, an effort to impose order, form, and meaning on the facts of an existence. One useful observation of critics of autobiography is that the way autobiographers understand and construct their lives is informed by available models as well as by the details of their experience. In other words, there may well be connections between nar-rative forms employed in autobiography and forms that appear in other cultural contexts.

Again, the models of "classics" have typically been described in terms of relatively few alternatives not generally applicable to women's lives or to those of working-class people. For example, in her recent, provocative analysis of autobiographies of Western European literary men, Susanna Egan deduces what she sees as the significant narrative forms that shape and lend meaning to these accounts for both author and reader. In particular, she argues that literary autobiographers employed four kinds of fictional narrative patterns: the myth of paradise lost (the usual "shape" childhood takes), the heroic journey (youth), conversion (characteristic of maturity) and confession. Egan suggests that the use of common fictional forms adds shared meaning.[9]

Now, if one were to qualify this model as appropriate for an understanding of the life structure of many European male professional writers, Egan's analysis would be convincing. But underlying her account is an implicit universal psychology that grounds the meaningfulness of these accounts and these metaphors in a general process of psychological development. According to Egan, the narrative forms in autobiography and the fictional forms to which they refer make sense precisely because they correspond to a universal psychological reality. Once again, the urge to create universal models leads to the privileging of the experiences of upper-class males. Although Egan's search for connections between literary fictional forms and narrative forms embedded in autobiography is provocative, the search for universals in this fashion is certainly misplaced.

What shape do working-class autobiographical narrative structures take, and what are the models (literary and otherwise) that inform them? One thing is pretty clear—few of these autobiographers seem to have read either the *Confessions* or *Dichtung und Wahrheit*, although some of the more educated workers in France were familiar with Rousseau's political treatises.[10] In other words, the models that shaped literary autobiographies cannot be taken for granted. Without going into great detail here on the history of popular culture, I merely want to point out the nature of the cultural chasm that separated "the people" from their social superiors. The period of emergence of bourgeois autobiography as an established form— the late eighteenth and early nineteenth centuries—has been characterized by the historian Peter Burke as the period in which educated Europeans created the concept of "the people" as a category different from themselves to be either denigrated or romanticized as exotic or natural.[11] This creation, Burke argues, coincided with the solidification of new cultural class barriers. The search for literary or broadly cultural models embedded in working-class autobiographies must be conducted with an eye toward their relationship to these class cultures.

One connection that seems worth exploring in popular autobiography is the connection to oral forms of narrative—storytelling, parables, street theater, and the like. Many of the earlier popular autobiographers were apparently inveterate storytellers, often the children and grandchildren of storytellers as well. Many seem to have had the prodigious memories that often accompany such habitual storytelling. Indeed, although the earliest working-class autobiographers were produced in an epoch when popular literacy was on the rise, several of these autobiographers learned to read and write only at a fairly advanced age.[12] If reading plays a conspicuous role in the lives of most of these people, there were nevertheless a great number who lived lives altogether on the margins of literate culture. Moreover, the influence of oral forms shows up in the episodic and anecdotal quality of many of the autobiographical texts.

The best example is perhaps that of Norbert Truquin (b. 1833). Truquin dated his memoirs 1887, when he was fifty-four years old. By this time he had obviously learned to write, but there are indications throughout the book that reading and writing came late in his life. Although his dating is not too precise, it is suggested that he remained illiterate in his late twenties, could not yet write at the time of his imprisonment for political activities (he would have been thirty-seven at the time), and could barely read in 1870. Nevertheless, by the early 1850s (his twenties), he had become an active propagandist for a particular version of Utopian Socialism, had developed his own elaborate plans for socialist colonization, and attempted to win converts to his system by the use of pointed storytelling and parables. Thus his illiteracy neither cut him off from the political culture of his time nor prevented his subsequent evolution into an autobiographer.[13] But it did shape the telling of his story. His autobiography, like that of many other working-class autobiographers, is a series of adventures and pointed anecdotes.

This public, indeed explicitly propagandist, storytelling exemplified by Truquin appears to have been primarily a male form.[14] Nevertheless, proletarian autobiographies are filled with women storytellers, too, even if their narrations occur in less public settings. Mothers and grandmothers often play the role of informant by their telling of family histories. For example, the French writer of peasant-worker origins Rene Bonnet (b. 1905) recalled evening village gatherings in the following passage:

> They would talk about the old ones who were long dead and who had livened up the veillées in the old days. It was at these veillées in the shepherd hut that I learned to know and love my ancestors. . . . It was an exceptional favor for us little ones when Mama Riette would agree to tell us a story. . . . Mama Riette was a born storyteller. . . .[15]

Alternatively, the "gossip" in which, for example, Madeleine Henrey's otherwise timid mother loved to indulge, is clearly the source of her rich account of her own childhood and the neighborhood in which it occurred. Henrey indicates that her first memories begin around age three; the first four chapters of her autobiography, which recount earlier events in her own life and that of her parents, must have been based largely on her mother's stories, as is suggested in the opening paragraph of the auto-biography:

> I was born on 13th August 1906 in Montmartre in a steep cobbled street of leaning houses, slate-coloured and old, under the shining loftiness of Sacre-Coeur. Matilda, my mother, describing to me later this uncommodious but picturesque corner which we left soon after my birth, stressed the curious characters from the Auvergne and from Brittany who kept modest cafes with zinc bars. Behind these they toiled. . . .[16]

Henrey's life, like that of Truquin, is structured around events she lived or heard recounted. It is simply a chronological sequence of things that happened to and around her.

Other plebeian lives read like picaresque, self-portrait as lovable rogue, with its roots in earlier oral literary forms and connections to the eighteenth-century novel.[17] I'll refer here to a single example, that of the windowmaker Jacques-Louis Ménétra (1738–1803). Ménétra's autobiography is a long series of often humorous anecdotes about his adventures, proceeding from encounter to encounter. Often his irreverence for social norms, his anticlerical humor, and so forth emerge from the anecdotes. Still, there is no sense of linear development. Also of significance is the explicitly sexual character of many of the anecdotes, a trait that distinguishes Ménétra's autobiography from most bourgeois autobiographies and links it to picaresque, to contemporaneous fiction, and to later working-class autobiography. For example, Ménétra describes the following encounter:

> Time passes I had even almost forgotten when one Sunday leaving my apartment I meet mother Pinard a book under her arm She stares at me I say hello She tells me she is going to mass I respond that I had heard a good sermon from her husband She tells me that it is by no means necessary to listen to it that she does what she wants and is the mistress of her will Good I tell her if that's the way it is would you like to come and refresh yourself in my room. . . . She comes up We accommodate ourselves She is pleased promises to come often and hear the mass in this manner[18]

Notably, while the persona of the sexual adventurer recurs in many subsequent male working-class autobiographies, I have not yet found a working woman's autobiography that could be characterized as picaresque. By way of contrast, the autobiography of Susanne Voilquin (b. 1801), who emerged from roughly the same social milieu as Ménétra, includes discussion of a sexual encounter, but in far different terms. The account follows that of her mother's death. She suggests that pressures from her fiancé to initiate sexual relations combined with her grief for her mother produced illness and hallucinations:

> I was at the end of my strength, I no longer was thinking; therefore, the new attempts of this man achieved the success that he wanted. From this moment I was his! . . . In the days that followed, he dried my tears with his kisses and calmed my conscience with his vow to marry me as soon as possible. . . .[19]

Furthermore, the narration of the third part of Voilquin's *Souvenirs,* which recounts her travels on behalf of the Saint-Simonien socialist movement, centers on the fourteen "stations" she visited on her trip around France—a deliberate use of the structure of the Christian journey to the cross—before embarking on her difficult trip to Egypt.

Some popular autobiographers use the anecdotal form more deliberately. The *Mémoires* of Valentin Jamerey-Duval (1695–1775) read like the adventures of a real-life *Candide.* They tell the story of the wandering life of a young peasant boy who in his travels through *ancien régime* France encounters the world's irrationality. For example, here is the description of young Jamerey-Duval's first encounter with the knowledge of war:

> My incredulity was equal to my ignorance. It is true that this martial and murderous glory, which immune to justice and reason had placed the Alexanders and Caesars among the demi-gods, was at that time completely unknown to me. Nature, which teaches nothing foreign to her, had given me no notion of that science whose simple theory is offensive to her, at least when its goal is not our own defense or that of our country.[20]

As this one passage illustrates, the author employs an ironic tone in his account of himself as young. He also continually uses distancing language that suggests the extent to which he has progressed since the time recalled. In this respect, Jamerey-Duval's account, indeed that of a peasant who left his class of origin to become a scholar and librarian, resembles more closely the linear pattern of development idealized in middle-class male autobiography.

Jamerey-Duval's autobiography is, in fact, one of the earliest examples of a form that would be repeated—that of the working-class "success story." Later autobiographers, for example Eugene Courmeaux (1816–?), who also made the transition from French peasant to librarian, and Bruno Bürgel (1875–?), the German worker-turned-astronomer, also use their narratives to establish their intellectual credentials even while they recount, for the benefit of intellectuals "born" to the class, the trials and tribulations accompanying their trajectory.[21] Perhaps what we see here is an explicitly working-class version of the *Bildungsroman,* attesting the progress of personal development but attuned to its social and psychic costs as well. But, again, this is largely a male form. With the exception of the occasional work such as Angela Langer's *Stromaufwärts,* a fictionalized autobiography depicting the social and intellectual ascent of a servant, "success stories" of women autobiographers generally entail either marrying up or becoming profes-

Adelheid Popp *(seated, second from right)* and members of the Women's Committee, Austrian Socialist Party, 1917. Popp, who wrote the first Socialist woman's autobiography in German, later edited a collection of autobiographical writings by her women colleagues in the Austrian Socialist movement.

sional writers; either route could be and often was pursued without a conscious effort at self-improvement that would then subsequently structure the life account.[22]

In contrast to these anecdotal forms, many socialist autobiographies of the later nineteenth century follow a structure that is a variant on the theme of progressive development. Many of the autobiographies of socialist men, following the suggestion of the scientific socialism then current, are consciously intended to be accounts of the transition from helpless object of history to active subject, through socialist activism. While not centered on the evolution and exaltation of individual personality and intellect, they nevertheless underscore the role of self-improvement or education in the broadest sense for a decisive transformation in their lives. Among women socialists, interestingly enough, this structure is also quite common. For example, the autobiography of the Austrian socialist Adelheid Popp (b. 1869) recounts Popp's successive stages of enlightenment and optimism despite her struggles, while that of Jeanne Bouvier (b. 1865), an active French syndicalist, is one long account of her laborious and dedicated self-education under the most trying of circumstances. Bouvier presents her life in three parts. The first recounts her childhood, the second, her conversion to syndicalism, and the last, entitled "How I Became a Writer," centers on her prodigious self-education.[23]

THE AUTOBIOGRAPHICAL IMPULSE

The sorts of accounts listed above suggest the variety of structures that shape working-class autobiography, although the list is by no means exhaustive. I would like to turn now to a brief exploration of the connections between the forms of the autobiographical stories and the conditions under which they were written. First, since the diffusion of literacy skills affected both the production of and audiences for autobiography, the contours of popular literacy obviously shaped the chronology of working-class autobiography. Growing popular literacy provided a necessary precondition for the emergence of the genre, but the ability to read and write in itself provided no particular incentive to write or read autobiography. The chronology of production of working-class autobiography points to the embeddedness of the genre in particular historical circumstances.

The most striking feature of the history of working-class autobiography is its synchronization with the history of working-class political and labor organization. If the middle-class autobiography appeared as the genre par excellence of the individual, the working-class autobiographer was usually enmeshed in collectivity. Roughly half of the several hundred published autobiographical texts written by nineteenth-century French and German working-class people were written by political or labor militants. Fluctuating levels of production of autobiographical texts, as well as the proportions written by men and women, and by people in different jobs and regions, reflect to a large extent the political and organizational history of working people. In part, this is because political organizations often provided both the skills and the access to publication facilities that the production of autobiography required. But perhaps more essentially, political commitment provided working people with a level of self-awareness, and possibly a narrative framework as well, that could structure a life and also might motivate the very act of writing.

For skilled workingmen, artisanal organizations and the established stages of artisanal formation—especially apprenticeship and journeyman status—provided the main structure of early life and the shaping experience most often recounted in memoirs. The formative impact of travel itself, framed by the organized artisanal network of stopover points, journeyman hostels, educational institutions, and so forth, fed a subculture that encouraged intellectual exchange, storytelling, political organization, and eventually memoirs. Furthermore, the stages of training could also provide a developmental framework distinct from but in some points analogous to the progressive line that structures many middle-class male accounts. The journeyman's *tour de France* and the German equivalent, the *Walze*, are the centerpiece of countless artisan life tales detectable as early as the late eighteenth century and persisting through the first half of the twentieth century. It should be pointed out that this artisanal subculture was exclusively masculine, indeed often misogynist; women workers, who lacked the professional organizational framework of the male artisans, did not produce a similar autobiographical literature.[24]

Even clearer, perhaps, is the impact of socialist organization on the production of working-class autobiography. By way of illustration, the early history of French popular autobiography could almost be written as a subhistory of French socialism. Susanne Voilquin, mentioned earlier, wrote her memoirs to recount her experiences in the Saint-Simonien movement and to record her disputes with the male leadership of it. Norbert Truquin was also involved in Utopian Socialist agitation. In the same year that Truquin published his autobiography, so did the Republican Socialist Sebastien Commissaire (1822–?), who recounted both his personal life and his political activities. The anarchist tradition also produced its autobiographers, such as Henri Tricot. Then, of course, came the great wave of working-class political narratives by the Communards involved in the insurrections of 1870–71. Some of these were fairly restricted political memoirs, but others were full-fledged autobiographies. Victorine Brocher (1838–1921), a Communard and anarchist exile, structured her autobiography around the chronology of rebellion that punctuated her life. Activists in the late-century French Socialist party and syndicalist movement continued the tradition, if at attenuated levels of production. Even as women fared better or worse within these movements, so too women's autobiographies reflect their presence or absence in the various branches of the French left.[25]

The German chronology looks somewhat different. After a much slower start, restricted largely to artisanal memoir, working-class autobiography flourished under the encouragement of the Socialist party only after its relegalization in 1890. The next two decades, however, witnessed an unprecedented and subsequently unequaled period of vitality in the genre. Not only did well-known socialists such as August Bebel publish their autobiographies during this era, but so did many relative unknowns who saw themselves, or were seen by their editors, as living exemplary socialist lives. These accounts ranged from those of "classic" proletarians such as the factory worker M. Theodor Bromme, to that of Franz Lüth, agricultural laborer and socialist propagandist. Often bearing titles like that of Nikolaus Osterroth's *Vom Beter zum Kämpfer* (From Pray-er to Fighter), these texts marked the passage from unwitting victimization to militancy.[26] Women, too, could redefine the meaning of their lives through the movement, although there was considerable debate over the place of women in socialism. Even as the presence of women in the German socialist movement began to grow, the first German-language autobiography of a working-class woman who was a political activist appeared in 1909 when Adelheid Popp published the anonymous first edition of her memoirs. And even as women were underrepresented in the movement, so were their autobiographical works but a small minority of the massive outpouring of socialist memoir literature.[27]

The discussion so far has suggested that working-class autobiographies often depart from narrative forms generally attributed to literary autobiography. Furthermore, working-class women's narratives generally follow different narrative logics than those of men. Finally, these narrative forms and the very impulse to write autobiography are closely connected with specifically working-class experiences and institutions that themselves reflect gender relations within the working class and class relations within the broader society and culture.

Still, the conscious employment of dominant cultural models in working-class autobiography is not to be ruled out entirely. For one thing, the prominence of working-class writers among autobiographers of course underscores the importance of literary history and editorial intervention in the production of working-class autobiographical texts. When there was a literary market for accounts of "how the other half lived," writers of working-class origin could expect favorable editorial response to marketable life stories, stamped by their voice of authenticity. The existence of a lively demand for working-class narratives not only provided writers with an incentive to write autobiography but also no doubt selected the sorts of autobiographical texts that would eventually see the light of day. Recent literary-historical scholarship has suggested the role of such literary fashion in the encouragement of popular autobiography in both contemporary France and turn-of-the-century Germany, and also provides some special caveats for interpretation of the texts so produced.[28] That such an influence was at work, however, is made explicit, for example, in the autobiography of the German waitress Mieze Biedenbach. Biedenbach's memoirs were written and published under the influence of a literary friend identified in the text as "Frederic." He gives her a copy of the recently published first-person account *Tagebuch einer Verlorenen* and suggests she write the same sort of thing. "The public has a great deal of interest in this sort of thing, and rightfully so," he tells her in encouragement.[29] Proletarian writers with an eye toward the literary marketplace may well have found both incentive for autobiography and models there, but these models may have molded working-class experience according to expectations of dominant culture.

Models drawn from dominant culture also appear in working-class life narratives in other ways—as distant goals, as unachieved aspirations, or as empty or deceptive claims. Many working-class autobiographies are at least in part structured by what their life was *not* and how it did *not* fit an implicit model depicted by the author as norm. In part, the prevalence of what has been termed "counter-narrative" reflects the particular character of the working-class family life and underlines its differences from the dominant model.[30] For example, Sebastien Commissaire admits in the preface to his *Mémoires* that he is not an appropriate subject of an autobiography. "Workers don't write memoirs," he claims. "Their lives pass in the workshops; the life of one closely resembles the life of others, a life of labor and privation."

Still, at age fifty-two, after delaying marriage and family because of political activities and subsequent imprisonment, he found himself with grey hair and very young children who "if he dies soon, may never know him."[31] Certainly here there is an echo of the concern to establish lineage that motivated some of the family concerns of the propertied classes, but set explicitly in the context of an "abnormal" life course.

The undercurrent of counter-narrative surfaces most strongly in accounts of childhood. Working-class autobiographers had strong opinions about what constituted a proper childhood, but most denied having had one. Orphan status, still so common in a world dominated by the bourgeois ideology of family, could in itself provide a motive for autobiographical self-exploration. For example, the anonymous German author who entitled his autobiography *The Memoirs of an Orphan Child* recounts his harsh orphanage childhood, particularly bitter for him since he knew his mother was alive but unable to support him. In fact, a huge percentage of the working-class autobiographers spent substantial proportions of their childhood with grandparents or other relatives or in foster homes. At times, the autobiographical accounts, especially of childhood years, are implicit protests against what is portrayed as the unfairness or impossibility of family life in working-class homes. One after another, the autobiographies recount growing up too fast, missing out on childhood, and, in the worst cases, suffering extreme brutality and abuse in the hands of caretakers. The cruelty of Lena Christ's mother or Adelheid Popp's father, or the tragedy portrayed by Heinrich Holek, who feels obliged to correct his father's memory of certain very painful events (his mother's infidelity, his father's contemplation of murder-suicide), marks the extreme differences between prevailing family mythology and the conditions that often affected working-class families.[32] But even where conditions were less harsh, childhood often appears in these accounts as something never experienced or as an experience to be regretted or exorcised. Only rarely is it depicted as an innocence or naiveté lost or an idealized dream. The impulse to write autobiography under these circumstances can perhaps be viewed as a product of the distance between the dominant norm and the lived reality. That is, this historical moment produced so many accounts of this form because so many autobiographers were affected by the clash between childhood as idealized in dominant culture and childhood as they had lived it. What this suggests is that prevailing mythologies may well have influenced self-portrayals, but in a manner far more nuanced and ironic than any universal cultural model would suggest.

Obviously, these comments are only a beginning. I have tried to sketch out the ways in which the history of working-class autobiography has been shaped by the social and political conditions in which working people found themselves, as well as by the variety of cultural models available from which a life could gain meaning and around which a life account could be structured. Even though the outline is tentative, the emergent lines of a chronology of working-class autobiography in France and Germany are becoming clear. In a sense, all of this work is prefatory to my eventual aim—analysis of these works in terms of their contribution to our understanding of the dynamics of class and gender relations as they played themselves out in individual life histories. Understanding how working people came to be autobiographers is only the first step toward a better understanding of how and why they structured their life accounts the way they did, and how they understood, and ultimately structured, their lives.

Notes

1. This essay is drawn from a book in progress on working-class life course and working-class autobiography. The book is based on about a hundred autobiographical texts written by French and German working-class people whose childhoods occurred before World War I. All translations from the French and German are my own unless otherwise indicated.

2. Recent literary historical studies that have influenced my thinking about these texts include S. Egan, *Patterns of Experience in Autobiography* (Chapel Hill: University of North Carolina Press, 1984); E. Jelinek, ed., *Women's Autobiography* (Bloomington: Indiana University Press, 1980); P. Lejeune, *Je est un autre* (Paris: Editions du Seuil, 1980) and *Le pacte autobiographique* (Paris: Editions du Seuil, 1975); M. Vogtmeier, *Die proletarische Autobiographie, 1903–1914* (Frankfurt/Main: Peter Lang, 1984).

3. J. J. Rousseau, *Les Confessions* (Paris, 1964), first published in 1782; J. W. Goethe, *Aus meinem Leben: Dichtung und Wahrheit* (Weimar, 1886), first published in 1811–1813.

4. W. Emmerich, ed., *Proletarische Lebensläufe* (Reinbek bei Hamburg: Rowohlt, 1974), pp. 14ff.

5. Jelinek, pp. 5ff.

6. There has been some especially useful work on the history of working-class autobiography in Germany. See Emmerich and Vogtmeier, cited above, as well as P. Frerichs, *Bürgerliche Autobiographie und proletarische Selbstdarstellung* (Frankfurt/Main: Haag-Herchen, 1980).

7. Emmerich, esp. pp. 14–22.

8. Although the focus here is on cultural models that inform autobiographical form, the book will address the question of how demographic shifts and gender differences in life-course patterns interact with cultural models.

9. Egan, pp. 35ff.

10. For example, J.-L. Ménétra refers to Rousseau's *Social Contract* and other texts. See *Journal de ma vie* (Paris: Montalba, 1982), p. 16. S. Voilquin also refers to reading Rousseau, and especially liking *Émile* and *Nouvelle Heloise*. See *Souvenirs d'une fille du peuple* (Paris: Maspero, 1978) p. 76.

11. P. Burke, *Popular Culture in Early Modern Europe* (New York: Harper, 1978).

12. Most German men could read and write at least minimally by the end of the eighteenth century. The *alphabetisation* of French men was accomplished toward the middle of the nineteenth century. In both countries, women's literacy lagged behind that of men. For women, basic literacy skills were widespread in Germany by the

middle of the nineteenth century, in France by the third quarter of that century. For an overview of trends in popular education and literacy in Western Europe, see M. J. Maynes, *Schooling in Western Europe: A Social History* (Albany: SUNY Press, 1985).

13. N. Truquin, *Mémoires et aventures d'un prolétaire á travers la révolution* (Paris: Maspero, 1977), originally published in 1888.

14. There is a suggestion in B. Taylor's study of women in British Utopian Socialism *Eve and the New Jerusalem* (New York: Pantheon, 1983) that a considerable number of these women were engaged in public propaganda. Though there are examples of French women such as Flora Tristan who traveled around giving public speeches on behalf of the socialist movement, this seems to have been less common on the Continent.

15. M. R. Bonnet, *Enfance Limousin* (Paris, 1954), p. 44.

16. Mrs. R. Henrey, *The Little Madeleine* (New York: E. P. Dutton, 1953), p. 1.

17. See Jelinek, p. 3, for reference to *vies scandaleuses* and early women's memoirs in England.

18. Ménétra, p. 189.

19. Voilquin, p. 84.

20. V. Jamerey-Duval, *Mémoires: Enfance et education d'un paysan au xviiie siècle* (Paris: le Sycamore, 1981), pp. 124–25, first published in part in 1784.

21. E. Courmeaux, *Notes, souvenirs et impressions d'un vieux Remois*, premiere serie, de 1817 a 1825 (Reims, 1891); B. Bürgel, *Vom Arbeiter zum Astronomen* (Berlin: Ullstein Verlag, 1919). For a more contemporary analysis of the ambiguity characteristic of working-class "success stories," see J. Ryan and C. Sackrey, *Strangers in Paradise: Academics from the Working Class* (Boston: South End Press, 1984).

22. A. Langer, *Stromaufwärts: Aus einem Frauenleben* (Berlin: C. Fischer Verlag, 1913).

23. Anonymous (A. Popp), *Jugendgeschichte einer Arbeiterin* (Munich: Ernst Reinhardt Verlag, 1909); Jeanne Bouvier, *Mes souvenirs ou 59 années d'activité industrielle, sociale et intellectuelle d'une ouvrière* (Paris: Editions Andre Bonne, 1956).

24. Examples include the well-known autobiography of Agricol Perdiguier *Mémoires d'un compagnon* (Moulins, 1914) and the early artisanal memoir of Christian Dobel *Auf der Walze durch den Balkan und Orient* (Stuttgart, 1916), first published in 1853. For discussions of the troubled gender relations that could characterize artisanal milieux in the late eighteenth and early nineteenth centuries, see J. Quataert, "The Shaping of Women's Work in Manufacturing Guilds, Households, and the State in Central Europe, 1648–1870," *American Historical Review* 90 (1985): 1127–48, and M. A. Clawson, "Early Modern Fraternalism and the Patriarchal Family," *Feminist Studies* 6 (1980): 368–91.

25. Voilquin, cited above; S. Commissaire, *Mémoires et souvenirs de Sebastien Commissaire, ancien representant du peuple* (Lyon, 1888); H. Tricot, *Confessions d'un anarchiste* (Paris, 1898); Victorine B(rocher), *Souvenirs d'une morte vivante* (Paris: Maspero, 1977), first published in 1909; J. Allemane, *Mémoires d'un combattant* (Paris: chez l'auteur, n.d.).

26. For Popp's autobiography, see note 18 above. A. Bebel, *Aus meinem Leben* (Stuttgart, 1910–1914); M. T. W. Bromme, *Lebensgeschichte eines modernen Fabrikarbeiters* (Jena: Eugen Diederich Verlag, 1905); F. Lüth, *Aus der Jugendzeit eines Tagelöhners* (Berlin, n.d.); N. Osterroth, *Vom Beter zum Kämpfer* (Berlin: Verlag Vorwärts, 1920).

27. For a detailed study of the place of women in the German socialist movement, see H. Niggemann, *Emanzipation zwischen Sozialismus und Feminismus* (Wuppertal: Peter Hammer Verlag, 1981).

28. For a discussion of this issue, see P. Lejeune, *Je est un autre*, and M. Vogtmeier, cited above, and M. J. Maynes, "Gender and Class in Working-Class Women's

Autobiographies," in *German Women in the Eighteenth and Nineteenth Centuries*, ed. R. E. B. Joeres and M. J. Maynes (Bloomington: Indiana University Press, 1986).

29. M. Biedenbach, *Mieze Biedenbachs Erlebnisse* (Berlin: Fontane, 1906), p. 2. The cited work appears to be fiction disguised as a journal.

30. This concept as employed here emerged during the discussion of L. Passerini's paper "Women's Personal Narratives: Myths, Experiences, and Emotions" during the conference on which this book is based.

31. Commissaire, pp. iv–vi.

32. A. Forel, ed., *Erinnerungen eines Waisenknaben* (Munich, 1910); L. Christ, *Erinnerungen* (Munich: Albert Langen, 1921); H. Holek, *Unterwegs: Eine Selbstbiographie* (Vienna, 1927); A. Popp, cited above.

POETRY AND TRUTH
Elisa von der Recke's Sentimental Autobiography

Katherine R. Goodman

To read an autobiography, one must know the fictions it engages. No more or less than men, women have fashioned the stories of their lives from the ready-made images at their disposal. Indeed, all of us tend to lead our real and daily lives guided by these ready-made images. But successful autobiographers have also broken with those fictions, manipulated and altered them, thus revealing important and genuine experiences from their lives. Just because an author speaks through conventional imagery does not mean that it has been adopted uninventively or even that it does not express some genuine experience. While the genres autobiography and novel may be more closely allied than we have liked to admit in the past, watching an author manipulate conventions reveals a great deal about a real life and its author.

One case will stand for many. When the Prussian aristocrat Elisa von der Recke (1756–1833) recorded in 1793 the story of her marriage, and in 1795 the story of her childhood, she did not intend the manuscripts to be published before her death.[1] As the daughter of two Junker families and formerly married into another, she presumably determined that her tales exposed her family to an embarrassing degree. Left in her testament to different libraries, the manuscripts were not published until the beginning of the twentieth century. The generous details of her education and marriage are of intrinsic historical interest, but if as readers we look for subjective insights into her experience, we find an extraordinary example of an autobiographer's craft at manipulating fictions.

The manuscript under consideration here is the one she wrote first, the narration of her unhappy marriage to Georg von der Recke. Unlike the later narration of her childhood, this portion of her life is told in epistolary form, an unusual choice for autobiography. In the main the letters are addressed to Caroline Stoltz, the governess of Recke's younger sister. However, in my view, their authenticity as letters is somewhat suspect, and the form itself therefore suggests the conscious adaptation of the conventions of epistolary novels for autobiography.

These letters relate the events of Recke's marriage in far too connected a fashion to have been genuine missives to a friend. No piece of information is missing, as it usually would be in a collection of letters. Scenes are described or explained in more detail than is normally the case in letters. No subjects are raised which are not relevant to the story of her marriage. There is no mutual exchange of pleasantries. It is questionable whether the relationship of Elisa von der Recke to Caroline Stoltz was actually as intimate as these letters suggest.

The most likely explanation for these inconsistencies is not that Recke simply edited her letters, but rather that she used her diaries when writing this story. For the style of the autobiography is far more suggestive of Recke's diaries than of her letters. Recke's real letters do not describe scenes in detail. Rather, in kaleidoscopic fashion they open a variety of topics ranging from philosophy to literature to health. In her real letters her sentences appear more spontaneous; they are shorter, with frequent dashes and exclamation marks. The story of her marriage, however, is told in carefully considered sentences which often vividly recreate a particular scene. Her diaries are replete with concrete detail. Furthermore, while we possess neither the original manuscript nor any diaries from the period of her marriage, other of her diaries bear witness to constant rereading and rewriting.

It is probable, therefore, that the choice of epistolary form was just that— a conscious choice—and if we ask the reason, the most likely is that Recke opted to imitate the epistolary narrations of women's lives popular just then in fiction. Authors such as Richardson and Rousseau had virtually made the telling of women's troublesome and amorous adventures synonymous with the epistolary form. The sentimental heroine opened her heart to her best female friend, her own better self, in letters. Especially in Richardson's versions and (as Ruth Perry has amply analyzed) in other earlier British variations, the heroine's most intimate self was under siege—as was Elisa von der Recke's.[2] However, in her case the villain was no aggressive suitor but rather her boorish husband—surely a daring invention in sentimental novels.

Although raised to shine at social gatherings, Elisa von Medem was coerced into marrying a man who expected her to spend her time managing his estate, something for which she had neither interest nor training. When he did not ridicule the talents she had developed—reading, conversing, dancing—he forbade her them. Even after she bore him a child, a girl, he continued to abuse her. She refused further intimacies until he treated her with respect. Behind her back, however, Georg complained of her to her family. According to Elisa, he also lied about the situation, blaming her entirely. Because of these machinations and intrigues, her own rather large and imperious family frequently sided with his bullying. Nevertheless, it was against her wishes that they separated and finally divorced. He paid her interest on her dowry for the rest of his life, and she never remarried.

The conflict in this marriage was a complicated one and no doubt was due in part to Recke's ideas of marriage culled from reading. Relatives suggested from the beginning that Elisa had read too many sentimental novels—and believed them. When she objects to marrying Recke because she does not love him, the stepmother (who had first introduced her to sentimental novels) tries to impress her with the fact that love and honor are found only in novels and plays (p. 157). Since a woman who loves her husband will always be under his control, only a wife who can maintain some distance from her husband's wishes will be able to exercise any freedom. Therefore, according to the stepmother, who had no difficulty separating life from fiction, she had best *not* love her future husband. An aunt and uncle tell Georg von der Recke that the stepmother had turned Elisa into a "fool and the heroine of a novel" ("Närrin und Romanheldin") (p. 174). And Georg himself comments once about her language that it is "a truly sentimental stage language" ("eine wahre empfindsame Theatersprache") (p. 180), and another time that she had studied "the language of novels quite thoroughly" ("die Romanensprache recht gut") (p. 186).

Indeed, not infrequently Elisa describes herself in a scene which seems more appropriate for a sentimental novel than a letter or even autobiography. Of herself in church she writes, for instance: "I supported myself on my arm, gazed up at the blue heaven above, listened to the pious song of the peasants . . . and so, heavily moved, I prayed to God above . . ." ("Ich stützte mich auf meinen Arm, sah zum schönen, blauen Himmel empor, hörte den andächtigen Gesang der Bauergemeine . . . und so flehte ich ganz bewegt zu Gott empor . . .") (p. 198). The prose is so typical of sentimental novels, and the perspective is so close to a third-person narration that it is difficult not to imagine the real influence of contemporary fiction.

Georg von der Recke is portrayed as the opposite of the ideal sentimental hero: he has no time, for instance, to accompany her on evening walks. He not only rebukes her for reading and dancing, he objects to her domestic theater performances. He is reckless with her feelings, and his brutality is emphasized when he taunts his dogs to kill her cat before her very eyes. He cannot give her the "intimate love of the soul" ("innige Seelenliebe") she desires because he does not understand it (p. 163). He even manages to force her to break off correspondence with one of her dearest friends. Since for Elisa matters of the flesh are low (p. 204, also p. 296) and kissing men on the mouth is unpleasant (pp. 176, 186), when George approaches her in intimate moments she finds it repulsive. Refusing him conjugal rights is therefore in line with her "character." In all of these situations, Recke's unwanted advances are described as those of a "Lovelace" might have been: occasions to be avoided, sometimes cunningly. To make the situation worse, Recke's entire family participates in intrigues to make her his captive.

Elisa von der Recke had wanted to play the role her training and her background had suggested to her—that of a virtuous and sentimental heroine. It was a role her stepmother had introduced to her by letting her read novels. But it remained a fiction for her stepmother, for whom it was essential not to marry any man a woman might love, because then he would be able to dominate her. Elisa asserts that she does not want to rule in the house as her stepmother would have her do. She has no desire to become the "gallant woman of the world" ("galante Weltfrau") her stepmother encourages her to become (p. 363). Instead she desires "domestic happiness" ("häusliches Glück") (p. 106) and mutual love and respect.

The stepmother believes it is a duty to share a husband's bed, and the rest is of no consequence. Elisa feels it would be neglecting a duty "to give yourself to the person who injures you in an unspeakable way and thus distances himself from your heart. But nothing releases us from our duty to secure the peace and tranquility of the person to whom we are bound" ("dem sich zu überlassen, der einen auf unsägliche Art kränkt und so unser Herz von sich entfernt; nichts aber entbindet uns von der Pflicht, für die Ruhe und Zufriedenheit dessen zu sorgen, mit dem wir in Verbindung stehn") (p. 331). The point of contention is her right to her own body. It is a right connected with her most intimate understanding of her "self," so that if she is not respected as a person she will not relinquish it. For the rest she feels bound by marriage vows and her own sense of duty, and she continually attempts to meet all of Georg's other wishes. She urges her angry stepmother to give in to Georg's wish not to have his bride perform in any more theatrical productions. She gives up dancing, and tries to learn domestic economy. She gives up visiting her parents and writing her friend for a time, and she reassures that friend, "I will be happy if I see him happy" ("ich werde dadurch glücklich sein, wenn ich ihn froh sehe") (p. 179).

She would appear, therefore, not only to have written the story of her marriage as a sentimental novel, but also to have lived the role of sentimental heroine in the face of adversity. When Recke and her own family press for a divorce, she resists them, holding out for her own image of herself as a dutiful and sensitive mate and mother. She acquires a martyrlike attitude toward her fate, one derived from sentimental fiction. From this point of view one could consider that her self-image had been formed within the new bounds of sentimental literature, that she was prey to new domestic images of women projected by men. Indeed, since the life Georg von der Recke proposed she should be living was much more active, less sheltered, less "feminine," one might be inclined to view her as having capitulated in her own oppression.

Such a picture of this eighteenth-century noblewoman portrays her as far more passive than she was. To view her storytelling only in relation to the sentimental epistolary novel in general does her an injustice. We get quite a different picture of her if we consider her relation to three texts she mentions specifically in her autobiography. Two of these are sentimental novels, and one is a historical document. One is a sentimental novel by a woman who had already challenged some of the genre's conventions. Two are by men: one a sentimental novel she rejects as an example of herself, and one a description of an action undertaken by a man which she takes as an example for herself. Her handling of these texts reveals that Recke is carefully selective in the images she adopts for herself. She does not passively accept ready-made images but, rather, actively recombines what she finds.

After her marriage, cut off from all society on Georg's isolated estate, she resolves to continue reading to strengthen her understanding. Given the fact that this narrative was most likely constructed with the aid of diaries and was not narrated from one distant point in time, it is possible to observe the impact of various works as she read them, for without question these books influenced her real-life actions. Of great interest for us, however, must be not only the particular choices for models but what specifically she took from each of them.

In the very year of Recke's unhappy marriage, a novel appeared in Germany which would give the sentimental heroine more opportunity to act. For a woman such as Recke, Sophie von la Roche's *Geschichte des Fräuleins von Sternheim* (1771) contained a fictional model that sustained and encouraged. Recke read it in 1772. The editor of Recke's papers had already noted similarities between la Roche's heroine and Recke's narration of her experience (pp. 230–34). Indeed, they were similarities which had not escaped Recke either, as she inclined to view her own experience through the interpretive lens of Sophie von Sternheim: "Oh! Sternheim was much better, much more lovable and more unhappy than I. I will try to imitate her virtues, but I can never become as happy as Sternheim was in the end! For ah—Recke has no similarities with Seymour!" ("O! die Sternheim war viel besser, viel liebenswürdiger und viel unglücklicher als ich. Ihre Tugenden will ich nachzuahmen suchen: aber so glücklich, als die Sternheim am Ende wurde, kann ich doch nie werden! denn ach—zum Seym[o]ur hat Recke gar keine Anlage!") (p. 230)

Why should Elisa von der Recke be so taken with this particular sentimental novel? In the tradition of Richardson, whose works most strongly influenced la Roche at this time, the sentimental heroine is a passively suffering, essentially virtuous woman whose own family is at least partly responsible for her misfortunes. She is the victim of intrigues whose baseness she can hardly imagine until she is confronted with it. She has few resources upon which she can call for sustenance and guidance. However, Sophie von Sternheim is a young woman of considerable inner strength and plentiful resources.[3] In moments of deepest despair, she acts—and acts with dignity. She had been educated in both intellect and heart by a father of the most noble character. When he dies, she falls into the hands of scheming relatives at court. They desire to install her as a well-placed mistress of the local ruler for their own ends. When a masked friend (the virtuous Seymour) reveals the plan to Sternheim, she knows she must leave.

But she will not leave her relatives with the wicked Derby (who has pretended virtue) until they are married. She is decisive and cautious. But she is fooled. And when she discovers the marriage was conducted by an impostor, her despair almost overcomes her. Still, she recovers by assuming a different name, applying for a position in a well-intentioned household, where she is soon encouraged to begin plans for an educational institution for women without independent means. She recovers her self-respect and sanguinity on her own initiative. Then, visiting in England, she is abducted by the same villain she had thought she married and who now fears her revelation of his evil deeds. She nearly dies in a shack in a desolate region before kindly neighbors rescue her. Lord Seymour (the masked friend) has finally learned the true nature and strength of her virtue, and, since she had loved him from the beginning, they marry. This is no young woman of uncertain principles or virtue. Even while forced to live in that shack, she begins educating Derby's illegitimate daughter by another victim of his evil deeds. By inclination she hated this creature, and yet she overcame this emotion to begin caring for this child.

When Recke read this novel, one year after its appearance, she must have been struck by certain parallel facts. Her mother had also died when she was very young, and like Sophie von Sternheim, Recke claimed she secretly wept in front of the picture of that tender, virtuous mother. Recke claimed for herself passion and talent for the great skill of von Sternheim, dancing. And she, too, became the victim of relatives who wanted to marry her off for their own motives. Both possessed female relatives who denied them the pleasure of reading on the assumption that it would make them less malleable. Although we can never know the degree to which it was so, it certainly was very likely that reading la Roche's novel influenced the perspective with which Recke viewed her personal history—as well as her own self.

For it seems unlikely that the principles she enunciates as those guiding her behavior were not at least strengthened by reading that first important novel by a German woman writer. In her own life, then, while a victim in reality, she opted for the self-respect and principles of virtue modeled for her by von Sternheim, who may have been victimized but was never a victim. Like von Sternheim, she expresses her intimate self in correspondence with her soul friend, Caroline Stoltz. She tells her that Recke expected passion of her, but that physical contact was unpleasant for her. Sternheim had said the same in her relationship with Derby. In both cases the villain (Derby/Recke) finds the virtuous heroine's desire to talk and reason tiresome and bothersome. Both heroines emphasize the importance and value of moral lessons learned in adversity. These enhance their nobility of soul, which in turn keeps "the wicked one" at the desired distance. It was less von Sternheim's famous lessons on charity than her clear sense of cheerfulness in adversity and the fulfillment of one's duty under all circumstances that captured Recke's imagination.

Cheerfulness in adversity and fulfilling one's duty appear, at first reading, to be virtues of passivity. For both these heroines, however, such sentiments were grounded in a healthy respect for themselves. For both of them, virtue and attention to duty were not only a means through which to intimidate the undesirable man but also a way of securing the approval of the external world and, at least as important, their own self-respect. This behavior became both heroic and a means of survival. Georg von der Recke clearly recognized the defiance residing in his wife's virtuous stance.

Indeed, seen in this light, Recke's adherence to her marital "duties" of providing friendship and comfort for a husband who does not respect her (while withholding her person and her self) gives her an authority her stepmother could never have achieved through domestic manipulations. The model of Sophie von Sternheim (which, in contrast to that of Clarissa or Pamela, contains precisely this element of authority and power) came to Elisa von der Recke in a moment of need. It would be a wonder if she had not seized it for herself, both for her life and for the narration of it. Recke's undoubted projection of herself into von Sternheim's character and situation ultimately worked itself out in reality. At moments like this, fiction becomes reality and real women sentimental heroines. But, by the simple, daring act of identifying her husband with the sentimental villain, Recke turned the conventions (including la Roche's) against themselves. Her virtuous authority can be (and is) applied against a restrictive domestic situation.

What cannot be emphasized sufficiently is that the model of von Sternheim was a choice. For Elisa von der Recke, Sophie von Sternheim represented a possibility she *wanted* to make her own. Indeed, while selecting some of von Sternheim's virtues, she rejected (or ignored) others. She did not choose, for example, to portray herself in possession of that heroine's famous and great charity and magnanimity. Nor did she choose the passive Clarissa or Pamela—or Lotte, the indecisive and passive sentimental heroine in Goethe's *Leiden des jungen Werthers* (1774).

In 1775 the young poet Gottlob David Hartmann arrived in Neuenburg, the Reckes' estate. Of sentimental tendencies himself, he soon fell in love with the beautiful young mother, Elisa von der Recke. Together they read for the first time Goethe's new novel. Hartmann read it ten times. And in a letter to the famous pietist theologian Johann Kaspar Lavater (22.2.1775), Hartmann effusively describes the difficulty of his situation, which he claims to experience as that of Werther's: a sensitive young man desperately and hopelessly in love with a motherly young woman (Lotte/Elisa) who is already married to a man who does not know how to appreciate her. The power of fiction to shape self-images appears to be great.

Nor can the parallels have escaped Elisa von der Recke, who seems to have secretly returned the affections. However, her reactions to the book reveal the moment of choice in the appropriation of such images. For despite the obvious similarities, she censures Lotte severely for her behavior and takes her as a negative example. Recke's virtue demands that

Lotte should have sent Werther away the moment she suspected the conflict in the situation. And, while Recke fails to send Hartmann away immediately, she does finally ask him definitively to leave. Although in Hartmann's case no suicide ensues, the tragedy is not averted. For, as if life really did imitate art, it was not long before Hartmann succumbed to illness and died. Recke's expressions of sorrow make her pain apparent, and the choice of virtue clearly brings loss as well as power. For Recke the pleasure of company she sorely desired was overshadowed by her desire for respect—from herself and others. Interesting in this regard, for it is not self-evident, is that Recke gave no thought to identification with Werther. Like her, after all, he was a sensitive young person, whose talents and desires social convention restricted. Perhaps the kind of unfettered individualism Werther sought was too dangerous a concept for women to even entertain, perhaps it was not something they considered a positive good. In either case Recke chose virtue and self-respect by accepting one model and rejecting another. She had made certain of the ideals of Sophie von Sternheim her own.

On at least one other occasion, readers of this remarkable autobiography are allowed to observe Recke in the process of selecting a model, another that aids her in the articulation of her self-respect. This time it comes not from a fictional text but from a historical one. And this time the desired identification crosses gender. It occurs as she faces the difficult confrontation with her husband about the nature of their marriage and her demands. On June 9, 1776, Recke reports reading about Johann Kaspar Lavater's efforts to rid Zurich of a tyrannical magistrate named Grebel (p. 356). In an anonymous letter, he and a friend had demanded that Grebel reverse, within two months, all the injustices they perceived that he had perpetrated on the city populace, or they would expose and accuse him publicly. When Grebel remained silent, they distributed an anonymous pamphlet throughout the town. Eventually Grebel was forced to leave, and Lavater and his friend were hailed as heroes in the cause of justice. Recke observes: "With how much noble candor he opposed the magistrate, so powerful in Zurich!—how he spoke to his conscience!—Ah!—how small!— how hesitant I seem compared to Lavater!—and how little I have to fear if I speak to my lord clearly and openly!—he risked his life and I—I make timid detours to avoid the displeasure of my relatives!" ("Mit welcher edelmüthigen Offenheit erklärte er sich gegen diesen in Zürch [*sic*] allmächtigen Vogt!—wie spricht er ihm ins Gewissen!—Ach!—wie klein!—wie zaghaft erscheine ich mir gegen Lavatern!—und wie wenig habe ich zu fürchten, wenn ich gegen meinen Herrn eine reine, klare Sprache führe!— er wagte sein Leben, und ich—ich mache kleinmüthige Umwege, um mich dem Unwillen meiner Verwandten zu unterziehn!") (pp. 356ff.)

Recke learns the unseemly virtue of speaking out against perceived injustices from this theologian. But it is doubtful whether Lavater would recognize his influence in Recke's adaptation of his "model" behavior to domestic affairs. From this point on she clearly, staunchly, and calmly articulates her demands for respectful behavior before her husband will be entitled to approach her intimately again. This is the point that leads ultimately to his expelling her from the estate and her acquiescence to Recke's, and eventually her family's, plea that she agree to a divorce. Once again a text (albeit this time a historical text) produces a stance in the autobiographer the consequences of which are borne out in reality. And this time the model *is* a male. As Recke modulates it for her own purposes, however, Lavater's principle of nonviolent rebellion is no longer carried out in the realm of local politics; it is carried out in the realm of domestic politics. This is no longer quite the same as Sophie von Sternheim's cheerfulness and fortitude in adversity. Recke acts in a principled way to remove herself from an adverse situation.

Elisa von der Recke made history. She was famous in her own day both with rationalists and with pietists. Her account of being taken in by the conjurer Cagliostro caused suspicion of the charlatan wherever he then went. Enlightened minds, including none less than Catherine the Great, thanked her for her exposure of his trickery. And, after her divorce, she wrote and published religious poems and songs. By no account was she an ordinary woman, and yet dealing with the events in her personal life surely required more strength than breaking any of those other barriers. The support of rationalists and pietists was at least some reward for breaking the constrictions against a reputable woman's putting her name before the public in print. But there was little or no support for divorced women.

Elisa von der Recke not only divorced her husband, she wrote about it. At that time neither the significance of this life event nor that of its telling should be taken for granted. In the upper classes, marriages of convenience could virtually enslave a woman. The pressures to accept the choice of husband for a woman were great. For what was a woman who had a reputation for disobeying parental authority to do? If educated and obstinate, her chances of marriage were weakened. It was not certain whether her family could or would continue to support her without a husband. And there were no employment opportunities for women, at least no steady ones, and none which would not involve a severe loss of social position. Elisa von der Recke had been married off to Recke because her parents wanted to leave all their land to the sons. Recke, whose estate was large, was prepared to marry her with a relatively small dowry. Her parents did not initially support the divorce. However, even before things had advanced that far, they were plotting her next marriage. This time Elisa von der Recke steadfastly refused, and she was lucky her husband agreed to pay her interest on her dowry. Naturally the social stigma attached to a divorced woman was also great. Recke needed to muster incredible resources to withstand the assault of husband, family, and society. It is clear that she derived unusual inspiration and support from sentimental novels and from historical accounts.

Almost more daring was the public telling of her story. To be sure, Recke did not allow the publication of these manuscripts during her lifetime. But she left them with libraries. While only the manuscript of her childhood was left with explicit instructions for publication, surely the implicit assumption regarding the story of her marriage was that it, too, would be published. When both manuscripts finally appeared in print over a century later (in 1902), the editor found certain passages about marital relations so bold that he omitted them—and at least one critic expressed relief that he had done so. Thus, even at the beginning of our own century, the telling of this tale of marital discord—especially in its realistic detail—was scandalous.

It should not surprise us if Recke expressed herself by means of the form, language, and images of the texts from which she drew strength. They gave her legitimation and authority, and it does not seem unreasonable to admire the ingenuity with which she molded those images for her own self. Her choice of the epistolary form was unusual, but was no doubt motivated by the sentimental novels which inspired her. In actuality this autobiography is dominated by Recke's letters, and her correspondent is given little voice. The form therefore seems mainly a device which permits her to express thoughts and feelings more appropriate to contemporary novels of domestic affairs than to the more objective forms of autobiographical writing about professions of the time. No man, to my knowledge, availed himself of the epistolary form of autobiography, but Recke is not unique among women at this time in choosing this form to narrate her life story.[4]

Insofar as the implicit ideal in sentimental fiction was domestic bliss, Recke turned that ideal against itself (all the while upholding it). This very ideal became the principle by which she disrupted her own oppressive domestic reality. It is a startling innovation on the form to imagine the husband in the role of the villain. Writing in that genre, but explicitly rejecting its weak heroines, Recke reached outside it and found a model in public life which she adapted for her quiet, domestic rebellion. Recke took what she needed and deftly manipulated the possibilities from which she chose. Therein lies the creative expression of her experience.

This should not be construed to mean that Recke faithfully expressed the reality of her situation. We can be quite sure that she exaggerated and distorted at the same time that she rallied these images to her support. Marriage as portrayed in sentimental novels may never even have been a goal for her. She once told her stepmother that she would rather not marry at all than marry Georg von der Recke. And she never remarried after her divorce. Instead she traveled for a time throughout Europe with her close friend Sophie Becker, visiting famous people she admired. And we know how she mourned the death of that friend. Maybe she found with a woman the soulful intimacy she sought.

Even if the conventions of the sentimental novel *were* that far from expressing her sentiment, in Recke's modifications they expressed enough to make it a valid vehicle for her dislike of that marriage and her desire for soulful intimacy. And the strong, active models she chose in the place of weaker ones of ambivalent character were, in Recke's modulations, no doubt more appropriate for her character. Though an author may speak through the language and conventions of her time, she is not therefore totally expressed by them. While there may be no absolute freedom, neither is there absolute imprisonment. Elisa von der Recke's autobiography evinces a strongly directed ability to combine and reshape conventions of her time. The force of that ability speaks to her unique character.

Notes

This article contains material reworked from chapter 2 of the author's book *Dis/Closures: Women's Autobiography in Germany between 1790 and 1914* (New York/Bern: Peter Lang, 1986).

1. Elisa von der Recke, *Aufzeichnungen und Briefe aus ihren Jugendtagen*, ed. Paul Rachel (Leipzig: Dieterich, 1902).

2. Ruth Perry, *Women, Letters, and the Novel* (New York: AMS Press, 1980).

3. Ruth-Ellen Boetcher Joeres, "'That Girl Is an Entirely Different Character!' Yes, but Is She a Feminist?" in *German Women in the Eighteenth and Nineteenth Centuries: A Social and Literary History,* ed. Ruth-Ellen B. Joeres and Mary Jo Maynes (Bloomington: Indiana University Press, 1986), pp. 137–56.

4. Please see my book, cited above, for more information.

CONSIDERING MORE THAN A SINGLE READER

Elizabeth Hampsten

In the beginning was the word; the word was with God, the word *was* God. The creation of experience and the language to describe it are one, each powerful, mysterious, and fearful. Yet the poet John of the Gospels imagined the creation of both language and matter as, essentially, a masculine wonder; in the Middle Ages, a poet was called a "maker." The words of women, other myths tell us, are likely to be mean, trivial, and not trustworthy. Women gossip; they talk too much and seldom tell the truth. Their hold on language is weak—unstressed syllables at the ends of lines of verse are termed "feminine." Women's speech is also said to take on demonic powers, as with the chanting witches in *Macbeth*. If Shelley is correct in declaring poets, at least male ones, "the unacknowledged legislators of mankind," women's relationship to the power in the word may well be even more daring, for it keeps threatening to contradict women's essential weaker state.

The renaissance in women's writing of the last twenty years has drastically challenged the mythology of creativity: women are writing, and being written about, as never before. The consequences can be radical to women's lives, since we know that the word *does* make flesh: forming the words that describe experience creates another experience, the literary work. This transformation does not deny experience; it forms another to add onto the first. We are nearly gods when we write, a state not permitted within the usual mythology of femaleness.

If these observations are not mistaken, it is reasonable to assume that women who have distinguished themselves as published writers are conscious of opposing the myths or conventions against their success. We can suppose that they were aware, at least, of impediments, and may have protested against them. But what of women who, generally, have accepted a fairly traditional way of life, and yet, while not actually saying that they aspired to be "writers," have written, and often about themselves? The literature by such women is growing in volume and importance; letters, diaries, and reminiscences written in the past are being uncovered and published, and women in the present day are finding public acceptance for articles and autobiographical essays, even fiction and poetry, that may first have been intended only for family and friends.

129

These works are essentially narrative and autobiographical; they tell stories, and at their best, they move swiftly through events in chronological time. One senses that the stories are ones that have extraordinary power for the individual writers, something like the fascination that made Coleridge's Ancient Mariner hold every third wedding guest in thrall. They are what I would call focal tales that may be told again and again, but without advancing a development of character or plot, as might an episode in fiction, or venturing self-analysis, as might the autobiography of a more self-conscious writer. When these writings attempt exposition, it too often relies on cliché and received opinion. Commentary seldom becomes them.

Scholars can, of course, read such writings in manuscript libraries or acquire them more informally, and will apply to them whatever diligence they require. But occasionally a work appears—possibly with a title such as "My Life"—that might speak to a wider audience, but one nevertheless with limited patience. Such a work invites collaboration, a partnership between writer and an editor/critic who can extend the writing from the private to a more public audience, in an arrangement that may well need negotiating. When I have entered into such collaborations myself, I have found writers sometimes prizing sections that I thought sentimental, and wanting themselves to remove references to events only because they were unpleasant. One woman allowed me to publish all of her grandmother's diary except a description of surgery she had undergone—the family was Christian Scientist, but the grandmother nevertheless had had the surgery, and had written about it in detail. Another woman removed sentences from her own description of her father's physical violence toward her mother. Some writers feel obliged to praise, and to suppress whatever they cannot speak well of.

With such endeavors come ethical considerations, such as the matter of "informed consent," that are similar to those confronting the use of oral testimony. Some scholars are troubled that, even after an "informant" has approved a text, agreed to publication, and written her permission to be quoted, the person may still not truly understand the implications of what she or he has said or written, and the "use" to which it is being put. I know of no entirely happy solution, no guarantee that we can be "clean," as I have heard some scholars long to be. The problem is not limited to social scientists conducting interviews, or to editors and critics presenting written texts. The dilemma is one of writing itself: as we appropriate the power of the gods in words, can we help but cannibalize the lives of others?—to the extent that we dare have anything serious to say. The mere desire to give form and therefore meaning to others' lives or their writing is, if you think too much about it, forbiddingly arrogant. We should be warned by the Pygmalion myth.

I think I have read enough of these essentially private writings to realize that their considerable narrative strength seldom sustains itself for long, but comes in short spurts of clear, crucial episodes. The whole is not properly a "life" at all. "My Story (An Autobiography)," by Mary Anna Albrecht Burckhard, now living in a nursing home in South Milwaukee, Wisconsin, tells of her parents' travels from the Ukraine to south-central North Dakota, and of her growing up on a homestead farm. She describes the punishment she and a brother received after constructing and lighting a shotgun shell while their parents had gone to town.

> Upon arriving home from the trip to town with a new stove, chairs, cupboard, and bed, our parents took one look at us and Mother screamed asking what happened. We must have looked a sight. They gave us both the third degree. I said Joe did it, and Joe said I did it. My dad did not decide what to do about us until he unhitched the team of horses and put them away. Then the final judgment was made—punishment would be a good razor strapping, no supper, and we would have to sit on a chair all the next day, not able to do anything. In addition, we would not get any of the candy and cookies they had brought for us from town. Mother did give us some bread and milk, but we could not have butter or syrup on the bread.
>
> My mother tended to our burns very gently and in no time we were as good as new, scheming and planning for our next adventure. Before we were finally released from our prison, however, Mother and Dad both sat in front of us and lectured us on the terrible things that could have happened to us for being so foolish. We had to promise never to try any more stunts like that again. Of course, even if Joe and I decided to try some foolish thing again, our younger brother, Bill, who was a big tattle tale, would probably tell on us. So we never tried anything worthwhile while Bill was around.[1]

"My Story" evolves in small increments barely connected to one another—rather, Mary Anna Burckhard focuses on details, one by one, in a nearly encyclopedic manner. Some details are riveting: "We made the shell and then decided to set it off by lighting a match to it. First we held the wooden farmer matches at arm's length, but the powder would not ignite. Joe moved closer but still could not get it set off. Enough of that. I took a lighted match and plunged it into the shell." Others appear to be there because that is the way she remembers things happening, like the list of purchases from town. In neither case, however, do these details particularly move the story forward. Events take place sequentially in time, but not in relation to each other. (The betrayal by the brother Bill is not referred to again.) She reports no reaction to her mother's standing by with salves, so that one wonders whether it occurred to the children that their mother might have tried to prevent such punishment, or that the makings for shotgun shells should not have been left within the reach of children. The calculated manner in which the father is described deciding upon the punishment, after he had unhitched the team, and its description in the passive voice ("punishment would be") are chilling but seem to pass almost unnoticed by the narrator. The episode that follows is a long account of the father's being caught in a snowstorm alone with horse and buggy, told in scrupulous detail (presumably from his report) but unconnected to the man who beat his children with a razor strap.

When Mary Anna Burckhard is not able herself to observe or participate in the events she describes, the writing takes on a somewhat bookish tone. There are several caught-in-a-blizzard accounts that she has to have written from the reports, such as that of her father wandering around with his horse-drawn stone boat (a sled with a box farmers used for removing stones from fields): "He was always scanning and searching the countryside in the darkness and swirling snow, looking for a farmhouse light or just anything that he could guide on. Way back then, however, the chance of seeing a farmhouse light was very slim. In those days in this wide prairie land, ranches and farms were few and far between, often miles apart." For direct observation here, she substitutes details that might apply to anyone lost anywhere; there is little necessity for information about distances between houses, or the clichéd phrase "this wide prairie land." The story was important because it happened to her father, and, possibly, because blizzards are obligatory to prairie winter mythology, but it cannot be said that they help to make this "her" story. It would not be difficult for an editor, however, to help her do so by reducing second-hand accounts to a few summary sentences, omitting unnessary information, and concentrating on the strong observations that *are* hers.

My second example is (as of the winter of 1987/88) in the process of preparation for a volume of essays on the history of women in North Dakota. In response to a news release from the project editors, Lucille Gullickson of Center, North Dakota, wrote (March 2, 1987) to say that she wished to write about "Hazel Miner . . . the 16 year old Oliver County farm girl who gave her life to save the lives of a younger brother and sister when caught in a late March blizzard on their way home from a country school." The letter states that the girl's "heroism became a legend" and the subject of a "poignantly beautiful ballad" by a popular singer.

Gullickson's subsequent proposal (March 17) was a fictionalized scene in the Miner household:

> The morning started like any other. It was warm for March. The sun rose, red against the bright blue sky as the stars faded into nothingness. Hazel was up early to help her father with the chores before school.
>
> As she sat on her milking stool she nestled her head against the soft flank of the old milk cow. She was still sleepy, and yawned as she aimed a stream of warm milk at the open mouth of the big black cat who sat waiting for his breakfast. Hazel loved the early morning chores, and the easy banter with her father as he fed and harnessed old Maude for the trip to the nearby school house.[2]

"And I can go on," Gullickson concludes a page later, "recalling many of the events of that fateful night—from newspaper accounts, from the memories of the two surviving children, neighbors, as well as persons who helped with the search."

In response, I asked her to avoid the appearance of fiction—that was not to be the intent of the history book—and instead to compile as many accounts as she could find of that event, using the newspapers and family and acquaintances she had mentioned. She identified herself as editor of the weekly *Center Republican* and said she was completing a degree in English at a local college. And, she wrote, she had "a personal knowledge of the area where the tragedy occurred (I live only two miles away) as well as a personal friendship with family members." Lucille Gullickson, I thought, was well positioned to glean information from a number of sources that would not be available to anyone else. But I was less sure that she would be interested in an analysis that went beyond, to my mind, enshrining an unhappy accident (that may have been the result of simple carelessness). The story of Hazel Miner has indeed become legend in the state. She is referred to as the "Angel of the Prairie," and in the 1920s schoolchildren were urged to form "Hazel Miner Societies" and collect money for an orphanage.[3] The tragic/heroic view is not questioned anywhere that I have found (although sometimes one comes across criticism of teachers who allowed children to start home from country school in a storm).

To date, Lucille Gullickson's first draft essay about Hazel Miner supplies a good deal of material for an analysis as to why the child's story is so powerful. She includes the inscription on Hazel's tombstone, the text of three articles from the *Center Republican* detailing the episode and its aftermath, an interview with a woman who remembers, as a child, Hazel and her brother and sister being brought into the women's family's house to thaw out, a version of the story by the brother who survived, and the words to "The Ballad of Hazel Miner" composed by Chuck Suchy of Mandan, North Dakota.

The interview with the neighbor, a woman named Anna Starck Benjamine, works particularly well in incorporating some of the color with which people have told the story, but the words, appropriately, are Anna Benjamine's, not (as in the fictional version) Gullickson's: "The weather had been beautiful, melting snow and running creeks. Bright March sunshine. It looked like spring was really here. Then one evening it started raining, got colder, and turned to snow by morning." The details, as Anna said she remembered them, carry a conviction that second-hand reporting would not—"the sound of Hazel's outstretched arms as they brushed against the furniture as they brought her into the house, and took her into my parents' bedroom . . . the crackling sound as that of frozen laundry being brought in off the clothes line in winter." Anna Benjamine, but not Gullickson, can say effectively about the surviving children: "The pain of their frozen limbs, when they got into the warm house, must have been terrible." These observations came from the four-year-old who had been "sitting in the east window with my grandfather" watching. We even can feel confident when she tells about Mrs. Miner "sitting in a rocking chair and just rocking and rocking," and telling of a dream in which Hazel says to her, "I was cold. Mama, but I'm not any more."

Lucille Gullickson's opening and closing paragraphs seemed to me to depend too much upon received opinions. Nevertheless, there also were sentences there that I thought effective for an introduction. Below are Gullickson's opening and closing sentences, and my emendations for a first paragraph:

Southeast of the Court House in Center, North Dakota, on the green lawn of the courtyard, stands a six-foot stone memorial. Its inscription reads:

[Closing paragraph] The Consolidated School has now become a modern home, with a new highway running past. The area, beginning at the school, and reaching about to where the highway runs south, some ten or fifteen miles, is known to locals as the "blizzard belt." Because of the way the land lies, blizzards sweep the area relentlessly. Those who travel the area often will undoubtedly sometime find themselves caught in a blizzard. Then thoughts turn to Hazel Miner and her awful ordeal. Even in a warm car we feel such a sense of panic. We learn a little of the fears she must have known. And there are those of us who feel her spirit may have been guiding us when we finally reach the safety of our warm homes. We say a prayer of thanksgiving.

Because of the way the land lies around Center, North Dakota, the fifteen miles between the consolidated school and the place where the highway turns south is known to locals as the "blizzard belt." It is famous for being the place where Hazel Miner died, and is commemorated by a six-foot memorial in the courthouse lawn that reads:

Lucille Gullickson's variety of sources reveal many details, with no two versions exactly alike. Two accounts say the father came for the children and told them to wait for him. According to the son, Emmett, the horse started on her own; the newspaper suggests that either the horse ran away or the children may have urged her. Emmett describes lying under coats, and wanting Hazel to get under the cover, but she refused. There is no way for us now to know whether even Hazel herself, described by Gullickson as "a great lover of children, who never hesitated to bring their troubles to her and found her always helpful and sympathetic," might have imagined a martyr's death for herself, even as she nagged the other two children to stay awake and keep moving their hands and feet against frostbite. To begin to understand the making of a powerful regional myth, Lucille Gullickson's collection is invaluable.

Mary Anne Burckhard and Lucille Gullickson's writings demonstrate a dilemma often present in the writings of women who did not suppose a public audience: the parts are so sharp we cannot forget them, but the whole is too unformed for us to know what to make of it. This dilemma cannot always be entirely resolved—you can't make silk purses out of sows' ears (although for all I know, nice *sows'* purses may be made of sows' ears). Without claiming too exaggerated a metamorphosis, I think it is possible nevertheless to enter into a friendly collaboration with writers like them— to nudge along their best moments of writing, and make what bridges one can over gaps and omissions. I am suggesting not a great deal more than what more practiced writers already do for each other—we read, talk about, argue, encourage, mock, correct, cross out, and otherwise engage our imaginations in the work of a friend or two, and cherish those who do the same for us. It is an intimacy like no other.

What we call "writing" is a contract between reader and writer—each needs the other, even when both may be the same person. "Good" writing is a shorthand term for whatever best reaches us, what moves and stirs our mind because it convinces us we are discovering the "truth" about another life. If arriving at that effect is our primary motive, if we think that what some women have written is so compelling that we must do almost anything to have it read, then we may need to invent ways to make new contracts between writers and readers. "My Story" and the martyrdom of Hazel Miner invite the collaboration I am speaking of. I believe these stories, in spite of their gaps and improbabilities, and want to nudge them along, hoping to make them more truly what they are.

Increasingly over the last fifteen years, books and articles have appeared devoted to women's private writings. Julie Roy Jeffrey's *Frontier Women: The Trans-Mississippi West, 1840–1880* (1979) was one of the first books to use women's diaries to investigate their experiences on the trails west. Jeffrey quotes from diaries to illustrate general observations about travel experiences, but she does not particularly concern herself with these writings apart from the information they contain—as works of literature on their own—and for that reason her study seems to me incomplete. Thus, to show that "marriage [did not] necessarily dull tender feelings," Jeffrey writes of a woman who "described her husband as 'my first and only choice. The man to whom I had first given my heart and conscience. The man with whom I had sacrificed my home and friends, the man with whom I had shed tears and shared his gladness and with whom I had shared many difficulties and by whom I had borne eight children'" (p. 67). I wish there were more: Jeffrey does not say whether this Susannah Willeford habitually wrote in so literary a manner, or whether her entries became mannered only on such a special topic as praise of her husband. The sentences in the quotations suggest that Susannah Willeford had heard those phrases before—in sermons, in romantic novels, and in prescriptive writing, all telling her what love and marriage were supposed to be, none of which is to deny her actual admiration and affection for her husband. Yet sharper attention to the context of the quotation might show that it does more than illustrate women's "tender feelings" in marriage.

Joanna L. Stratton's *Pioneer Women: Voices from the Kansas Frontier* (1981) reproduces extended quotations from autobiographies that her great-grandmother, Lila Day Monroe, had collected from women who settled in Kansas. Monroe's intention had been to publish these essays as a book, a project she never completed. Stratton extrapolates from the writings illustrations to such topics as "Daily Life on the Prairie," "Indians," or "The Frontier Church." Her great-grandmother, I think, had a better idea, for with the entire texts, we might have interpreted for ourselves the nature of these women's experiences. Stratton intervenes both too greatly and not incisively enough. Thus she paraphrases and quotes from a woman named Lilian Forrest, who she says "tenderly described" a young boy's encounter with Indians who visited his house: "'A band of so-called "Noble Red Men" arrayed in all the paraphernalia of savage life'" arrived, and the child "'played the role of hospitality to the entire band of wild, gay-looking strangers,'" as oblivious, evidently, as Stratton herself to the racism of the description (p. 51). Stratton comments only that "not all experiences were as carefree as little Laddie's with the Indians." Her not saying more is as distracting as her using the passage merely to illustrate "the warmth and candor which many children displayed toward their Indian neighbors."

True, the spare, laconic style of some women's writing can appear to reveal little beyond plain facts. Glenda Riley and Carol Benning have described "the 1836–1845 Diary of Sarah Browne Armstrong Adamson of Fayette County, Ohio" as one of the "treasure troves of information" uncovered in the current interest in women's writing.[4] They glean from the diary considerable information about the Adamsons' farming operation near Bloomingburg, Ohio, and about Sarah's strong feelings toward her children, who had moved to Iowa. The authors emphasize facts: "While Sarah paid for staples for baking, canning, and preserving with money earned from the sale of her butter, eggs or goose feathers, her husband and sons bartered cattle and hogs for farm equipment, borrowed and loaned money or food, and hauled goods for friends and neighbors within at least a fifty mile radius" (p. 286). Riley and Benning also take note of the emotional elements of the diary: "When Sarah's daughter and grandchildren succumbed to an unidentified illness after reaching Iowa, their deaths were a tremendous blow to Sarah. Her grief recurred with poignant regularity in her diary and poems. The approximately five-hundred mile distance between Sarah and her children became increasingly unbearable to her. Sarah and her husband eventually joined their family in 1850" (p. 287). One entry reveals the death of Sarah's stepdaughter: "'Rec'd Hanna's letter bearing the melancholy news of our dear Mary's death,'" to which the scholars comment: "Sarah's 11 August entry concerning her stepdaughter Mary's death may appear callous, but actually speaks more to her haste than her heartlessness," and then they point out that later in her life Sarah wrote poetry "that exhibited a depth of feeling seldom reflected in her early diaries" (p. 282).

There is more going on here than haste, I think. Sarah's language changes between two kinds of entries: those about what the authors call her business and her interest in economic affairs, and those about her worries over the children. The first sort—"Higgins returned from Cincinnati," or "paid the tax"—almost never subordinate or include modifiers. If someone else's activity is being reported, then she lines up subject-verb-object; if the activity is hers, she begins with the verb. In passages of "deep feeling" (which I would say are very present), Sarah expands to subordination and adjectives, as in the sentence about Mary's death. She mourned her first husband and the departure of a son with several rhetorical embellishments: "This day 30 years I buried my Armstrong and this day my William has started to IOWAY with H. Walker another bereavement for me to endure" (p. 296). Repeating "this day" and adding the appositive phrase is rather different from the style of entries that typically read "bought at Furgusson Tea Coffee Sugar pd bill 5.89."

Sarah virtually composed her diary in two languages: one for work and business; the other for affairs of her heart. The contrast makes each kind more arresting and important, the two parts of her life that vied against each other: "Must I record again the departure of my dear Higgins Sidney Mary Jane and little William and sweet little Sarah Ann. Together with my beloved Charlotte Sydne Cassann Sarah Jane my dear Black-eyed Mary Catherine O for fortitude to bear the heart-rending painful dispension. May the God of peace go with them. O may we meet where all this parting will at an end" (p. 298). The "treasure trove" that Benning and Riley say they found becomes richer by including the manner of writing with the matter.

Other books have published private writings of nonliterary women: the Feminist Press, for instance, has issued *With These Hands,* edited by Joan M. Jensen; *The Maimie Papers;* and most recently, *A Day at a Time: The Diary Literature of American Women from 1784 to the Present,* edited by Margo Culley (1985). These books reaffirm the fact that if we are to know women's lives, we should not stop with published fiction, poetry, and other public literature. These are bare beginnings; a review essay by Susan N. G. Geiger in *Signs*[5] argues for paying more attention to life histories of women who are not part of Western European literate cultural traditions—for instance, life histories of African women in slavery and enslavement, of Native American and Eskimo women, of Chinese women across several generations and political systems. In our desire for true women's history, we have had to invent ways not only of finding those "lives" but of making them known as well, and we have realized along the way that the usual methods—publishing "the best that has been thought and said"—not only have usually excluded women but may be inadequate to their work. It is as though we are learning all over again how, in the beginning, there really was the word.

Notes

1. *Plainswoman,* November 1987.
2. Letters and manuscript drafts in the possession of Elizabeth Hampsten and the ND History of Women Project.
3. *North Dakota Children's Home Finder,* Fargo, N.D., January 15, 1921.
4. *The Old Northwest: A Journal of Regional Life and Letters* 10 (Fall 1984): 285–306.
5. "Women's Life Histories: Method and Content," Winter 1986.

NINETEENTH-CENTURY BLACK WOMEN'S SPIRITUAL AUTOBIOGRAPHIES
Religious Faith and Self-Empowerment

Nellie Y. McKay

Acknowledgment of the significance of black women to all aspects of the life of the Afro-American community, and recognition of the role of the spiritual or conversion narratives of the ante- and postbellum periods are among landmark advances in recent Afro-American scholarship. Little need be said here of the part that feminist scholarship and black feminist scholars have played in facilitating this new awareness of the importance of gender in the making and interpretation of a people's history. On the other hand, it is more difficult to understand why, in spite of the pervasiveness of the cultural influence of the Afro-American religious tradition, early studies of the black autobiographical narrative tended to focus mainly on the heroic and political dimensions of slave narratives (male), to the exclusion of the dynamic power of the spiritual or conversion narratives. Fortunately, the new scholarship, in quest of a more fully developed intellectual understanding of Afro-American life, recognizes and has begun to explore the spiritual and secular importance of black religious faith in eighteenth-and nineteenth-century black men's and women's narratives.[1] Such study has more than historical implications, and the narratives of twentieth-century black women and men continue to reflect the profound impact that the early religious traditions of the nineteenth century have had on their individual and collective lives. Using autobiographical writings of two black women of the nineteenth century, I shall examine in this essay the roots of the tradition of black women's engagement with the spiritual life of the community, the roles they assumed within that religious framework, and the extent to which faith in the "divine" gave expanded meaning to their lived experiences.

The current flowering of Afro-American autobiography and autobiographical criticism is not undeserved. Afro-American prose writings began with autobiography: the slave, conversion or spiritual, and con-

For My Students at the Harvard Divinity School, Fall 1986

139

fessional narratives, preeminent from the middle of the eighteenth century through the middle of the nineteenth. In spite of major changes and developments, the form continues to hold a central position within the twentiety-century black American literary tradition.[2] Scholars of the evolution of black traditions in writing point to a number of reasons for the popularity of the personal narrative over other literary forms among Afro-American writers in the early years. Not the least of these were indeed the politics and propaganda it directed toward the outside world and the internal sense of order and control it bestowed on a group whose external world demanded subservience and dependence on others. For as Pamela S. Bromberg notes in another context, the "self-generated and self-motivated [narrative] . . . tends . . . toward a unity of point of view and coherence that makes it . . . patterned and meaningful," not disordered and purposeless, in conflict with "coincidence—the unforeseen, random, [and] unpredictable"—in human experience.[3] Moreover, the appeal of the personal narrative for blacks also lies in the challenge of critic Albert Stone's theory of autobiography as literary convention and cultural activity: imagination and history.[4] As Andrews notes, the nineteenth-century black writer, in telling his or her story, had to be sufficiently imaginative to avoid the pitfall of boring "facts," even while he or she remained true to the personal history.[5] In the final analysis, autobiography connects the writer to her or his individual self as well as to collective human existence. In black autobiography, to a greater degree than in white, author and white reader, with separate racial identities within the same culture, are forced toward a common reading of experience.

In this respect, eighteenth- and nineteenth-century blacks who told their own stories forced a different relationship between Afro-Americans and the dominant culture. Escaped slaves who condemned the "peculiar" institution by indicting its atrocities in writing, and spiritual narrators who claimed equal access to the love and forgiveness of a black-appropriated Christian God could not be nonpersons in the eyes of the white world. Their narratives compelled a revisionary reading of the collective American experience, as specific situations and individual acts of memory and imagination yielded to identifiable patterns within the larger cultural context. And while the centrality and importance of the individual life initially motivates all autobiographical impulse, in black autobiography this "act of consciousness" in the present bears the weight of transcending the history of race, caste, and/or gender oppression for an entire group.[6]

The spiritual and slave narratives, one religious and addressed mainly to the black community, the other secular and intended for a white readership, offer profound second readings of the American and Afro-American experiences against prevailing white American views in their time. Clearly, the authors of these narratives wanted more than to create and recreate the self-in-experience in literature. In establishing their claims to full humanity, they wanted their words to change the hearts of the men and the women whom they reached. Robert Stepto reminds us that in the Afro-American slave narrative these claims sought validity in the "moral voice of the former slave recounting, exposing, appealing, apostrophising, and above all *remembering* his ordeal in bondage."[7] Similarly, in his argument for the significance of the spiritual narratives, Andrews maintains that they are "models of the act and impact of biblical appropriation on the consciousness of the black narrator as bearer of the Word."[8]

Other scholars have ably demonstrated that the rhetorical aims of early Afro-American autobiographical narrative focused on the authentication of the black self in a world that had denied that self humanity. As the form evolved through the mid-1800s, it revealed more clearly the nature of creative tensions between the black self and white cultural assumptions of that self in relationship to the dominant white society, and between the black individual and his or her psychological needs beyond survival.[9] In the slave narrative, the writer's concrete quest was physical freedom, while literacy—the ability to articulate that quest through writing—intimated a less restricted self, socially and otherwise. For spiritual autobiographers, the escape from sinfulness and ignorance of a worthwhile self and the achievement of salvation and knowledge of God's saving grace bestowed a fundamentally positive identity.

Much has been made of narrative differences and meanings in early black autobiography based on severe antebellum legal and extralegal strictures against black literacy. Critics of black narrative and autobiography have fully discussed the loss of authorial authority to the amanuensis-editor and the use of authenticating documents by whites, such as appended prefaces, letters, and the like, to give historical validity to the narrator. Historians, anthropologists, and literary critics, among others, agree that the narrative written by the subject of the text has a higher "discursive status" than the dictated narrative, edited and shaped by another, especially one outside of the experience. Consider, then, the significance of the fact that the first relatively autonomous black narrative was a spiritual narrative, published in 1810.[10] In addition, almost all of the spiritual narratives published through the 1860s were relatively autonomous documents. Their largest distribution appears to have been within the perimeters of the black church and at revival meetings. While most lacked the immediate overt political value of the slave narratives (i.e., they seldom clamored for abolition), they presented readers with a radical revision of prevailing white myths and ideals of black American life. Spiritual narratives were written by ex-slaves as well as freeborn blacks and provide a valuable cross-sectional view of nineteenth-century Afro-American intellectual thought.

As noted earlier, critical evaluation of black women's autobiographical narratives, past and contemporary, is rapidly becoming a substantial part of new Afro-American scholarship.[11] While the major concern for all black people in America has always been the issue of race, the narratives of black women present a more complicated dilemma than those of their male counterparts. In the search for self, issues of gender are equally as important as those of race for the black female, a matter black men usually overlooked. Consequently, as male slave and spiritual narrators sought autonomy in a world dominated by racist white male views, black women writers demonstrated that sexism, inside and outside of the black community, was an equal threat to their quest for a positive identity. Black women use the personal narrative to document their differences in self-perception as well as their concerns for themselves and others, their sense of themselves as part of a distinct women's and racial community, and the complexities of the combined forces of race and gender for the only group beleaguered by both.

In all categories of writing, considerably fewer nineteenth-century texts by black women than men survive. Most of these are spiritual narratives. While the majority of women who wrote were Northern and freeborn, all— former slaves or free women—felt "called" to a mission that transcended the mundane activities of their daily lives and manifested their first loyalties to a being more powerful than humans. Most were itinerant preachers and/or missionaries who traveled extensively in America and abroad, with or without the sanction of the established black church. Their stories focus on their religious convictions, on their willingness to respond to a calling that demanded they overcome formidable personal and societal hindrances in the process, and on a consciousness of the authority that came to them in the service they carried out. Nor is it surprising that religious black women of great personal power and authority emerged from their communities. Often referred to as the glue that has held the black church together, black women within this institution developed the "independence, self-reliance, strength, and autonomy" that the dominant culture little suspected they possessed.[12] Nineteenth-century black female spiritual autobiographies vividly demonstrate this claim in their delineation of women's participation in the ideological conflicts of their religious communities—in their insistence on the validity of the doctrine of ecstatic experience and the rights of women to the clergy.

This essay focuses on two representative spiritual narratives by Northern antebellum black women who claimed authority largely on the basis of their ecstatic religious experience and the fundamental right of women to self-determination: Jarena Lee and Rebecca Cox Jackson. Lee never mentions the latter, but Jackson notes one meeting between them in Philadelphia in 1857. Apparently, the women had disagreed vigorously at earlier times, most likely over religious matters, and Jackson claims that Lee had been "one of her bitterest persecutors." In 1857, however, the meeting was amicable. Jackson attributes this to the "Lord's doing," and the "answer to her prayer." According to Jackson, Lee "spoke lovingly" to her, read from the Scriptures, sang, prayed, bestowed a blessing on Jackson's house, and left her "with love."[13]

Lee was an itinerant preacher with affiliations to the AME church. She

Mrs. Jarena Lee. Preacher of the A.M.E. Church. Aged sixty years. Philadelphia, 1844. (From *Religious Experience and Journal of Mrs. Jarena Lee,* Philadelphia, 1894.)

claimed fame for her astonishing record of traveling thousands of miles—many of them on foot—across the border states, Ohio, and Canada, to dispense her message. In 1835, for instance, she covered more than seven hundred miles and preached almost as many sermons. Jackson, on the other hand, began her religious career independently of approval from organized religion and traveled only moderately within the North Atlantic states. Both women claimed gifts of vision as one confirmation of their faith. In their journals, kept over several years, they wrote of their experiences of faith and mission. These narratives illuminate the differences that a strong religious faith made in their lives and their perceptions of the freedom they achieved through that faith. Both emphasize the women's search for Christian perfection, the highest state of salvation in life; the process of their development as leaders; their challenges to male authority; and their unfaltering belief in the authenticity of their special gifts of power through vision.

The black female autobiographical tradition begins with Lee's narrative: *The Life and Religious Experience of Jarena Lee, a Coloured Lady, Giving an*

Account of Her Call to Preach the Gospel. Revised and Corrected from the Original Manuscript, Written by Herself (24 pages), published in 1836.[14] Lee printed a thousand copies of her text, paying the cost of thirty dollars herself, and sold them at camp meetings and other church gatherings. She believed that her story, a record of God's work through her, would be a useful tool to lead others to him. In 1839 she printed another thousand copies, and presumably dispersed them in the same way. In 1844 she tried without success to convince the book committee of the AME church to publish an expanded version of the narrative. Against the church's rule forbidding traveling preachers to publish books or pamphlets without its approval, *Religious experience and journal of Mrs. Jarena Lee, giving an account of her call to preach the gospel* (97 pages) appeared in 1849.

Rebecca Cox Jackson, twelve years younger than Jarena Lee, kept journals of her religious experiences from 1830 to 1864. She died in 1871, and her words remained unpublished for more than a hundred years. *Gifts of Power: The Writings of Rebecca Jackson, Black Visionary, Shaker Eldress*, edited by Jean McMahon Humez, appeared for the first time in 1981. The existence of Lee's and Jackson's works, an immediate record of the women's experiences, demonstrates that black women felt it was vital that they preserve documentation of their personal convictions and spiritual leadership. Both Lee and Jackson had almost no formal education and no social privilege. Although she could read from the Bible by the time of her conversion, Lee claims to have been to school for approximately three months. On the other hand, Jackson purports to have been wholly illiterate but to have prayed for and received the "gift" of literacy in her search for autonomy after her conversion. This was an extraordinary blessing, since it not only enabled her to read the Bible for herself but freed her from what Humez calls the "editorial tyranny of her more [literate] privileged" preacher-brother (*Gifts*, p. 19).

Following their conversions, Jarena Lee and Rebecca Cox Jackson began their ministries as members of Holiness groups within the Methodist faith.[15] These groups, which also existed outside of Methodism, held firmly to a belief in justification—the recognition and acceptance of the power of God to forgive sins. Beyond that, they reinforced the women's commitment to seek sanctification, the controversial doctrine of "the blessing of perfect love," the ability to strive constantly for a higher "experience of divine grace" (*Gifts*, p. 5): to be in harmony with the will of God. Largely female in composition, the "praying bands" met in each others' homes. In these "relatively intimate, highly participatory, democratic religious gatherings in the familiar world of women friends," the members were encouraged to develop their "spiritual talents and speaking skills" within a safe and protective community (*Gifts*, p. 6). In describing a group of which she was a member, Jackson comments on the presence of women who were "gifted either in prayer or in speaking" and notes that meetings were conducted "as the Spirit of God directed," with members having "[equal] liberty to move as they felt" (*Gifts,* p. 102). Initially refused permission to preach by the church, Jarena Lee held prayer meetings in such groups, at which she spoke as the spirit moved her and exhorted before more public audiences. Around 1821, requests for her to preach came from far and near and transformed her into an itinerant preacher. By then, Bishop Allen approved her activities, although she was never ordained.

Rebecca Jackson belonged to no formal religious groups until she joined the Shakers. Before that, rather than seek the approbation of the Christian church, she disapproved of much that it did: "I saw that these churches were not the Lord's, and neither were these people serving the Lord in the way which was acceptable to him. Therefore I labored among them for the good of souls" (*Gifts,* p. 103). On the other hand, she struggled within herself for confirmation of the authority to preach, for a long time not trusting the "inner voice" prompting her in that direction. She feared that Satan was leading her into the sin of presumptuousness. Her narrative suggests that she regularly attended weekly prayer group meetings of women (the Covenant Meeting), and in 1831 she became a leader. In time, she assumed voice and authority beyond the prayer group.

While Jarena Lee's life was outer-directed, Rebecca Jackson's was inner-directed and depended heavily on her reliance on the efficacy of her dreams, the gift of foresight, waking visions, and an inner voice. Lee's motivation to print her journals—giving herself voice and authority within the established religious community—does not apply to Jackson. Although her narrative implies a reader, we have no indication that Jackson attempted to publish the materials during her lifetime.[16] Why then, keep a journal of these experiences? One might surmise that as a black leader in a predominantly white religious group, she intended her record to confirm her racial presence and leadership among the Shakers, except that the preciseness with which she records the dates and events in her life in the 1830s indicates that she began to keep journals several years before she knew of the Shakers, and more than a decade before she joined them. Unresolved (and perhaps ultimately unresolvable) issues such as this emphasize Marilyn Richardson's astute observation of how little we know of the intellectual thought of black women in the nineteenth century—to say nothing of whether still-undiscovered black women's journals and other writings exist from that period.[17]

What is certain, however, is that the desire to read and interpret the Bible on their own was one that propelled women such as Lee and Jackson toward the competence that made it possible for them to keep records of their civic and religious activities. On this level, literacy was power bestowed on the self by the self. Philosophically, their achievements in writing are further proof that for black women as well as men, there was a close relationship between freedom and literacy in the minds of eighteenth- and nineteenth-century Afro-Americans. Spiritual narrators participated in the quest for literacy and gained the freedom to assert their relationship to God by their ability to read and expound on the Bible through their own powers of understanding. In this and other ways, their literacy negated some of the most debilitating effects of race and/or gender oppression and enhanced their self-respect and sense of autonomy.

Although she was not a slave, Jarena Lee, born in Cape May, New Jersey, in 1783, was the child of very poor parents. At age seven she was sent out to "service." Her parents, she tells us, were "ignorant of the knowledge of God" and gave her no religious instruction. No doubt she, and other black women like her, were deeply affected by the general wave of religious revivals that swept New England in the late 1700s and early 1800s after the American Revolution. This places Lee's consideration of her preconversion self as a "wretched sinner" within the larger context of women's religious conversions in the nineteenth century. Much like white women caught up in the fervor of such awakenings in this period, black women were more convinced of their membership in the collective sinfulness of the human condition than of their guilt in having committed particular sins.[18] Thus Lee, a young, poor black woman, more sinned against by the conditions of her life than guilty of sins of her own, could bypass feelings of alienation and estrangement that her race, class, gender, and social circumstances dictated and feel joined to the fallen state of all humankind, as needful and worthy of divine forgiveness and salvation as all others, no matter how outwardly different their life situations were from hers. Once converted, black women (and men), as members of the community of believers, felt themselves equal before divine authority, for, as Lee later noted, citing St. Paul's letter to the Romans, and including herself among the blessed, "as many as are led by the Spirit of God are the sons of God" (*Sisters*, p. 48).

In a dramatic moment in 1804, when the Reverend Richard Allen, later the bishop of the AME church, was preaching in Philadelphia, Lee was converted:

> My soul was gloriously converted to God. . . . it appeared to me, as if a garment, which had entirely enveloped my whole person . . . split at the crown of my head, and stripped away from me, passing like a shadow, from my sight—when the glory of God seemed to cover me in its stead. (*Sisters*, p. 29)

Four years later she received the gift of sanctification. Some four or five years beyond that, an inner "voice" called her to preach. Lee's response (common among black women evangelists of the nineteenth century) to the "call" was to deny her ability to carry out such a mission. But like the Old Testament Moses, who hesitated to assume responsibility to deliver the Children of Israel out of Pharaoh's Egypt, she was assured by the "voice" that words would be put into her mouth and that her enemies would become her friends (*Sisters*, p. 35). Still not obeying the call, she married a minister in 1811 and moved to an outlying township of Philadelphia, where she supported his ministry until his death six years later. Then, convinced of the authenticity of her call to the great work of preaching to save souls, she left her two young children and began her public career. She traveled extensively through the country, addressing black and white audiences, condemning slavery, preaching the gospel, and saving souls. Initially, she met with opposition from black male church leaders who disapproved of women as preachers, but she eventually gained the support of many of them. For a number of years she enjoyed a successful evangelistic career. In spite of her lack of formal education, she mastered the Scriptures and was an intelligent, effective carrier of her message. Sustained largely by unfaltering faith, she later wrote:

> I have been fed by his bounty, clothed by his mercy, comforted and healed when sick, succored when tempted, and everywhere upheld by his hand. (*Sisters*, p. 41)

Rebecca Cox Jackson, also a free black woman, was born outside of Philadelphia in 1795. Jackson's journals reveal almost nothing about her life before 1830, when, she says, she became a "new creature" to carry out the will of God. Her father, it seems, died around the time of her birth. Until age thirteen, when her mother also died, she lived alternately with a grandmother and her mother. Subsequently, she went to live with a brother eighteen years her senior. He was a minister, a prominent figure in one of Philadelphia's most well known black churches, and a widower with six children. When she married, Jackson and her husband lived under her brother's roof. She was housekeeper for her brother, his children, and her husband and also earned her living as a seamstress. She appears to have had no children of her own.

Between her mother's death and her conversion, Jackson's external situation appears relatively safe and comfortable. Although there was a good deal of racial unrest in the city between 1829 and 1849, Philadelphia had a growing free black community with its own religious and social institutions. Even before she married, because she lived with her brother and had a respectable trade, Jackson, no doubt, escaped many of the indignities that black women who lived with white employers suffered. Like Lee, she felt in her youth that her life was full of sin and that the religion she was familiar with offered no salvation. In 1830, during a severe thunderstorm, Jackson, who until then had feared thunder and lightning, experienced conversion. Like Lee, she described the event as well as the contrasts between the sinful and redeemed selves in dramatic language. Of the former state she wrote:

> My sins like a mountain reached to the skies, black as sack cloth of hair and the heavens was as brass against my prayers and everything above my head was of one solid blackness. Then, the old gave way to the new: . . . the cloud bursted, the heavens was clear, and the mountain was gone. My

spirit was light, my heart was filled with love for God and all mankind. And the lightning, which was a moment ago the messenger of death, was now the messenger of peace, joy, and consolation. (*Gifts*, p. 72)

Not only did she feel that her sins were forgiven, and that the peril of the moment, "the expect[ation] of every clap of thunder to launch [her] soul at the bar of God," had passed, but she immediately lost her phobia, and thunder and lightning became sources of God's redemptive power.

During a revival the following year, Jackson received the gift of sanctification and began her preaching career in the homes of fellow believers. As a result of her conversion, she felt called to practice celibacy, although she was married. "I saw clearly," she wrote, "what the sin of the fall of man was." She claimed that at the moment of that recognition, had she owned the earth, she would have willingly given it all away to once again become "a single woman" (*Gifts*, pp. 76–77). Jackson's decision to reject sexual love occurred several years before she knew of Shaker doctrine on the subject. She made claims for sexual abstinence on the basis of her implicit belief that after conversion her body was no longer her own but had become a vessel dedicated to a higher-than-human will. To maintain its consecrated state it was necessary, she said, to free it from the desires of physical lust. Yet the decision is a powerful manifestation of self-assured empowerment. It is reasonable to think, as Jean Humez does, that by invoking her religious conviction, Jackson (consciously or unconsciously) used that conviction (the only one she had) to reclaim control of her body (*Gifts*, p. 17).

Although closely associated with the AME church as a child, and later through her brother and the "believers" whom she knew, Rebecca Cox Jackson never joined the church. Her religious life continued through direct personal intercourse with the Holy Spirit, with whom she made a pact at the time of her conversion to "obey in all things, in all places, and under all conditions" (*Gifts*, p. 85). This communication continued immediate through "secret and continual prayer," which she called her "wall of defense" (*Gifts*, p. 82). Focusing intently on interior reality, she was able to use the power of God to her best advantage when she sat still and waited for instructions from her inner voice. Listening within herself became the most active and demanding process of her life. Her "gifts of power," her wisdom, knowledge, foresight, and the power to heal, came to her not from human sources but "by faith and humble prayer and holy living and . . . being led by the Spirit of the true God" (*Gifts*, p. 99). She noted that she would "inquire of the Lord from day to day to know His will" required of her, adding: then, " 'I put my hands to work and my heart to the Lord' with a double resolution to do His will" (*Gifts*, p. 85).

Although outside of the church, Jackson had major confrontations with it from the beginning of her ministry. These, she said, separated her "further from the professed Christian world" even as she came "closer to the Lord." Her insistence that humans could attain salvation through grace and deliberate resistance to sin met opposition from laity and clergy. Most church members felt they could be saved only by the "merits of Christ," and not by their deeds. She disputed this as an evasion of personal responsibility to struggle for individual righteousness. As a result of her opposing doctrinal position, her refusal to join the church, her criticism of its laxities, her insistence on her immediate access to God, the validity of her leadership, and her position on celibacy, ministers and leaders saw her as a divisive force within the religious community. In 1837, church leaders, all male, accused her of heresy but denied her request for an interdenominational trial on those charges. While this event seems to mark the end of her relations with her family and the church, she interpreted the refusal of the leaders to confront her, in a forum in which she could defend herself, as a personal victory over them. In the early 1840s she belonged to a small group of religious Perfectionists who lived near Albany. Although these people had separated themselves from their churches in search of the holy life, Jackson found that "they lived in the flesh, like all the churches . . . and were all unjust, to God, to Christ, to His Spirit, and to His Holy cause" (*Gifts,* p. 184). She stayed with and admonished them for a short time; then in 1843 she committed herself to the faith of the Shakers, the people whom she believed "to be the true people of God on earth" (*Gifts,* p. 171). As a group, their way of life and religious beliefs were compatible with her own. Jackson took up residence with them in 1847 and lived in their community in New York State until 1851, when she returned to Philadelphia to organize a mostly black, mostly female Shaker society there. That small community lasted forty years beyond her death.

Jarena Lee and Rebecca Cox Jackson, women of different dispositions, conducted very different ministries. Lee concentrated on her external life and struggled with the male hierarchy of the black church, choosing to work within its structure. Both women's narratives record ecstatic experiences, but Lee's are more illustrations to prove spiritual authority. Her text is impressive for its overt feminist qualities: her rejection of the traditional woman's place as wife and mother, her determination to defy gender biases against women's spiritual leadership, and her physical ability to carry out the ministry she did.

Jackson, on the other hand, believed that the most important aspects of her experiences were connected to her visionary abilities. The strength of her text resides in the rich details of its descriptions of spiritual experiences. Although her public career was important to her as an example of the truly redeemed, Jackson's main priority was the continual searching out and verification of the sacred force which guided her actions, which she was determined to obey in all things. Throughout her religious life, she made frequent use of such traditional ascetic methods as fasting, weeping, praying, and going without sleep for long periods of time as ways of altering and heightening her consciousness, of sharpening her visionary gifts.

Free black women in the nineteenth century were not cut off from each other or other people in the world, and they were not silent. Supportive communities enabled them to know that external, oppressive authorities were not all-powerful, and that they were not completely powerless. The small prayer groups afforded women like Lee and Jackson an opportunity to display their "gifts" of speech and thought, and gave them the encouragement of their peers and the confidence to move beyond their intimate circles. In these woman-centered groups, women living in a male-dominated world, aware of the disadvantages of race and their lack of education, did not restrain their speech or apologize for their feelings. They explored the power of words and used them to express developing thoughts. For those who could read, even in rudimentary ways, language and literacy came together for them in the reflection that occurs when the oral and written traditions meet and mingle. They spoke and listened to each other and shared and expanded their perspectives on experience.

Lee and Jackson are joined as black women in the nineteenth century whose religious faith enabled them to achieve a sense of autonomy and selfhood that otherwise would have been impossible for them. Other women, such as Sojourner Truth, Maria Stewart, and Frances Harper, were able to combine the religious and secular gospels, and to leave other kinds of powerful imprints on the pages of history as well.[19] One important aspect of these writings that survive is what they teach us about major differences between three groups of nineteenth-century black women. Sojourner Truth stands virtually alone in her accomplishments. Perhaps one of the most powerful orators of her day, she never achieved literacy, so others had to record the intellectual legacy of this extraordinary woman. On the other hand, women such as Stewart and Harper had the advantages of formal education, which gave them additional options and their own peculiar vision of life and freedom.[20] Jarena Lee, Rebecca Cox Jackson, Amanda Smith, and others, denied education or other opportunities for public life, fought the battle for selfhood and independent black womanhood on the only grounds available to them—the religious frontier, where they challenged the boundaries of race and gender in nineteenth-century white America.[21] Religious faith meant self-empowerment; and in their hands, the spiritual narrative turned the genre of autobiography into a forceful weapon to express and record another chapter in the history of black women's liberation.

Striking aspects of these narratives include the challenge they mount to conventional women's roles and male authority in their time. Their faith gave them the self-assurance they needed to search out the positive identity that other circumstances in their lives denied. In their quest they ran headlong into the opposition of men and social customs at home and in the church. Lee was a widow with two small children, one only six months old when her husband died. Her behavior shatters the stereotype of the selfless black mother. Her itinerant evangelistic career lasted more than thirty years, and her absences from home took place during some of the important early years of her children's lives. Yet, she makes it clear that she had no maternal anxieties about leaving them for extended periods of time, and this and her struggle against the church fathers for affirmation of her ministry, on the basis of gender equality, place her in the forefront of women's struggle over fundamental issues of female autonomy.

In Jackson's case, even without children of her own, she had traditional household responsibilities to her husband, her brother, and four of his children. Her conflicts with her family began shortly after her conversion. Predictably, her husband responded with open hostility to her decision to be celibate; but for her gift of foresight, his attempts to do her bodily harm on this account would probably have been successful. On the other hand, the intensity with which she gave herself to her spiritual inclinations and yearnings was equally a source of family disruption. Of early in this period, when she tried to fulfill her obligations to herself and her household, she wrote:

> I sewed all day, . . . [saw] that the house was kept in good order, done all their sewing, keep them neat and clean and took in sewing for my living, held meeting every night in some part of the city, then came home. And after Samuel would lay down, I would labor oft times till two or three o'clock in the morning, then lay down, and at the break of day, rise and wait on the Lord. . . . And fasting the three days, Monday, Tuesday, Wednesday—at evening of each day I would take a little bread and water. This brought my system low, yet I had strength to do my daily duty. (*Gifts,* p. 86)

Only her conviction of a divine calling enabled Jackson to stand up to the opposition of her brother and her husband at home, and of the church on the outside. In her own defense against black male authority, she claimed, like Lee and others, that God was the authority and power behind her actions. But as both Jean Humez and Alice Walker conclude, Jackson's narrative is a study in conscious self-control, "an assertion of the power and reality of her inner sources of strength and knowledge" (*Gifts,* p. 2). Walker describes her as "a woman whose inner spirit directed her to live her own life, creating it from scratch, leaving husband, home, family, and friends, to do so."[22] Seen in this light, Jackson's ability to concentrate on her interior reality was the source of her inner authority. Her constant intense periods of prayer and contemplation as she awaited instructions to act were dialogues with self: an assertion of the power of her inner reality. Not surprisingly, before coming to Shakerism, she believed implicitly in a four-person Godhead: God the Father, God the Mother, Christ the Bridegroom, and his Bride, each having equal power and authority.

My argument for the significance of these texts rests on premises that black spiritual autobiographies were one vehicle through which nineteenth-century black writers sought spiritual healing from oppressive social conditions and gained literacy and power in the language of the dominant culture. For men and women, the genre permitted black people the freedom to "elaborate" on the Book of Books, "the white text, in a black voice, and through a black perspective."[23] To a certain degree, the political and economic freedom sought by the fugitive slave was grounded in the black spiritual autobiographer's claim that black people were fully human, with as much right to spiritual salvation as white people. Black spiritual autobiographers recorded the process by which they were saved from sin, and recognized and celebrated the new empowered selves who emerged out of their conversions. Like the slave narrative, the spiritual autobiography gave black women in nineteenth-century American life an opportunity to expand the genre beyond the boundaries set by black men. They used it to express female identity through the religious faith that gave them direct access to God in the Self—the highest authority; this knowledge imbued them with pride, self-respect, and control over their intellectual lives. In the face of other inhumane circumstances, they believed that in the "democracy of saved souls" all "were on an equal spiritual standing *with them* before the Lord" (italics mine; *Sisters*, p. 19). In bypassing and defying the place that white people and black men allotted them by asserting their right to control their perceptions of themselves and their assumptions of full selfhood, they declared an independence of spirit that made them outspoken feminists of their time. In the words of Alice Walker, we need to receive them as gifts of power in themselves.

Notes

I owe special thanks to Deborah McDowell, who first suggested that I explore the lives of Jarena Lee and Rebecca Cox Jackson for this essay. In addition, many people read or listened to this paper in its early drafts and offered encouragement and/or helpful suggestions for its improvement. I specially thank Constance Buchanan, Director of the Women's Studies in Religion Program at the Harvard Divinity School, Carol Christ, Riffat Hassan, Alexandra Owen, and Chava Weisler, Research Associates at the Divinity School 1986–87, who read, listened, and gave me positive and supportive criticism. I also thank Warner Berthoff, Randall Burkett, St. Clare Drake, Nathan Huggins, and Werner Sollors for their sensitive and helpful comments. Especially for encouragement and fellowship I am grateful to Victoria Byerly, Katie Canon, Marion Kilson, Deborah McDowell, Marilyn Richardson, and Mary Helen Washington.

1. See William L. Andrews, *To Tell a Free Story: The First One Hundred Years of Afro-American Autobiography*—a groundbreaking book on early Afro-American autobiography. This text includes the exploration of male and female slave and spiritual autobiographies. Andrews also deserves special credit for his work in *Sisters of the Spirit: Three Black Women's Autobiographies in the Nineteenth Century*, the first anthology to focus specifically on black women's spiritual experiences.

2. In addition to the slave and spiritual narratives, there were the male "criminal" confession narratives in the eighteenth and nineteenth centuries. These were stories recorded from testimony given before the subject's execution. Perhaps the most famous is *The Confessions of Nat Turner*, but others such as *The life and confession of Johnson Green, who is to be executed this day, August 17, 1786, for the atrocious crime of burglary; together with his last dying words,* a broadside published in Worcester, Massachusetts, were not unusual.

3. See Pamela S. Bromberg, "The Development of Narrative Technique in Margaret Drabble's Novels," p. 179.

4. Albert Stone, *Autobiographical Occasions and Original Acts: Versions of American Identity from Henry Adams to Nate Shaw,* p. 5.

5. Andrews, *To Tell a Free Story,* p. 2–3.

6. Stone, p. 10.

7. Robert Stepto, *From behind the Veil: A Study of Afro-American Narrative,* p. 3.

8. Andrews, *To Tell a Free Story,* p. 64.

9. See ibid., pp. 32–60, for an extended discussion on this subject.

10. George White, *A brief account of the life, experiences, travels, and gospel labours of George White, an African, written by himself and revised by a friend* (New York: John C. Totten, 1810).

11. As a large number (reprints and new works) of black autobiographical texts have become available for classroom use (in contrast to their paucity even five years ago), critical essays and longer studies of the genre keep pace with other scholarship in Afro-American literature and history. Among longer works in progress are at least two books on black women's narratives.

12. See Cheryl Gilkes, "'Together in Harness': Women's Traditions in the Sanctified Church," pp. 678–99. Although the essay refers specifically to the Sanctified church, these qualities have been hallmarks of women's groups among all sects within the black church.

13. See Jean McMahon Humez, *Gifts of Power: The Writings of Rebecca Cox Jackson, Black Visionary, Shaker Eldress,* p. 262. All other references to Jackson's journal come from this text. Humez's fine editing of the journals deserves special commendation. In addition, her excellent introduction to the work provides a good deal of information on Jackson and others in the context of black women's spiritual lives in the nineteenth century.

14. Jarena Lee, *The Life And Religious Experience of Jarena Lee, a Coloured Lady, Giving an Account of Her Call to Preach the Gospel: Revised and Corrected from the Original Manuscript by Herself,* in *Sisters of the Spirit: Three Black Women's Autobiographies in the Nineteenth Century,* ed. William Andrews. Further references to this narrative are taken from this text.

15. According to Humez, her research revealed that black and white groups of women assembled in small prayer groups seeking the "blessing of perfect love" as early as 1819 in New York. Rebecca Cox Jackson refers to her mother as belonging to such a group when she (Rebecca) was a girl. Amanda Smith, another black female spiritual autobiographer, reports that in the 1890s she saw modestly dressed (somewhat like Quakers) Methodist women in Philadelphia, New York, and Baltimore who were known as "Band Sisters." See Humez, p. 315.

16. Often in Jackson's text after she relates an event, she will write—as though aware of a lack of clarity for the reader—"I should have said first . . . ," and then will relate a previously omitted incident that bears on the point she wants to make.

17. Marilyn Richardson pointed out to me that we know very little about the intellectual thought of black women in the nineteenth century: of what they read and with whom they discussed important issues of the time. In some cases, we are unaware of the accurate pronunciations of their names.

18. See Barbara Leslie Epstein, *The Politics of Domesticity: Women, Evangelism, and*

Temperance in Nineteenth-Century America, pp. 45–65, for a discussion of white women in the religious movement of the late eighteenth and early nineteenth centuries.

19. Only recently have we begun to address issues of differences among the lives of nineteenth-century black women. Economic and educational status varied widely between them, and were factors that influenced individual vision and individual perceptions of options.

20. Maria Stewart, born in Boston, was an articulate black feminist abolitionist who is credited as the first American woman to speak from a platform to a "promiscuous" (men and women together) audience. See Marilyn Richardson, ed., *Maria W. Stewart: America's First Black Woman Political Writer, Essays and Speeches* (Bloomington: Indiana University Press, 1987). Frances Harper was a feminist abolitionist writer (poetry, fiction, and nonfiction prose), public speaker, and educator. Her novel *Iola Leroy,* which focuses on black life during Reconstruction, was first published in 1892.

21. Amanda Berry Smith was born of slave parents in Maryland in 1837, but was freed after the death of her mistress, who shortly before had experienced religious conversion. The Berry family moved to Pennsylvania, where at age eight Amanda went to school. Her evangelistic career began in the late 1870s with a trip to England. Later she went to India and then to Africa for eight years. Smith's narrative, *An Autobiography: The Story of the Lord's Dealings with Mrs. Amanda Smith, the Colored Evangelist,* was published in 1893.

22. Alice Walker, *In Search of Our Mother's Gardens,* p. 79.

23. Andrews, *To Tell a Free Story,* p. 54.

Works Cited

Andrews, William L. *To Tell a Free Story: The First Century of Afro-American Autobiography, 1760–1865.* Urbana: University of Illinois Press, 1986.

————, ed. *Sisters of the Spirit: Three Black Women's Autobiographies of the Nineteenth Century.* Bloomington: Indiana University Press, 1986.

Bromberg, Pamela S. "The Development of Narrative Technique in Margaret Drabble's Novels." *Journal of Narrative Technique* 16, no. 3 (Fall 1986): 179–91.

Epstein, Barbara Leslie. *The Politics of Domesticity: Women, Evangelism, and Temperance in Nineteenth-Century America.* Middletown: Wesleyan University Press, 1981.

Gilkes, Cheryl. "'Together in Harness': Women's Traditions in the Sanctified Church." *Signs: Journal of Women in Culture and Society* 10, no. 4 (Summer 1985): 678–99.

Humez, Jean McMahon, ed. *Gifts of Power: The Writings of Rebecca Jackson, Black Visionary, Shaker Eldress.* Amherst: University of Massachusetts Press, 1981.

Stepto, Robert. *From behind the Veil: A Study of Afro-American Narrative.* Urbana: University of Illinois Press, 1979.

Stone, Albert. *Autobiographical Occasions and Original Acts: Versions of American Identity from Henry Adams to Nate Shaw.* Philadelphia: University of Pennsylvania Press, 1982.

Walker, Alice. *In Search of Our Mother's Gardens.* New York: Harcourt Brace Jovanovich, 1983.

PERSONAL NARRATIVES, DYNASTIES, AND WOMEN'S CAMPAIGNS
Two Examples from Africa

Marcia Wright

Any two women can be compared. The questions that will arise are, what significance is there in the comparison, and what larger generalization can follow? In linking the two cases of Christina Sibiya and Mary Leakey, I endeavor to work on conceptual problems in the handling of personal narratives while also discerning the scope and value of comparison of these two persons.[1] For the purposes of this comparison, I draw coordinates from moments in a life cycle—widowhood, separation from husbands, refocus on sons, and change in class status. Christina's life story and Mary's autobiography do contain parallels, in that each displays passionate determination in pursuit of a cause, troubles with a husband who was a public personality and somewhat larger than life, and partial resolution of the contradictions of female dependency by bonding with a son in the place of a husband. The centrality of family and motherhood and the initiative of these two women as key actors in campaigns of legitimation give a dynastic coloration to the cases.

Certain distinctions between autobiography, life history, and biography are necessary to the present discussion. Autobiography implies the greatest degree of self-control; life history is often a mediated account composed by another person but retaining the perspective of the subject; and biography is a study of the focal person informed by many sources and external criteria of significance. Plainly, life history is a combination of efforts and agendas of the subject and of the composer. Within this ambiguous middle group, interpretive judgments will be made as to whether the text is more autobiographical or biographical.

CHRISTINA SIBIYA

This critical exercise must be applied immediately in taking up the text of *Zulu Woman*. The life story of Christina Sibiya, I conclude, is to be placed on

155

the side of autobiography; that is to say, the subject propels and shapes it more than the interlocutor-biographer. The personal narrative thus permeates the structure as well as the content of the published book. Without doubt, a lengthy life story of an African woman would not have been published, especially in its second paperback edition, were it not for its combination of power, sex, and drama. That the power was royal and tribal made it exotic. That the setting was South Africa in the industrial age made it accessible.

Kingship among the Zulu has been an object of political study from the 1840s onward, and the reputation of Shaka, the empire builder of the early nineteenth century, has spread far beyond South Africa and the affected parts of southern Africa. Royal women have received attention both where they functioned with a degree of autonomy as rulers and subrulers, and as officeholders or important persons in the court of the kings. Around the time Christina narrated the story of her life, in 1934, well-rehearsed tales of royal women of the past in Natal and Zululand were communicated in a collection of life and career sketches, *Daughters of Africa*.[2] A lengthy pseudo-autobiography of Queen Mkabi published in the early 1960s drew heavily on the material supplied by a princess who was Christina's contemporary.[3]

Commoner women among the Zulu and other peoples of southeastern Africa in the twentieth century have been described as hemmed in by extreme sexual stratification at an ideological and practical level.[4] Royal princesses, on the other hand, enjoyed a degree of civil status and property ownership. They were also keepers of dynastic lore, in which their female predecessors figured as censors of misrule and active conspirators to eliminate rulers who became too despotic. *Zulu Woman* contains very little evidence bearing upon the ordinary woman, perhaps the wife of a migrant worker, and equally little about the princesses. It best exposes the situation of the *kholwa*, the Christian-educated African elite of Natal and the royal household of the Zulu monarchy at a critical time in South African history, the interwar years. At this time, a new synthesis came into being: advanced segregation as the state's policy of social management, and neotraditionalism among the Natal elites. Royalist sentiment flourished during the powerful upsurge of traditionalism. Although the honor had become increasingly hollow, the importance of queens, princesses, and the office of Great Wife, the ritual consort and mother of presumptive heirs, became strategically important.[5]

Christina Sibiya was born in 1900 to a Christian (*kholwa* in local terms) family living on a mission reserve in Natal Colony, South Africa. Her personal narrative was recorded in 1934 by Rebecca Reyher, assisted by a young man from a Natal family long associated with magistracy and the administration of African affairs. Together they visited the Zulu reserves, letting it be known that Reyher was interested in the daily life of women.

Christina presented herself as an informant and told her story in an intense and continuous way. Reyher says of these encounters:

> We established a working procedure. Christina came and talked, slowly, sentence by sentence, while Eric translated. Occasionally, we interrupted her to ask a question, but seldom. At first, she was awkward, overdressed, self-conscious. Then she began to come in everyday clothes, at seven in the morning, and stay until way past her bedtime, and the words flowed from her. By the end of the day, with time out only for meals, Christina was tired and drowsy, Eric was an automaton, and I was cramped, with my shoulder and arm still aching from taking notes. (1970), p. xiii)

The outlines of Christina Sibiya's life assume memorable dimensions beginning when she was eight and her parents separated. She was the second-born and the eldest daughter of the four children born following a Christian monogamous marriage. In 1908, her father was expelled from the mission reserve because he took a second wife. Christina's mother, Elizabeth, remained on the land controlled by Norwegian Lutherans, protected and sympathized with by the church to which she adhered with rigorous conviction. Determined to preserve her status as her husband's sole legitimate wife, regardless of their separation, she sent Christina and her other children with regular wifely tributes of beer. Christina thus glimpsed non-Christian "kraal" life from a strained and adversarial standpoint. When she was ten, she moved to the mission school, earning her board as caretaker of the missionaries' infant. She became more insulated from the ordinary nonformal education of daily life but excelled in the ways of Christian culture, to the point of being appointed at the age of fifteen as the teacher of a simple village school at Babanango, twenty miles distant (Reyher, chaps. 1 and 2).

Solomon, who was to become Christina's husband, was the presumed heir to his father, Dinizulu, who had died in 1913. There was a rival, however, and Solomon's faction was not entirely secure in the succession to Usuthu, the division of Zululand over which the uncrowned kings were allowed to rule as chiefs, or in the kingdom at large, where the civil war of the 1880s had left legacies. The northern chiefs, led by the Buthelezis, remained to be reconciled to the central kingship. Before his ritual installation as chief of Usutu, which had to follow the formal period of mourning, he became betrothed to six women, each representing a political alliance. His choice of Christina did not have this explicit purpose and was presented in her narrative as a love match. Its dynastic political implications will be discussed below. Clear from the narrative is the calculation that in making Christina his first wife, Solomon signaled a certain Westernization in himself and in the leadership of his female retinue. The segments of the story always contained cross-currents, however. She was courted by correspondence but was also commandeered by Solomon, by a unilateral declaration first to the evangelist, then to the Norwegian missionary. After sexual consummation, a marriage celebration was carried out at the kraal of Christina's father, with her reluctant mother also present, but with all the Christian girls secluded. The honor of marriage to the king was offset by an understanding that the kingship could never be reconciled with Christian monogamy (Rehyer, 1970, p. 51).

Between 1918 and 1925, she bore four children, two male and two female. Over the same time, Solomon became more and more ensnarled in the political dilemmas of his position, especially the entrenched opposition of the northern Zulu factions. The number of his wives increased rapidly, and jealousy among them and between the "mothers" of the royal kraals created countless problems for Christina, who struggled to maintain her status as first (executive) wife and favorite. A test of her marriage took place shortly after the birth of her first child, when she pleaded for the right to remain with it rather than attend Solomon on his continuous journeying. The concession was won, but as soon as the infant was weaned, Christina returned to the personal service of the king. Surrendering her child to a "mother" who was brought from another royal settlement to establish the baby in a separate household, Christina occupied the king's residence and regulated the affairs of the junior wives who were being continually added to the community (Reyher 1970, p. 82).

Reflecting the personal narrative, the next charged passage in the book concerns the sudden death of Christina's elder son, Herzon, who stayed behind when she was absent. Solomon blamed poisoning, a common form of "witchcraft" prompted by jealousy, caused, he believed, by a false rumor that he had pointed out the young boy as his designated successor. Christina became obsessed with the danger to her other children. She had a breakdown and recovered, only to be punished during a rage by Solomon against his wives when he charged that one had engaged in adultery. The attendant beating, provoked by her defense of the wives collectively, was followed by Solomon's open apology, but the sequence provided the final justification for Christina's departure from the king's household (Reyher 1970, pp. 172ff., 289ff.).

She fled to Durban and took employment as a domestic worker at a lower wage than she might have commanded as a shop assistant, because the latter position would have made her easier to trace. After a period of anonymity, however, the king's agents discovered her whereabouts. They brought a case before the local magistrate demanding that she be returned according to recognized customary law, which denied a wife legal right to move or act on her own initiative. The king's case failed because he had never delivered the ritual cow representing the opening of the household to a bride, marking the formal conclusion to the prolonged marriage proceedings (Reyher 1970, pp. 198ff.). While the magistrate could not find against Christina, who thus became technically an unmarried woman with certain freedom, he did order her to return to Solomon's court and seek a settlement there.

After Christina had waited for a long time, the prime minister finally arrived to participate in a public hearing as to whether she had the right to leave and go "wherever I want to." The life history at this point underscores the unusual initiative in the case:

> Never before had a King's wife been given a trial at the instigation of the wife. Wives had been tried. Wives had had charges of adultery brought against them. . . . Never, though, had a case been brought up of a wife who simply wanted to leave the King and wished to have the case tried publicly to decide that issue and that issue alone. (Reyher 1970, p. 214)

The array of tactics used by those who sought to impugn or persuade her included suggestions that she had already taken or intended to take another man, which would have made her the guilty party. A friendlier advocate for the king proposed in a private conversation that she go on living under the royal wing and engage in adultery, which everyone knew was a practice common among the host of neglected "wives." Quite sensibly, Christina asked who would protect her if she accepted this compromise. Lastly, the "mothers" asked her how she could be separated from her children, for the right to any degree of access to them would be extinguished if she won (Reyher 1970, pp. 210–18).

Solomon ultimately refused to render a verdict and thus granted Christina the de facto right to live apart, undisturbed. She was ostracized, however, and utterly dependent upon her own economic activities. In 1933, when Solomon died, she was excluded from a formal place in the mourning ceremonies, and she could not claim the political assets that should have been hers as Solomon's first and favorite wife (Reyher 1970, p. 226). A regency was established to care for the affairs of the kingdom, and they selected a young heir apparent who was not Christina's son, although in 1934 their choice was unknown, and Christina as well as her extended family had hopes.

The conversion of the personal narrative into a book took more than a decade. Reyher states that what she wanted to convey was not the difference but rather the commonalities between seemingly distant portions of humanity. Ingenuously, she asserted that "these Zulus . . . were not different from my New York and Maine friends, only a lot more interesting" (Reyher 1970, p. vii). She empathized with the women of Zululand who had little autonomy, endured severe domestic subordination, and lacked protection as individuals under the law. It was not her inclination to go deeply into the history of Zulu women, and she did not realize how and why authority had been preoccupied with their control.[6] The life story more explicitly reflects the unfolding history of the Zulu as a modern ethnic group coping with cultural contradiction: Christina's *kholwa* Christianity conflicted with her duty to Solomon as husband and king.[7]

Upon reading the manuscript in 1947, Ruth Benedict, as a professional anthropologist, was struck by a certain lack of balance and awareness of the larger political economy within which Solomon was operating. Benedict underscored the contradictions that colonialism had brought to Zululand and saw Christina as politically naive: "She knew little of the real dilemma [Solomon] had to face: his right hand trying to keep intact loyalty and fidelity within his tribe and his left hand ensuring the steady stream of black laborers necessary for the Witwatersrand mines" (Reyher 1970, p. ix).

How congruent were these interpretations with the intentions of the subject? In the postscript to the second edition, Reyher reports how after 1948 she learned that Christina had engaged in an active campaign to gain official South African recognition for Cyprian (Seaprince in the narrative), her surviving son, as the heir to the Zulu kingship. She claimed that Solomon had written a letter in which he made this designation. Cyprian was chosen by the nationalist regime and reigned for twenty years until his death in 1968, using his privilege to see that Christina was buried beside Solomon. Yet when Reyher returned to Zululand in 1951, she was dismayed to discover that Cyprian was ignoring what she believed to be the lessons of Christina's life, which called for greater consideration of wives. Following more in his father's footsteps, Cyprian had in that year brought a case against his second wife, charging her with one occasion of adultery, for which she was spending three months in prison, her plea of neglect having brought no mercy (Reyher 1970, p. 240).

Reyher had been less in control of her text than she imagined. Insufficiently informed to be a full biographer, she had led Ruth Benedict also to underestimate her subject when Benedict wrote in 1947:

> The entirely personal lenses through which Christina always looked out upon her life makes the whole Zulu story of the last generation the more vivid. We see through her loyal and innocent eyes the disintegration of the ties which bound the King and his well-to-do subjects, the growing recklessness of the King, and the strange shapes Christianity took when earnestly lived by the Zulu. (Reyher 1970)

In turning up at Rebecca Reyher's doorstep in 1934, Christina Sibiya could not be certain of the ultimate possibilities and outcome of the succession question, but she was doubtless aware that she was shoring up her son's claims by talking to a friendly foreigner who was an intimate of the white magistrates. Her selection of information effectively built a case for legitimacy by various rules and value systems, including her status as first wife and potential Great Wife, her recognition among the royal women as one who was able not simply to enjoy her special favor but ultimately to suffer with and for the more oppressed of them, and her acculturation and adherence to Christian ideals.

Christina's narrative as conveyed by Reyher neglects to inform the non-Zulu reader of the many resonances in the political history of the Zulu kingdom of the name "Sibiya," by which she was known in the royal household and by the "mothers." Her own father may indeed have been a man of no political consequence. The salient issue is why bridewealth did not have to be paid. The text declares that it was postponed because nonpayment to kin of other wives would have had dire political consequences. The Sibiyas, on the other hand, were tolerant of the debt and later reluctant in giving sanctuary to Christina (Reyher 1970, p. 219). Such behavior reflects their record as stout loyalists who had begun to intermarry with the Zulu leaders even before the kingdom assumed regional importance.

In royal traditions, the Sibiya clan leaders figured throughout the ascent of the rulers from petty chiefship to subordinate chiefship to hegemonic chiefship and kingship. They contributed wives to the Zulu royal family, delivered their people as a friendly client population to the military and political core of the aggrandizing Zulu state, and consequently figured among the important councilors at the court. Mntaniya Sibiya, granddaughter of the Sibiya ruler Ndaba, had become Chief Jama's Great Wife. When Jama died, her unmarried daughter Mkabayi served several times as regent and also commander of her own division of warriors and territory under Shaka. She and other office-bearing royal women owned cattle and were thus exempted from the general rule by which commoner women did not control herds (Gollock, 1932, pp. 24–25; Cowley 1966, p. 191).

Langazana, the fourth wife of Senzangakona, was chosen from the Sibiyas of Gazu. The death of her only son in battle with the Boers in 1858 removed any possibility of conniving for his succession. She lived to a very great age and died only in the 1880s. The ritual stool of the Zulu dynasty, the Nkata, was alleged to have been in her custody until it was destroyed by the British in the 1879 war against the kingdom (Cowley, 1966, pp. 212–13).[8] Sibiya men associated with the Zulu rulers were not so long-lived, but they formed with the royal "mothers" an important core in dynastic, and thus in kingdom, politics. The strength of the maternal Sibiya line prompted Cecil Cowley to designate it a junior branch of the royal family (1966, p. 220).[9] The Sibiya clan's significance in the monarchy must be understood in light of the active roles of their women members as royal wives and sisters.

Thus, when the heir to the Zulu throne in 1915 chose a Sibiya woman as his first wife, he affirmed a central dynastic alliance. Given that Christina was ostracized by the court, her campaign must be seen in association with a party that supported Solomon. That Cyprian, or one of his brothers, the descendant of Sibiyas, would succeed to the kingship was something that some councilors anticipated from the time Christina became Solomon's first wife. In her epilogue, Reyher admits that she could not ascertain the reasons he was eventually chosen or pin down the existence of the letter from Solomon to Christina designating him:

> Did the Government lean toward Christina because Cyprian and his followers were amenable to the official plans to make Zululand a Zulustan? Is this a sensitive political area enshrouded in political intrigue as Zululand traditionally has often been? I do not know. The story told me seemed to fit in with Christina's character as I had known it, to emphasize her essential nobility, and on that basis I accepted it. (1970, p. 240)

To go outside Christina's narrative as conveyed in *Zulu Woman* in order to suggest dynastic features is to recall that Reyher called Christina a skillful teller of tales. Resonances in Christina's own love story of certain well-known episodes in royal romances harking back more than a hundred years may have been coincidental, but they would not have been lost on a Zulu audience (Reyher 1970, p. xiii). Christina also played to the Western features of African elite and colonial values when she emphasized to Reyher that she was an educated Christian woman who was courted by letters. Essentially, she invoked the Western equivalent of ritual material, documents. Such means of legitimation were vital in the context of political strategizing within the modern South African state.

MARY LEAKEY

Mary Leakey's *Disclosing the Past* was written as several facets of her life had reached closure. Her husband, Louis, was dead, and her three sons were launched on their own careers in archeology, natural science, and politics. She had to retreat from the isolation of Olduvai in the Serengeti Plain of Tanzania to the comparative comfort of Langati near Nairobi in Kenya because of the deterioration of the supply situation at Olduvai and in Tanzania generally; her own more limited physical capacity, owing to the loss of sight in one eye; and a recognition that after so many years of fieldwork, it was necessary to write up the findings of several important and protracted "digs" (1984, p. 210). The relationship of the personal narrative to the overall task of writing up is palpable.

> *Disclosing the Past* was composed with the assistance of Derek Roe:
> With the possibility in mind that one day my life story might be written, I had—over the past several years—taken to jotting down memories as they came to me. The result was a sizeable pack of index cards arranged in no particular order. From these, Derek helped me piece together the full story of my personal and professional life. (1984, p. 9).

The linkage of personal and professional life is central to this remarkable autobiography, in which a more and more embracing professional identifi-cation followed upon a personal relationship with her husband, Louis Leakey. In the concluding portions of the narrative, strong commitments to ideals of science determined personal choices. At seventy, Mary changed her earlier opinion about autobiography, and no longer believed that it was "rash and arrogant to feel that one's life story was worth inflicting on other people" (1984, p. 11). Having seen merit in the project, which her son Richard had proposed to her, she structured it in three parts, "Early Life," "Partnership with Louis," and "Assertions of Independence." She was able gently to mock herself as a person captured by her discipline, even in presenting evidence within an autobiography:

> Archaeologists often divide things into three stages, usually "lower," "mid-dle" and "upper" if they are thinking stratigraphically. Afterwards, of course, they argue that the whole thing was continuous anyhow and that the divisions are arbitrary and for convenience only. (1984), p. 13).

Mary Leakey's early years were spent largely on the Continent, where her parents lived successively in Italy and France, wherever her father, an artist, decided to settle for a time to paint. She was born in 1913, named Mary Douglas Nicol, remained the only child, and received her education almost exclusively at home. Taking after her father, she had a talent for drawing and enthusiasm for ancient remains, rock paintings, and arch-eological sites. He died when she was thirteen, and she returned with her mother to live near, and later in, London. There she followed up her earlier rejection of systematic teaching by a governess, managing to exit quickly from two convent schools and any steady instruction by tutors (1984, chap. 3).

Beginning in 1930, she pursued her "self-appointed training in archae-ology" by being accepted as and becoming a regular team member on seasonal excavations directed by Dorothy Liddell. Between summers, Mary attended lectures and started to make drawings of finds she had helped to dig out. These caught the attention of Gertrude Caton-Thompson, whom she liked at once and on hindsight described as "the epitome of that remarkable breed of English ladies who for archaelogy's sake would go out alone into harsh desert environments and by determination, skill, expertise and endurance achieve discoveries of major and permanent importance" (1984, p. 39).

In 1933, Caton-Thompson introduced Mary, then a young woman of twenty, and Louis, a rising star of archeology in his mid-thirties. Soon after Mary took on the task of illustrating his data, they became emotionally attached, and after a short while Louis decided to seek a divorce in order to marry her. Their open relationship scandalized many of his circle and family as his separation and divorce slowly proceeded. In the interval before their marriage in December 1936, she made her first visit to East

Africa, the scene of Louis's fieldwork, where he had also been reared. He did not introduce her to his family, and after the marriage Mary had to contend with their initial disapproval (1984, pp. 32, 45–46).

From 1937 to 1950, Mary might best be described as the junior partner, working on successive sites and having children. Three sons born during this period survived; a daughter died shortly after her delivery. Mary Leakey's ability to knit together various strands in her narrative is well illustrated by the section on *Proconsul,* where she reports that this discovery of a very early fossilized skull came in time to make a splash at the First Pan-African Congress of Prehistory and Palaeontology, in which Louis was a prime mover. She had gone along, although the expedition aimed to unearth material on the Miocene period, which was "never . . . one of my major interests." Nevertheless, it was she who actually sighted the first evidence, a tooth of *Proconsul:* "one of the most spectacular discoveries of my entire life" (1984, pp. 98–99). Phillip, the third son, was self-consciously conceived as part of the celebration of the discovery of *Proconsul,* which indeed proved to be an important turning point in the Leakeys' career of verifying early (hominid) man in East Africa.

When in 1951 the Leakeys went to Kondoa-Irangi in Tanzania to study the sites of rock painting and record the paintings themselves, Mary became the principal investigator. From this personally gratifying interlude, she turned to large, protracted excavations, more and more concentrated at Olduvai, where in July 1959 she recognized an exposed part of a hominid skull, which became known as Zinjanthropus and brought the Leakeys into the spotlight in the Western world, and especially in the United States (1984, pp. 108–109, 188ff.).

The spotlight was mostly on Louis, the spokesman and showman, who became increasingly occupied with public appearances and enjoyed celebrity status while Mary stood back. By 1967, Richard Leakey was beginning to assert his independence as an archeologist and to challenge his father in various arenas:

> By the end of 1968 my own necessary path, for Louis's good as much as my own, had become clear in my mind. A new campaign of excavations could be begun at Olduvai whenever I was ready. . . . One did not go to Olduvai just to live: one went to work and live. (1984, p. 148)

From 1968 onward, Mary became increasingly separated from Louis, for whom she lost professional respect as he made scientifically irresponsible claims and turned to the companionship of adoring young women. After his death in 1972, she continued with her excavations, coming up with significant new evidence at Laetoli near Olduvai, where fossil footprints established the dating of erect, bipedal hominids. She remained committed to technical and scientific standards, which, even while she became accustomed to the spotlight left empty by Louis, prevented her from making large generalizations about the origins and early evolution of the human species (1984, p. 211).

For Mary Leakey, the term *campaign* is familiar. Above all it describes a program for developing an archeological site, entailing careful plans for the excavations, arrangements for housing and feeding professionals and workers in what are often remote places, and securing the material means to support the work. These specific campaigns became part of the unfolding saga attracting wide public interest, because this archeological work "concerns the human origins that are common to the whole human race" (1984, p. 11). To establish a record of early man also entailed defensive measures, for others attempted from time to time to move in on territory that the Leakeys had staked out. For example, Mary wrote of Charles Boise, an adopted Briton, American by birth, who doubled his gift "when he heard via Louis that an American expedition with impressive financial resources and led by Wendell Phillips, was seeking to move in on the West Kenya Miocene deposits" (1984, p. 97).

Campaigns of excavation, preservation of hegemony over territory, and scientific legitimation, yes; feminism, no. Mary Leakey did not see her story as a contribution to women's liberation. Commenting about the occasion when she received the Gold Medal of the Society of Women Geographers in Washington, she wrote that it was a high honor, but added:

> There was a certain undercurrent of Women's Lib . . . for which I carry no banner, though quite often people seem to expect me to do so. What I have done in my life I have done because I wanted to do it, and because it interested me. I just happen to be a woman and I don't believe it has made much difference. (1984, p. 193)

Autobiography was nothing new to the Leakey family. The narrative of Louis's early years, published in 1937, described his upbringing as the son of missionaries, his special attachment to the Kikuyu people, and his emergence as an archeologist, who by the end of 1936 had led four expeditions in East Africa, sponsored by British learned societies, colonial-oriented foundations, and the Kenya Colony government. Material bearing upon Louis's first marriage is virtually absent, although female apprentices and team members are mentioned by name and given their due for discoveries.[10] The second volume, covering the period 1932 to 1951, treated Mary's increasing professional contributions to their partnership.[11] This volume does not deal with domestic relations and children, however, portraying as it does a career rather than a life.

Richard Leakey, his father's rival and successor as an internationally known and well-supported scholar of early humans, also wrote the first volume of an autobiography when he was in his mid-thirties. With a chapter entitled "Out of My Father's Shadow," he describes his achievement of professional autonomy.[12] In early 1968, he accompanied his father to

America, on what Mary describes as the "usual fund-raising pilgrimage," to report to and solicit continuing support from the research committee of the National Geographic Society.

> Without consulting Louis in advance, he . . . asked for the grant to be given to him to go with a separate expedition to explore his new East Turkana area, leaving the Omo joint expedition to the French and Americans. This bold stroke threw Louis completely off balance and he argued forcefully against it, though it was just the kind of tactic he might himself have deployed in earlier days. The outcome was significant: Richard's arguments won the day. (M. Leakey 1984, p. 147; R. Leakey 1983, pp. 93–94)

There was no doubt of Richard's ego and ambition as he proceeded in a campaign to gain control of the National Museum. To this end, he played the cards of Kenyan nationalism and did so, when necessary, against his father's position. Nevertheless, the sense of dynasty is inescapable, as when he asserts: "From 1960, Olduvai became the cornerstone of our family activities" (1983, p. 54).[13] Olduvai and Zinjanthropus were what raised the Leakeys, but especially Louis, the popularizer and lecturer, to the heights of funding.

Mary Leakey speaks of campaign in the sense of a calculated assault upon and defense of archeological sites. Her larger campaign, however, was to secure the honor of archeology as a rigorous science, and she practiced it as such both in partnership with Louis and then by herself when she had become estranged from and highly critical of him. The rupture in the marriage and partnership took place concurrently with Richard's coup at the National Geographic Society early in 1968. Although Mary did not suffer the physical punishment that had precipitated Christina's final withdrawal from the royal household, her assertion of independence contained its own drama. For the preceding year or more, the folly of Louis's involvement in a search for evidence of early humans in southern California had led to disagreements. Late in 1967, the Leakeys were nominated for honorary degrees by the University of Witwatersrand, in Johannesburg. Louis decided to refuse as a gesture against apartheid.

> He expected me to do the same. My own view was different. It was true that the University of Witwatersrand had ultimately been compelled to exercise racial discrimination in its admission of students, but it was doing so under strong protest, having spoken out boldly.
>
> So I told Louis I proposed to accept. He was furious about it. Again, instead of accepting a decision of his with unquestioning loyalty, I had opposed it with a reasoned judgement of my own. So I went ahead and on 30 March 1968 received what was, in fact, my first Honorary Degree. (1984, pp. 144–45)

An emphasis upon dynasty as a basis for comparison is unusual in a study lodged in the twentieth century and is not a conscious point of reference in either of the personal narratives under discussion. In the case of the Zulu royal family, dynastic considerations were to be expected, yet they were underplayed in Christina's account. Mary Leakey came from a bourgeois English family whose culture did not contain the successions to title and associated property that still perpetuated dynastic considerations among the aristocracy. Furthermore, the family circle of her youth had been composed almost exclusively of women, centering upon a maternal grandmother and several maiden aunts. These women had no regular economic activity and were relatively impoverished. The dynastic situation for Mary Leakey thus evolved as a consequence of her own marriage, the circumstances of colonial East Africa, the public importance of the archeological finds made by the Leakeys, and the ultimate creation of a family name and reputation.

The Leakey family had a name before it became associated with archeology. The church and the mission had been the arena in which Louis's parents gained status. He learned the Kikuyu language from his comrades as a child, became initiated into an age grade, and later figured as an "expert" on African life, maintaining a particularly unfortunate and propagandistic colonial bias with respect to the cultural roots of the Mau Mau movement of the early 1950s.[14] His background led to an intellectual career and political entanglements. Meanwhile, he and Mary developed an archeological gold mine at Olduvai, and he became a magnified figure, a celebrity in the wider world. His son Richard in time succeeded him as a field archeologist, an active contender for the limelight in declaring the course of human evolution and leadership over the National (Coryndon) Museum of Kenya. Within the new Kenya, he and his younger brother Philip, a member of parliament and junior minister, managed to build on the family name that began with their missionary grandparents.

Amid the campaigns of her sons in the nationalist arena and celebrity lecture circuits, Mary waged an autonomous campaign to see to it that the Leakey name stood for scientific rigor. This motive may have been the ultimate one behind the autobiography. The transition from suspecting the Leakey Foundation to embracing and influencing it can be offered as critically important evidence of how this overall determination had to be negotiated. In 1968, the L. S. B. Leakey Foundation for Research Related to Man's Origin was set up by Leakey's admirers:

> The Foundation from the start tended to have a second existence as an elite social club for the higher ranks of California hostesses, but there was no question of their devotion to Louis. (1984, p. 157)

After the great man's death, and Mary's activities at various symposia in the United States, the foundation turned to his widow to replace him:

> I was approached by the Leakey Foundation to undertake a lecture tour of
> the kind Louis used to give every year during the last period of his life. I
> agreed and the tour was successful enough for the Foundation to want it to
> become an annual occurrence: this really established the pattern of my
> visits to the States since 1977. (1984, p. 187)

Within the family, there were times of conflict, as when Mary, now the
senior partner in the archeological enterprise, felt compelled to publicly
diassociate herself from certain of Richard's claims. On the other hand, she
was able to support him in his disputes with Donald Johanson, who she
believed made unsound use of her own work (1984, p. 148, 180ff.). Mary
Leakey claimed, to the contrary, that designing grand schemes of human
evolution remained at best "an entertaining pasttime [sic] if not taken too
seriously, [for] in the present state of our knowledge I do not believe it is
possible to fit the known hominid fossils into a reliable pattern" (1984, p.
214).

As prominence and independence were thrust upon Mary, a lineage
claim from her own side took its place. It was contained in the introduction
the public orator made, in Latin, as part of the ceremonies conferring upon
her an honorary degree at Oxford in the summer of 1981. The citation's
final paragraph begins:

> Dr. Leakey has anthropology in her blood; one of her ancestors was John
> Frere, who published an article on the flints he found in Suffolk in 1797,
> the year before Nelson won the Battle of the Nile. So she is descendant,
> wife, and mother of anthropologists, but she has not been infected with the
> arrogance one might expect. She is like the modest Archedice
>   "Unto whose bosom pride was never known
>   Though daughter, wife, and sister to the throne."
> She takes no part in those public controversies to which the life of an
> archaeologist is prone. (1983, p. 199)

Dynasties are clearly the constructs of societies, and no less than the Zulu
storyteller, the Oxford orator played his part in merging "blood" with
classical and national elements.

CONCLUSIONS

The discussion of campaigns, dynasties, and personal narratives undertaken in these pages has taken up the invitation to engage in comparison
found in Ruth Benedict's preface to *Zulu Woman:*

> We see Christina, the inhibited little Christian schoolteacher, plunged as
> First Wife into Solomon's entourage, growing into wise adulthood as the
> warm and loving wife of the King and threading her capable and womanly

way among his wives' intrigues. Just because we appraise the full disin-
tegration that surrounded her, we respect Christina the more. We wonder
what "civilized" woman would have done as well. (Reyher 1970, p. x)

By substituting "Western white elite" for "civilized," the necessary elements
of status, culture, and context can be unpacked from the simple dualism
implied by this quotation, and thus the opening for comparison widens. My
comparison of Christina Sibiya and Mary Leakey has revolved around their
experiences as women intimately connected with powerful men and the
existence of a collective family interest in succession. These two women
asserted their independence but nevertheless had to become campaigners
bent upon assuring the legitimacy and good name of the family. In a sense,
the succession of their sons galvanized the campaigns, but these situations
matured after their declarations of independence, the ruptures of the
marriages, and the deaths of their husbands. As they became reengaged
with the public realm, each brought with her an explicit claim to her own
charter of descent or tradition of righteous resistance. In Christina's case,
the elaboration of her mother's separation and willingness to live without a
man in order to protect her standing as the legitimate wife served to
anticipate her own tale of chastity and suffering. For Mary, the emphasis
upon the devotion of forebears to art and archeology plays a similar part.

The concept of dynasty has provided a linchpin of this essay. It had to be
brought from outside the texts and the consciousness the narrators expressed to add to the formal structure of moments in the women's life
cycles and events of marriage and separation. It discerns a condition
atypical of twentieth-century global society. To make the two figures and
their personal narratives so comparable may in more abstract discourse
about social relations seem to be beside the point, even misleading, in the
face of oppressions shared by women and communities in a world where
economic privilege and color all too often coincide. Yet personal experiences, consciousness, and narratives do not conform to the categories of
such abstraction. What appears to be preindustrial in women's views of
their relationships is not a chronological lag but rather a persisting and
ideologically reenforced way of framing their roles as reproducers of
family in the cultural as well as the biological sense. Through the narratives
of two women, we are privileged to explore this process and also appreciate
the steps in changing consciousness and action.

Finally, beyond the surprising parallels to be pointed out in these super-
ficially disparate lives, what is the value of such an exercise? In terms of
critical considerations, it has been possible to suggest some of the problems
in the mediation of life stories and the value of grappling with the many
contexts from which the text arises. The life history can open vistas by
generating empathy, which can fire more exhaustive quests for explanation.
Text and context must in any case be brought into a measured relationship
in order to make judgments about the extent to which a personal narrative

and hence a set of purposes specific to the subject, here seen in light of campaigns, propel the final composition.

The full authorship of an authentic autobiography, as it is found in Mary Leakey's personal narrative, is desirable for its clarity and freedom from issues of who controls the communication. Such is the deceptiveness of life history in terms of authorship and control that only a short time ago, I concluded that those who undertook such mediation should do so only with an understanding that responsibility must be forced in one direction or the other, toward the self-control of autobiography or the overt externalization of biography.[15] The product of a more sustained comparison of Christina Sibiya and Mary Leakey is a change in this opinion. The lesson is in part a feminist reminder that women from seemingly distant places and cultures, especially wives and mothers, have had to struggle not only with their husbands but also with themselves as acquiescent figures who believed in the appropriateness of patriarchal authority with its extensions from private to public behavior. Christina would never have written her own autobiography in the sense that Mary Leakey did, drawing upon accumulated documents and the recollections of others to fix details and test recall. Without Christina's life story, appreciated as a self-propelled personal narrative, a biography of her would have been virtually inconceivable, let alone a comparison through which, by leveling certain differences, we can arrive at illuminating commonalities. Women's campaigns and dynastic strategizing are categories that will stand up in transcultural studies where power and family are intimately connected.

Notes

1. The comparison draws primarily upon Rebecca H. Reyher, *Zulu Woman* (1st ed., New York, 1948; 2 ed., New York: Signet, 1970) (references are to the second edition), and Mary Leakey, *Disclosing the Past: An Autobiography* (New York, 1984).

2. G. A. Gollock, *Daughters of Africa* (New York, 1932).

3. Cecil Cowley, *Kwa Zulu: Queen Mkabi's Story* (Cape Town, 1966). The reconstruction adopts the perspective of the Great Wife of Shaka's father, who lived on until the second part of the nineteenth century. This device draws on royal women's traditions and allows for a critical attitude toward Shaka, that illegitimate child, childless, despotic, and brilliant founder of the Zulu empire. Cowley's dedication to his royal patron reveals an important bias in his sources, although he used a variety of archives as well. It also has the quality of court praises: "To Princess Magogo, Daughter of Dinizulu, son of Cetshwayo, son of Mpande, Son of Senzangakona, King of the Zulus—Mother of Mangosuthu, Chief of the Abakwa Buthelezi—A princess, a cultured woman, an accomplished musician, the descendant of a line of Kings . . . " (p. iv). He failed to add, sister of Solomon.

4. See Denise O'Brien, "Female Husbands in Southern Bantu Societies," and Alice Schlegel, "Toward a Theory of Sexual Stratification," in A. Schlegel, ed., *Sexual*

Stratification: A Cross-Cultural View (New York, 1977). See also Karen Sacks, *Sisters and Wives: The Past and Future of Sexual Equality* (London, 1979).

5. Shula Marks, "Natal, the Zulu Royal Family, and the Ideology of Segregation," *Journal of Southern African Studies* 4 (1978). See also her "Patriotism, Patriarchy, and Purity: Natal and the Politics of Zulu Ethnic Consciousness," in Leroy Vail, ed., *The Creation of Tribalism in Southern Africa* (Berkeley: University of California Press, 1988).

6. See C. de B. Webb and J. B. Wright, eds., *A Zulu King Speaks: Statements Made by Cetshwayo ka Mpande on the History and Culture of His People* (Durban, 1978). See also H. J. Simons, *African Women: Their Legal Status in South Africa* (London, 1968), which shows how the codification of custom occurred in Natal and extended from there to elsewhere in South Africa. See also Martin Chanock, *Law, Custom, and Special Order: The Colonial Experience in Malawi and Zambia* (Cambridge, 1985), pt. 3, "Men and Women."

7. See Shula Marks, *The Ambiguities of Dependence in South Africa: Class, Nationalism, and the State in Twentieth-Century Natal* (Baltimore, 1968), which elaborates on her significant article noted above. Chapter 1, "The Drunken King and the Nature of the State," is about Solomon.

8. For a more encompassing historical account, see Jeff Guy, *The Destruction of the Zulu Kingdom* (London, 1979).

9. Needless to say, this evaluation served to enhance the "royal" quality of Chief Gatsha Buthelezi (Mangosuthu Gatsha Buthelezi).

10. L. S. B. Leakey, *White African* (London, 1937).

11. L. S. B. Leakey, *By the Evidence: Memoirs, 1932–1951* (New York, 1977).

12. Richard Leakey, *One Life: An Autobiography* (Salem, N.H., 1983), chap. 7.

13. For Leakey's discussion of National Museum maneuvers, see 1983, pp. 107ff.

14. L. S. B. Leakey, *Defeating Mau Mau* (London, 1954), *Mau Mau and the Kikuyu* (London, 1955).

15. Marcia Wright, "Femmes Africaines: Utilisation d'autobiographies, d'histoires de vie et de biographies commes texts de campagne," forthcoming in *Cahiers d'Etudes Africaine*. Both the earlier paper and the present one owe much to the advice and encouragement of the Personal Narratives Group at the Center for Advanced Feminist Studies, University of Minnesota.

TRANSFORMATIVE SUBJECTIVITY IN THE WRITINGS OF CHRISTA WOLF

Sandra Frieden

Transformation of individual consciousness, and ultimately of society, has always been the main agenda of feminism. Socialization works on consciousness to create what we experience as gaps in our identity—between private and public, between personal and political; and feminist theory and practice have sought to reconcile these false separations. Focusing on the construction of subjectivity, especially on the contradictions individuals are unable or unwilling to repress, feminists have used the "bad fit" of imposed social roles as an impetus for social transformation. Contemporary women's autobiographies, in particular, have had a consciousness-jarring impact on our understanding of the social basis of identity formation: subjectivities laid bare in the process of development reveal the power of society to press for conformity, to propel the construction of individual identity along the path of least social resistance.

East German author Christa Wolf departs from this path, and her writings serve as models of resistance. The works I will discuss (I am using English titles and editions, although dates given are for the original German-language publications)—*The Quest for Christa T.* (1968), *Patterns of Childhood* (1976), *No Place on Earth* (1979), and *Cassandra/Conditions of a Narrative* (1983)—directly address issues of identity formation and social change. Wolf's strategy is to provide a two-part model of countercultural consciousness: first, a narrated subjectivity which resists normative social values; and second, a narrating subjectivity which refuses the normative functions of literary conventions.

Christa Wolf, committed socialist and preeminent writer of East Germany, is now in her mid-fifties. As a chronicler of life experience for her country and her generation, she achieved international prominence with the 1968 publication of *The Quest for Christa T.*, a reminiscence of her childhood friend Christa T., whose never-realized attempts at self-fulfillment—whether in school, work, or family life—caused her to chafe continuously against the restrictive East German social model for women until her death from leukemia at age thirty-five. Much as Christa T.'s values ran counter to the prevailing norms of her culture, the work defies strict categorization as novel, biography, or autobiography according to conventional definitions. The foreword declares:[1]

> Christa T. is a fictional character. Several of the quotations from diaries, sketches, and letters come from real-life sources.
>   I did not consider myself bound by fidelity to external details. The minor characters and the situations are invented: any resemblance between them and living persons or actual events is accidental.

Under this pre-text of fictionalization, the work proceeds as an apparent biography by a friend whose memory fleshes out the letters and diary entries left by Christa T. and whose seeming purpose in reminiscing is to understand why another person might refuse to accommodate herself to society's expectations. By interweaving recollected "facts" with her own self-projections, Wolf depicts a life course which is not hers and yet is so imbued with her own subjectivity that the two Christas become only as separable and as contingent as the narrating and narrated "I." The first-person narration carries no quotation marks, ambiguously blends first-person accounts with direct discourse, and confuses self-address with words spoken to and by others. These formal ambiguities and syntactical intrusions of the narrating consciousness have confounded the placement of the work into a conventional category: it has been both "authenticated" as biography through the discovery of an actual "Christa T.," and declared to be covertly autobiographical.

In acknowledging her own shaping of events and characters, the narrator does not presume to convey an objective "truth"; rather, she acknowledges the frightening responsibility incurred by writing, both in terms of a "truthful" rendering of another's life and in terms of authorial projection. She says: "This is where the evasions begin. . . . But I can still see her. Worse, I can do what I like with her" (p. 4). What she is evading may be both the difficult work of separating self-projection from the motivations of "the other," and the temptation not to do so at all, but in fact to shape "the other" as she wishes. For if "the other" is different from any sort of self-projections imagined by the self, then what implications might there be, what changes in the self might be necessitated by such an acknowledgment? Rather than allowing such evasions to be cloaked by the pretense of objectivity, she renders visible those evasions she recognizes and leaves open the likelihood of others. This is the closest she comes to "truth," a comprehension of "the secret of the third person, who is there without being tangible and who, when circumstances favor her, can bring down more reality upon herself than the first person: I. The difficulty of saying 'I'" (p. 170). For Wolf, "authenticity" goes beyond the traditional (auto)biographical convention of verifiability or attempted objectivity. The authenticity she models for the reader is that of a consciousness intent on revealing its own self-deceptions, continuously questioning its own assumptions, and persistently redefining itself in, as, and apart from "the other."

In *Patterns of Childhood,* Wolf recalls the first sixteen years of her life, 1929 to 1945, in Nazi Germany. These recollections are occasioned by and inlaid into the account of the narrator's 1971 trip in the company of her family to the (now) Polish town in which she grew up, a retrospective level which allows the narrator to comment on the past with the tempered judgment of present-day hindsight. The description of this trip is, in turn, embedded in the diaristic account of the writing process (1972 to 1975) of this book. What results is a narrative strategy of three superimpositions linking past and current events, past experience with present understanding, and past self with present self-construction. Both the individual and social histories are summoned through the childhood memories of the adult, act upon the adult retrieving them, and are commented upon by the reflecting writer, who (re)views their significance within an ever-broadening spectrum of current events and moral values. For example, Wolf recalls her childhood enthusiasm for Goebbels's voice on the radio and school assemblies on the *Führer*'s birthday; these memories are then pointedly linked to her shock at the absence of Adolf Eichmann's name in her daughter's history book, and to her indignation over Watergate. In this way, Wolf uses her own life and work to lay bare the psychological and political consequences of socialization in its insidious dailiness: the cumulative and generally unfiltered (and therefore unquestioned) creation of a seemingly coherent identity through layers of every day's events, experiences, and impressions. Unless broken down, such an identity accepts as "truth" the circumstances of existence which maintain and nurture the status quo, however contradictory those circumstances might be. Wolf's book communicates the difficulty of breaking down and breaking through these layers of socialized consciousness and exposing their contradictions; and this message finds its appropriate expression in the dismantling of form.[2]

Some of the most apparent formal markers of conventional autobiography include the (more or less) linear narration of a chronologically structured life story; a claim to truth, often documented by "verifiable" data; and the unproblematic use of the pronoun *I* to represent a seemingly continuous past and present self, with scarce (if any) reference to the act of writing. Wolf disrupts these expectations of the reader in order to demonstrate her own sense of disruption, and also to present a model for a different way of perceiving the otherwise familiar. Wolf forces constant intrusions of the different temporal levels upon each other, rupturing a comfortable sense of a historical continuum in favor of an alienating discontinuity, modeling her own confusion as to how *that* past became *this* present, how *that* child became *this* adult. Claims to autobiographical "truth" within her painstaking gathering of substantiating documents are relativized by her own acknowledgment. In trying to recall her childhood, she says: "But what about the child herself? No image. This is where forgery would set in" (p. 6). Like the "evasions" in *Christa T.,* the "forgery" in *Patterns of Childhood* is inspired by fear: the fear of coming too close to "the abysses of memory" (my translation: *Kindheitsmuster,* p. 69), too close to an accounting for the illogic of her own development, which, once acknowledged, necessitates change. For if the linearity of her retroactively constructed life story dissolves upon confrontation with memory, then her basis for understanding herself and the world—and linear thinking itself—becomes questionable. Like the denial of biographical authenticity in the preface to *Christa T.,* the foreword in *Patterns of Childhood* disclaims autobiographical accuracy, but now it is clearly ironic:

> All characters in this book are the invention of the narrator. None is identical with any person living or dead. Neither do any of the described episodes coincide with actual events. Anyone believing that he detects a similarity between a character in the narrative and either himself or anyone else should consider the strange lack of individuality in the behavior of many contemporaries. Generally recognizable behavior patterns should be blamed on circumstances.
>
> C.W.

Without clarifying her point of reference, Wolf allows critics in the West to interpret these words as an attack on conformity in the East, and critics in the East to understand her words as an assault on a universal tendency to accede to the demands of authority. She achieves this ambiguity by casting the problem in the slippery category of autobiographical "truth." Rejecting conventional rules of pronoun reference, Wolf recreates and refers to her childhood self in the third person, with a different name, and addresses her adult self as "you." The "difficulty of saying 'I'" thus becomes the driving force behind the work, as she attempts to reconcile the past and present self, to enable the writing adult to refer to the childhood self as "I." The use of second-person address for herself is a strategy also designed to draw readers into the text, since the conventional understanding of "you" would be an address to the reader. Wolf's narrative strategies thus disrupt conventional readings of her life story in favor of an ongoing process of self-scrutiny: both content (her search for self) and form (the expression of that search) resist a comfortable or insulated familiarity. Wolf's counter-cultural perspective of the self draws out and questions assumptions buried within socialized consciousness, and reveals complex and contradictory connections between self, others, and events.

Wolf's *No Place on Earth* (1979) describes an imagined meeting between the writers Heinrich von Kleist and Karoline von Günderrode. An early Kleist biography claims the two might have met, and Wolf brings them together in the company of mutual friends for an afternoon tea party. The year is 1804. Kleist, still seven years before his suicide, is recuperating from nervous collapse and pondering his future as a Prussian bureaucrat. Günderrode, two years before her suicide, is a melancholy poet, published but of little renown, ridiculed for her "feminine verses," and friend of the eminent intellectual and literate Brentano family. These two casualties of an unyielding social order observe one another, participate politely in various conversational groupings, talk about their mutual melancholia, and depart with the other guests at the end of the afternoon.

No Place on Earth is published (in the German-language editions) without a genre designation and seems to be historical fiction, but the research underlying the quotations and the historical setting suggest a biographical study. Various other readings have been suggested: a utopian parable (or even an antiutopian parable), a critique of patriarchal culture, an artist's story, and a masked autobiographical statement of Wolf's uneasiness as a writer in East Germany and of her sense of being lost in a "transitional epoch." Wolf has further complicated the issue by her publication in the same year of Günderrode's works in the form of a "biography," *The Shadow of a Dream.* The empathy Wolf feels for Günderrode permeates this work, in which she follows rather closely the conventions of biographical form. Here she presents the life of Günderrode through a linear narration of chronologically ordered life events; information comes from letters, works, eyewitness accounts; and the attitude of the narrating biographer—while hardly as objective as scholarly historiography would have it—is more or less non/self-referential.

This form, however, was apparently inadequate to treat the content envisioned by Wolf in the Günderrode material, and in *No Place on Earth* she reshapes it, not in accordance with traditional biographical format but rather in contradistinction to it. *No Place on Earth* begins by moving through a dreamlike present into a seemingly dramatized version of the past.

> The wicked spoor left in time's wake as it flees us.
>
> You precursors, feet bleeding. Gazes without eyes, words that stem from no mouth. Shapes without bodies. Descended heavenward, separated in remote graves, resurrected again from the dead, still forgiving those who trespass against us, the sorrowful patience of angels or of Job.
>
> And we, still greedy for the ashen taste of words.
>
> (. . . .)
>
> Centuries-old laughter. The echo, monstrous, bouncing off innumerable barriers. And the suspicion that nothing more will happen but this reverberation. (pp. 3–4)

The title itself disputes historical accuracy: again (as Susan Lanser has suggested; see note 1), the disclaiming of verifiability is thoroughly ironic and more severe, since these events have occurred "no place on earth," and the tale is described as "a legend that suits us" (p. 4). The omniscient narrator inhabits the thoughts of first one character, then another, allowing pronominal references to spill over into the next figure's dialogue so that it is often not clear precisely who is speaking, or even if it is the narrator's words we hear. The book suddenly resumes the present-time frame at its conclusion, as Kleist and Günderrode return from their walk:

> Now it is getting dark. The final glow on the river.
>
> Simply go on, they think.
>
> We know what is coming. (p. 119)

The indeterminacy of this "we"—is it Kleist and Günderrode or the writer and readers?—makes a final appeal to the readers to see themselves in this setting, in Wolf's setting, in their own setting through Wolf's eyes. This strategy of pronominal ambiguity is further complicated by intertextuality: Wolf uses Kleist's and Günderrode's actual writings as sources for their words and thoughts, but blends these with her words and her own subjectivity. Her consciousness at once inhabits and is subsumed by those of her characters in a literary act of empathy; and yet she herself remains present as a narrating consciousness with the right to speak. This intervention in the text, as in the earlier works, models a subjective stance which opens itself up to the words/thoughts of others while not losing its own perspective.

Wolf's 1983 "story" *Cassandra* and the accompanying essays *Conditions of a Narrative* demonstrate her sustained dissatisfaction with genre prescriptions and her insistent reworking of form and content as a model of countercultural consciousness. In *Cassandra* the narrator stands before the gates of present-day Mycenae and says: "It was here. This is where she stood. These stone lions looked at her; now they no longer have heads" (p. 3). Against a sky that is "still the same," Cassandra, captive of Agamemnon after the fall of Troy, begins speaking in the first person, to tell to and for herself the causes of how she came to be there: "Keeping step with the story, I make my way into death." As the seer who is never believed, Cassandra knows that the gates will soon be opened by Clytemnestra, inviting her to follow Agamemnon to a bloody death. Out of her need to witness, she thinks and wonders: "What I grasp between now and evening will perish with me. Will it perish? Once a thought comes into the world, does it live on in someone else?" (p. 5) In *Patterns of Childhood*, Wolf wondered whether the lessons of one generation could be passed on to the next; in *Cassandra*, she traces the indifference of our entire civilization to the warnings of history.

Wolf addresses the issues raised in *Cassandra* explicitly and personally in the accompanying essays, which consist of a travelogue, a work diary, and a letter, all related to a trip to Greece and her research into the figure of

Cassandra and ancient matriarchal cultures. As with the Günderrode material, Wolf requires both a form into which she can project herself freely, and a documentary account of the process of appropriation, which is to say how she, Christa Wolf, assimilated the information which she found. Her subjectivized re-vision of the classic versions of Cassandra's story and of nineteenth- and twentieth-century archeologists' versions of ancient cultures unmasks the work of patriarchy in the omission of women's experience, and she attempts a subversive restructuring through her "different lens" (p. 232). Wolf relates contemporary concerns ranging from feminism to nuclear proliferation, and her reappropriation of history encompasses not only Cassandra but also the veiled and obedient Syrian wives on her plane to Greece, Nazi Germany, and late-capitalist America. Here, as in the earlier works, Wolf's insistent involvement with, or questioning of, the text speaks for the authenticity of her narration. The re-vision, she believes, is necessary to reveal a "different reality":

> To what extent is there really a thing as "women's writing"? To the extent that women, for historical and biological reasons, experience a different reality than men. Experience a different reality than men and express it. To the extent that women belong not to the rulers but to the ruled, and have done so for centuries. To the extent that they are the objects of objects, second-degree objects, frequently the objects of men who are themselves objects, and so, in terms of their social position, unqualified members of the subculture. To the extent that they stop wearing themselves out trying to integrate themselves into the prevailing delusional systems. (p. 259)

The concern with subjects and objects—with women as subjects and objects, with subjectivity and objectivity in narration—ties Wolf's works together. Wolf's writings infuse a female subject, whether an autobiographical self or a biographical or mythological other, with a distinctly and openly present-day, female consciousness. Her characters, and she as author, take on through the functions of narrative the role of active subject historically denied to women. Wolf insists that her writing lead to a sensitizing process in which the readers may become "conscious subjects" (*The Reader and the Writer*, p. 212). This insistent and engaged presence of the author in and with the text challenges the readers' conditioned "pseudo-objectivity," which would otherwise falsify and prevent a personal response to the text or the appropriation of its message ("Documentation," p. 98). She works against conventional forms of autobiography, biography, or fiction, rejecting their stultifying effects upon consciousness: "An ability to be 'authentic' . . . that comes only by renouncing the detachment afforded by definite forms" (*Conditions*, p. 301). Wolf relates this anecdote:

> An intelligent and cultivated poet told me he does not understand me; why should I no longer wish to accept the authority of the literary genres? After

all, they really are (he said) the objective expression of laws filtered out of
centuries of labor, the laws of what is valid in art, and by which we can
recognize and measure it. I was so stupefied that I could not answer him.
(*Conditions*, p. 278)

Wolf is always telling "life stories," the dailiness of women's lives, both
those details which would normally be recorded in history books and those
which would not. Through the life story, Wolf demonstrates the strength of
societal forces and institutions—schools, religions, governments, media,
social behaviors, and literary canons—as well as the acquiescence or resistance to them by represented and representative subjectivities. The author
breaks with traditional expectations of biographical and autobiographical
forms to model for the reader an involvement with and assimilation of
another's experience and perspective. Thus for her, biography becomes, as
Sara Speidel has described, a "narrative solidarity"[3] with another person's
perspective; and autobiography becomes an attempt to discover such a
"solidarity" within varying configurations of the self.

What is there about Christa Wolf's writing and its relationship to the
contexts in which she writes that is generalizable to the experiences of other
authors? I will now examine various aspects of the literary milieu of German writing of the 1970s for both its specificity and its broader ap-
plicability.

Under the slogan of "New Subjectivity," hundreds of autobiographical
(and biographical) works have appeared in both West and East Germany,
Austria, and Switzerland in the past fifteen years. Autobiographical accounts of wartime experience, in the tone of self-justifications and exposés,
did, to be sure, begin appearing immediately after 1945, and such works
corresponded in the public sphere to needs felt in the private sphere to
explain, if not justify, the self to the outside world. After 1970 however,
autobiographical writings became more intense and direct in their examination of identity and general sociohistorical context. Former National
Socialists now wrote their memoirs in an atmosphere which encouraged
confession rather than self-justification, a documentation of inner struggle
rather than an impassive accounting of events. Their children had had time
to come of age, both those socialized under Nazi rule and those born
afterward. These various age groups began to reassess the socialization
processes they had undergone, and publishing houses reacted to and fostered the autobiographical, self-analytical trend which drew writers and
readers from so broad a cross-section. Attempting to root out that which
had been sown either deliberately or unconsciously, the heirs of Nazi
Germany struggled as a society to find a sense of historical identity and
continuity while renouncing much of what the previous period represented.

The student movement of the late sixties had already begun its protests against what the students experienced as authoritarianism perpetuated and (unsuccessfully) repressed by the "parent generation." By the end of the 1960s, the Left had generated and popularized a code of values which privileged only the politically functional and, in its focus on such trans-individual, principally Marxist categories as class, base, and superstructure, denigrated any reference to or consideration of the personal realm of life. As a consequence, literature of the late sixties displayed a preference for documentary writing, for protocols and reportage that betrayed no inner feelings, no personal cases, but rather collective experience rendered objective. But political disillusionment arrived with the 1970s, and the now alienated students became suspicious of dogmatic, group-identified ideologies. Reacting against the reduction of individual experience to rarefied political paradigms, many sought understanding in the differentiated examples and models of individual histories, withdrawing increasingly to a world of "personal" rather than "purely political" concerns. Bolstered by popular psychology's emphasis on self-revelation as therapy and developmental life crises (Erikson, Laing, Wolfe, Lasch, Sheehy), they turned to autobiography as a means to explore and account for the individual's socialization by and resistance to the authoritarian forces of society. "Pseudo-objective" reportage thus evolved into a documentation of the inner world, told by the observing self in search of an individualized authenticity, and resistance to authority extended to opposing the authority of generic conventions. The acknowledgment of the limitation of perspective to one's own was considered more honest: authors turned to first-person narration to give specific voice to and overcome their own anguished sense of helplessness and to express their determination to expose any attempt at institutionalized manipulation—even their own.

Factors which influenced writing in the West during the seventies affected literature in the East as well, operating upon a somewhat different constellation of attitudes and conceptions. Reduced to simplest terms, the "I" of West German subjectivity was seen as narcissistic in the East, where the subjective "I" was officially obliged to secure an understanding of the relationship of the individual to society ("Documentation," p. 101). East German writers met with other programmatic prescriptions as well. The official historical background was declared to be *Neubeginn* (New Beginning): since, according to official pronouncement, Nazi history was not "their" history, writers were encouraged to approach the problems of the German past from the perspective of the outsider who could distantly observe and comment upon the problem of someone else's historical guilt (Linn, p. 52). Writers who chose to approach the problems of the (East) German present outside the mandated structure—i.e., explicit declarations of party support, the portrayal of dialectically resolved, nonantagonistic conflict, and the restriction of criticism of East German society to "atypical" elements (Nieraad, p. 313)—were encouraged to leave the country, or were sometimes "invited out." Stylistic authenticity and essayistic tendencies were encouraged to conform to a political standard of documentary realism. The tendency to dwell on the political rather than the aesthetic reception of a work (Linn, p. 54) generated a climate unfavorable to the experimental, subjective exploration of historical guilt or contemporary problems. A number of writers refusing to adapt to such restrictions are now in the West; others, such as Christa Wolf, have tempered their writing enough to be published and discussed, at least in private circles, if not in a public forum ("Documentation," p. 105). Wolf ponders such problems while traveling through Greece:

> The centering around the Logos, the word as fetish—perhaps the deepest superstition of the West, or at least the one of which I am a fervent devotee. Hence, the mere fact that I do not know the language gives me an inkling of the possible terrors of exile. When did it begin, this unfortunate habit of trying out foreign cities to see how it would feel to live there? The question is, When did the feeling of having a homeland disappear? (*Conditions*, p. 162)

The contemporary international women's movement was growing during this same period, affecting both East and West. West German women writers, politicized by the student movement and influenced by emerging American radical feminist writings, turned to life-history writing both as consciousness raising and as analysis of female socialization. Claiming the personal as political, they created a literary support system which would strengthen women through the affirmation and sharing of experiences and the detailing of their stages of socialization into patriarchal culture. While East German women's claims to equal rights and equal pay were built into their constitution, still the absence of women from the highest levels of leadership, the traditional domestic expectations placed upon women, and the lack of an infrastructure or support network for women in East Germany created needs which women writers addressed.

From conventional and unconventional autobiography to protocols, journals, letters, and confessions, from published protests to public outcries, women writers of East *and* West have attempted to span the gaps between public and private, between history and individual experience, between official myths of womanhood and women's lives. These writers took the responsibility for creating new vocabulary, new expressions, and new literary images which would give voice and substance within the world of literature to the new consciousness of women. They sought an articulation and a primacy of their own subjectivity, not only as a reaction against late-sixties "objectivity" or political dogma, but also as a countercurrent to traditional expectations of women and women's writing, and as a disruption of traditional forms of the patriarchal system. For some writers, disruption took place through the dislocation of experience into fantasy: fictional worlds evolved in which expressly fantastic contexts foregrounded clearly

contemporary issues. Other writers created ruptures in the public consciousness by writing explicitly about their own lives—childhood traumas,
divorce, lesbian relationships, mental breakdowns, abortions—or even
their revised views of recent (male) history. Women's speaking out was itself
a departure from the traditional restraints upon women's assertiveness and
daring; and the details which they revealed had a radicalism of their own.
As described by Evelyn Beck and Biddy Martin (pp. 136–38), these accounts were in a tone of "subversive realism": a disclosing of details so
overwhelming in their exactness and in their everydayness that a de-
mythologizing of women and their lives followed unavoidably. Despite
charges of narcissistic self-indulgence, it soon became clear that women
writers were describing much more than their individual experiences: they
were describing experiences of a community of women who found in the
public exchange a validating support system and a basis for critical (and
specifically political) thinking.

What do we see in this phenomenon that is generalizable to other societies and other times? The struggle of a community to understand its
past, and thus its present, has been carried on through means of a literary
form molded to suit its needs. The subjectivizing of public expression turns
an accounting of past and present into an accountability of the self for its
role in events; and the self is in turn shown as shaped by these events.
("Don't ask your contemporaries certain questions. Because it is unbearable
to think the tiny word 'I' in connection with the word 'Auschwitz.' 'I' in the
past conditional: I would have. I might have. I could have. Done it. Obeyed
orders" [*Patterns*, p. 230].) Women dealing with their socially and psychologically restricted role assignments, young adults recounting their struggles
with the authoritarian legacy of Nazi parents, and mature writers whose
recollections of childhood loyalties conflict with current values—all these
groups have turned to a chronological analysis of self, an attempt to
discover the logic of socialization and behavior within a set time span, that
of the unfolding of their lives.

The psychological necessity of recognizing and accepting the significance
of childhood experiences and impressions, and of acknowledging the roles
played by society in identity formation, has clearly been urgent for this
generation, as evidenced by the number and popularity of such accounts.
They are attempts to understand an earlier self—a self such as the young
girl who swears undying allegiance to the *Führer*. And this was Christa Wolf
(*Patterns*, p. 304). Often parents now themselves, these writers not only are
trying to explain their past to the next generation, and to warn them: they
are still seeking their own explanations. The openly autobiographical
nature of these works has undoubtedly been significant for both their
writing and their reception: the pain of the search and discovery of such
communally shared traumas could thus be released and mediated by the
acknowledged commonality of the experiences. The autobiographical format serves both the individual and the community in coping with a broken

sense of identity. The task of comprehending and overcoming the German past (both East and West), and of challenging the German present, was now to be pursued through the more readily accessible realm of personal experience.

While life-story writing may contribute to a society's sense of self-understanding, questions remain as to its potential for effecting social change. Contemporary life-story writing necessarily invokes traditions of structuring and understanding which affect present-day writing strategies and appropriation. Writing which describes and analyzes social structures and processes of socialization (an inherent part of life-story writing) for the purpose of social change (an inherent part of feminism) must deal with these traditions and assess their potential for undermining the project of change. One such tradition is the notion of a unified self as the basic structuring principle of autobiography. Because of its conventional grounding in a concept of the unified self, the consequences of using autobiography as an oppositional strategy for the women's movement must be considered. Autobiographical writings of earlier centuries affirmed the existence of the unified self, of coherence and continuity in the world. Addressing the individual as the primary source for initiating change, feminist countercultural practice has utilized life-story writing to subvert this earlier function and has called upon the subject to resist and overthrow the normative formulations of experience.

But postmodern criticism has reduced the concept of self to an illusory construct, at least for much of present theory, if not in current popular understanding. The constructed nature of the self, however, does not eliminate its functioning as a self-aware unit. In practice, which is to say, in the actual life world of writers and readers, traditional identification with a fragmented, disunified self may still take place, as even a "splintered" self will struggle to affirm its own experiences within a seemingly cohesive context. While such accounts have had a widespread appeal and have gained "grassroots" political support for the women's movement, this popular confidence in the ability of the "self" to witness and to narrate has for a time caused a rift between popular and some theoretical accounts of feminist subjectivity. Such critics have felt obliged to reveal in the popular model of autobiographical accounts the apparently illusory unity within a self which they see as a social and linguistic construct. They must ask whether the recourse to a traditional form does not automatically both engage the historical functions and incur the historical consequences of that form: namely, that by invoking a context in which the self successfully adapts (or the aberrant self maladapts) to society, writers also affirm the world-as-is, the status quo.

Life-story writing has always presented some models which differ from the norm; but these are dismissed as aberrations from the approved standards, or they are sensationalized, reproducing victimization rather than producing an exploration of options. Like all narrative, autobiography engages the momentum of narrative closure, a process which may lead to the repression of contradictions and the affirmation of false alternatives in the service of ideology. Although many examples of popular and literary autobiography have brought new perspectives to public awareness, and though some degree of social change has occurred, the similarity of the concept of the traditional unified self to the contemporary self as predominantly addressed within these works, as well as the ease with which such a form slides into false resolutions, may risk cooptation by limiting the scope of potential change.

Recent feminist theory has, in fact, questioned all use of narrative for women's oppositional writing. Teresa de Lauretis, for example, cites fairy-tale, myth, and folklore studies by Greimas, Propp, and Levi-Strauss to argue that Oedipal "logic," as a product of patriarchal culture, informs *all* established narrative structures.[4] In this argument, traditional narrative structure reenacts and dramatizes the male's struggle and search for identity, which is to say, his process of socialization. Thus, the movement of a subject(-hero) desiring (con)quest of an object(-princess) symbolically inscribes narrative with positions of specifically *male* desire. Images and points of identification for the subject addressed by the narrative are always "seen" through an Oedipal configuration, a point of view which presses the female reader into the service of a (male) subject who desires her-as-object. Notwithstanding the critique and revision of this scenario by numerous theorists (e.g., Chodorow 1978, de Lauretis 1984, Kaplan 1983, Mulvey 1975, Silverman 1983), this Freudian notion of women's "necessary" self-objectification is certainly inscribed in the canons of narrative, and in the processes of comprehending narrative as well. The question, then, remains whether and under what terms women can use language or images if the overarching mode of signification, as a form and process of patriarchal narrative, is grounded in female objectification.

Certain oppositional strategies employed in literary forms of autobiography reduce these risks and make possible a (self-)critical appropriation of alternative patterns of experience that entail neither a rigidly unified sense of self nor a "positive" model of female objectification. Such strategies may confront the seemingly inescapable Oedipal structure of narrative by addressing it directly. Autobiographical structure which resists convention on a formal level (insofar as it is recognizable through external or internal signals as autobiography) has consequences for the ways in which the depicted experience is appropriated. Appealing through "authentic" rather than fictional models, autobiography invites an adaptation of its given notions of self and experience.

However, a lack of resolution (closure) within the model presented for identification raises questions about that model and about the social constructions of self and experience. Appropriation, as a form of understanding, still takes place, but on terms other than those defined by dominant social patterns. The recognition of large social structures is rarely achieved in the individual instance: one woman, examining only her own life, can scarcely know that her arguments with prevailing values are echoed in other households. Rather, such recognition occurs as a function of sharing experiences and perceptions, so that (political) analysis takes place through consciousness raising or autobiography. The narration of such experience must be, on the one hand, sufficiently generalized to allow for widespread possibilities for identification, but, on the other, historically specific enough to maintain a basis in social and material realities. Concretized experience is thus made available for comparison and analysis (as well as for identification) on the levels of literary, sociological, psychological, historical, and political inquiry by virtue of its mediation through narrative.

Such oppositional strategies can be analyzed in both their structural and functional dimensions. Christa Wolf has reworked traditional autobiography by directly addressing "the subject in division" (de Lauretis, p. 28), revealing the ideologically concealed gaps in subjectivity and memory which inhere in traditional notions of autobiography. The insistent juxtapositions and interrelations of personal, local, and world events work to disperse experience (the construction of the self) over new realms, broadening the range of that which is to be appropriated. Her adaptations of traditional biography blend subjectivities, so that the "illusory" self becomes completely elusive and thus resists falling into the conventional understanding of a unified self or an objective analysis of "the other." The model she presents for identification is not that of a unified self but rather that of an insistently questioning subjectivity, a sense of self which, on the one hand, disregards the expected boundaries separating "self" and "other," and, on the other hand, acknowledges the differences between them. Her multiple use of forms—the rendering of (auto)biographical information into varied formats—prevents a fixation on conventional narrative functions of identification or closure. Combining narrative forms with open-ended essays, letters, and journal structures, she uses form and content to reduce and resist the powerful influence of patriarchal canons.

Other works emerging from the past fifteen years of autobiographical writings have explored structural practices which foreground contradictions within apparent unity, or expose the consciously constructed fictions within autobiographical "truth." Indeed, the very tensions between fiction and nonfiction which complicate autobiography's status as a genre may in fact be the source of a productive deconstruction of convention. Alexander Kluge suggests that the potential for social transformation resides in a conflation of forms, since the adherence to one (conventional) form plays into repression, prefigures the positions of desire and action to be inhabited by the reader. The integration and/or instrumental juxtaposition of different forms thus becomes a strategy for revealing contradictions through which the reader may render transparent and go beyond predetermined positions of response (Kluge, pp. 215ff.).

186 / NARRATIVE FORMS

In 1956, Georges Gusdorf described autobiography as a form of conscious communal discourse, a public act to preserve collective memory through time and to provide continuity between generations of a culture (Gusdorf, pp. 105–123). More recently, Elizabeth Bruss placed autobiography within a speech-act context, declaring its ability to "reflect and give focus to some consistent need and sense of possibility in the community it serves" (Bruss, p. 5). The "autobiographical act," as Bruss called it, is much less a private deed than a social performance: the placing of a text into a public forum, where it functions synchronically as a link among contemporaries and diachronically as a bridge between past and future communal expressions. That which is perceived as *individual* experience becomes a collective expression with the public act of autobiography, a voice which carries a sense of life at that time. Authors of autobiography offer their individual specificity to the community, where private experience is adopted and validated as community history.

Christa Wolf's participation in and witnessing of contemporary history do not in themselves make her and her writing unique; her insistence on the process of questioning, of establishing relationships for events and ideas across time and across boundaries, has created a space for the personal to confront the political, for daily experience to come into focus alongside "grander" events. The tasks of authors such as Christa Wolf are historically specific; the struggle may be played out and documented on an individual level, but the ratification of the struggle, the sense of communal identity, come through the voices of *many.* Contemporary autobiography presents an articulation, a documentation of life struggles performed *en masse,* evidence of both continuities and discontinuities between generations of a culture, a communal search for a voice, and of each voice for others.[5]

Notes

Portions of this paper have been revised from previously published or forthcoming discussions of autobiography and the works of Christa Wolf (see list of works cited).

1. Susan Lanser reads Wolf's forewords as irony directed at aesthetic problems of "truth" in representation and political problems of censorship (presentation on "The Difficulty of Narration" at the Women in German Conference, Racine, Wisconsin, October 13, 1979).

2. The notion of change as "a function of content seeking its adequate expression in form" is from Frederic Jameson (see list of works cited), page 328.

3. For this suggestion I am indebted to Sara Speidel's comments in an unpublished paper entitled "Borderlines: Christa Wolf and Autobiography."

4. De Lauretis, pp. 79–80. The Freudian account of the boy child's Oedipal development begins with love of the mother and turns to fear of castration as he realizes the implied threat to himself both by her lack of a penis and by the superior power (and superior penis) of his father. His way to successful adulthood requires conquering (t)his fear: he identifies with his father to compensate for his fear of "lack" and sets out to win a (different) woman to replace his mother as love object. Similarly, Freud's model of female Oedipal development presses the female into the service of the male as both negotiate the Oedipal stage. The female's process parallels and supports the male pattern; it begins, according to Freud, with an immediate perception of lack and an ensuing displacement of affection. This means that the female must accept her own "lack" and desire the father, i.e., the male who will provide her with a child as a substitute for the missing penis.

5. I am grateful to Richard Spuler for his thoughtful and repeated readings of this paper and his many insightful suggestions.

Works Cited

Beck, Evelyn Torton, and Biddy Martin. "Westdeutsche Frauenliteratur der siebziger Jahre." In *Deutsche Literatur in der Bundesrepublik seit 1965*, ed. P. M. Luetzeler and Egon Schwarz, pp. 135–49. Koenigstein/Ts.: Athenaeum, 1980.

Bruss, Elizabeth W. *Autobiographical Acts: The Changing Situation of a Literary Genre.* Baltimore: Johns Hopkins University Press, 1976.

Chodorow, Nancy. *The Reproduction of Mothering.* Berkeley: University of California Press, 1978.

de Lauretis, Teresa. *Alice Doesn't: Feminism, Semiotics, Cinema.* Bloomington: Indiana University Press, 1984.

Erikson, Erik. *Identity and the Life Cycle.* New York: International Universities Press, 1959.

Frieden, Sandra. *Autobiography: Self into Form. German Language Autobiographical Writings of the 1970s.* Frankfurt: Lang, 1983.

———. "'For God's Sake, ANYTHING But That!' Autobiography, Women's Films, and Countercultural Practice" (in German), ed. J. Fischer et al. Anthology on oppositional cultures (forthcoming).

———. "A Guarded Iconoclasm: The Self as Deconstructing Counterpoint to Documentation," ed. Marilyn Fries. Anthology on Christa Wolf (forthcoming). In German: "'Falls es strafbar ist, die Grenzen zu verwischen': Autobiographie, Biographie und Christa Wolf," in *Vom Anderen und vom Selbst*, ed. Reinhold Grimm and Jost Hermand. Koenigstein/Ts.: Athenaeum, 1982.

———. "'In eigener Sache': Christa Wolf's *Kindheitsmuster*." *German Quarterly* 54, no. 4 (1981): 473–87.

Gusdorf, Georges. "Conditions et limites de l'autobiographie." In *Formen der Selbstdarstellung: Analekten zu einer Geschichte des literarischen Selbstportraet*, ed. Guenther Reichenkron and Erich Haase. Berlin: Duncker und Humboldt, 1956.

Jameson, Fredric. *Marxism and Form.* Princeton: Princeton University Press, 1971.

Kaplan, E. Ann. *Women and Film.* New York: Methuen, 1983.

Kluge, Alexander. "On Film and the Public Sphere." *New German Critique*, no. 24–25 (Fall/Winter 1981–82): 206–220.

Laing, R. D. *The Divided Self.* London: Tavistock, 1959.

Lanser, Susan. "The Difficulty of Narration." Paper presented at the Women in German Conference, Racine, Wisconsin, October 13, 1979.

Lasch, Christopher. *The Culture of Narcissism.* New York: Norton, 1978.

Linn, Marie-Luise. "Doppelte Kindheit—Zur Interpretation von Christa Wolfs *Kindheitsmuster.*" *Der Deutschunterricht* 30 (1978): 52–66.

Mulvey, Laura. "Visual Pleasure and Narrative Cinema." *Screen* 16, no. 3 (Autumn 1975): 6–18.

Nieraad, Juergen. "Subjektivitaet als Thema und Methode realistischer Schreibweise." *Literaturwissenschaftliches Jahrbuch,* n.s. 19 (1978): 291–315.

Sheehy, Gail. *Passages.* New York: Dutton, 1974.

Silverman, Kaja. *The Subject of Semiotics.* New York: Oxford University Press, 1983.

Speidel, Sara. "Borderlines: Christa Wolf and Autobiography." Presentation at Modern Language Association Conference, December 1985.

Wolf, Christa. *Cassandra/Conditions of a Narrative.* Translated by Jan Van Heurck. New York: Farrar-Straus-Giroux, 1984.

———. "Documentation: Christa Wolf." Interviews in *German Quarterly* 57, no. 1 (Winter 1984): 91–115.

———. *Kindheitsmuster* (German version of *Patterns of Childhood*). Darmstadt/Neuwied: Luchterhand, 1979.

———. *No Place on Earth.* Translated by Jan Van Heurck. New York: Farrar-Straus-Giroux, 1982.

———. *Patterns of Childhood* (formerly *A Model Childhood*). Translated by Ursule Molinaro and Hedwig Rappolt. New York: Farrar-Straus-Giroux, 1980.

———. *The Quest for Christa T.* Translated by Christopher Middleton, New York: Farrar-Straus-Giroux, 1970.

———. *The Reader and the Writer.* Translated by Joan Becker. New York: International Publishers, 1977.

———. *Der Schatten eines Traumes.* By Karoline von Günderrode. Edited by Christa Wolf. Darmstadt/Neuwied: Luchterhand, 1979.

Wolfe, Tom. "The 'Me' Decade and the Third Great Awakening." *New York,* August 23, 1976, pp. 26–40.

WOMEN'S PERSONAL NARRATIVES
Myths, Experiences, and Emotions

Luisa Passerini

The themes singled out for consideration in this paper are drawn from research on the working-class life in Turin in the period between the wars, research largely based on oral sources. These are life stories of about seventy women and men, born between 1886 and 1920, stories generated by the request to "retell your own life," with supporting questions accompanying the narration.[1] This paper will address several aspects of the larger project: first, the symbolic importance and narrative function of rebellious self-images in women's life stories; second, the place of work in women's life narratives; and finally, general observations about the role of gender in narrative choices.

IRREVERENCE AND REBELLIOUSNESS IN WOMEN'S LIVES AND IN THEIR NARRATIVES

Carolina Griffanti, born in 1893, a worker for long periods at the Fiat automobile factory in Lingotto, told the story of her life in the presence of other women at the Fiat old people's home:

> I was five when my mother died, there were two brothers, one aged three and the other forty days old. My life is a bit too hard. (she is interrupted by tears)
> Another woman: Don't get upset, Carolina. Tell us about some of your larks as a little girl!
> Carolina: Once I was on the window-sill of the house—I was living in the countryside—I was eating bread and salami with a knife and there were the hens, you know, underneath it was like a poultry-yard . . . and then I was there eating and this hen jumped up to peck me, and I had the knife in my hand, and it went right through its back. Then all the hens ran off, eh! Another time, I was starting to go to school, but I was grandad's pet and anyone who told me off had better look out, whatever I did was fine for him, even if it was wrong. And that time they were in the country to work and I took my two brothers plus three or four from school and told them: "Be quiet, won't you?" My aunt had already taken down the salami to cook, I went there: chop chop chop, the next moment there was no salami left!

> Then I came to the end of the third year of primary school, because if I said: "I am not going," my grandad said: "She says she's not going, don't let her go any more. You stay at home now." And I didn't go and got into all sorts of things.

The narration adds two more instances in the same tone and then suddenly jumps to the conclusion of the life story:

> Then I got married, I was 25. We got along, then one fine day he left me, abandoned me, and went off, not of his own accord, because they carried him away, he was dead, he died in the night.

The incidents of the first sequence are designed to show that Carolina, when she was little, "got into all sorts of things." The story of the marriage, which follows on the picture of the willful child, does not represent the definite conclusion of rebelliousness but only its adaptation to new circumstances. Carolina's memory then goes back in time to meeting her husband, moves on to their son's death at the age of seven, and once again shifts back to an argument with her father over her marriage. The ultimate moral: "I was a bad one, wasn't I! But I don't know what (laughs). . . . I was full of the devil!"

The order of recall belies the "naturalness" which is implicitly ascribed to chronological order. The first beginning (her mother's death) to Carolina's life story, the "natural" one, does not stand up to the emotions it arouses. It is a beginning tied to autobiographical and psychological experience, while the other starting point suggested by the women present allows her to overcome her tenseness and establish an acceptable stereotype. The contrast puts us on guard against the mistake of confusing the latter with a depth of identity in the psychological sense; cultural and psychological identities here do not coincide.

It is interesting to note the readiness of the other women in the old people's home to listen to the stories they have already heard. Evidently this attitude rests on the habit of reciprocal narration, based, in turn, on family oral traditions. We can imagine that, when Carolina was already grown up, her aunt might have recounted stories of her daring exploits as a child during evenings spent with friends and relatives. Thus the story that Carolina transmits is not necessarily a simply individual one; rather, it has important collective aspects.

Despite the emphasis on rebellion, other attitudes and forms of behavior are revealed in the life story. Carolina also speaks about herself as an exemplary wife and mother, a conscientious and obedient worker, a devout Catholic, and, in politics, someone in favor of the status quo. The contrast reinforces the impression that irreverence is a narrative stereotype which does not so much point to real behaviors as project affirmations of identity on the symbolic plane. Carolina does not expect us to take at face value all the transgressive episodes which she uses to illustrate her childhood; she retells them not so much as facts but rather as metaphors, as narrative resources that convey an impression of her public image. At the same time, she also tells us about her conventional behavior, sometimes between the lines (if we can use this expression for oral discourse), sometimes under the stimulus of a direct question. (This last remark also points to the dialectics between a more or less free flow of autobiographic memory and the replies to questions.)

A major point of interpretation is that in Carolina's story irreverence has a great symbolic value. This becomes clearer if a centuries-old tradition of iconographic and verbal representation of women rebels is called to mind. Variations of the "disorderly" woman, or the woman "on top," or the woman able in some way to overturn gender roles have been illustrated and discussed with reference to much earlier historical periods.[2] The importance of these analyses lies in their recognition of the symbolic, rather than simply reflective, character of representations, and, at the same time, in the recognition of their potential influence on forms of actual behavior. Natalie Zemon Davis has hypothesized that "the play with the various images of women-on-top kept open an alternative way of conceiving family structure" (p. 143).

If today we find affinities in the individual stories with that age-old image, we too can conclude that such individual mythology may draw its power and *raison d'être* from the very fact of not being "true," but rather from acting as a source of inspiration, encouragement, and excitement *in the face* of a different social reality. In such a case, the rebel stereotype recurrent in many women's autobiographies would not primarily aim to describe actual behavior, but would serve a markedly allegorical role. It could be the means of expressing problems of identity in the context of a social order oppressive of women, but also of transmitting awareness of oppression and lack of integration, and hence of directing oneself to current and future change. The historical translation of the myth can change from time to time and through contact with different life experiences, but its force as a utopia of freedom and innovation continues through the epochs.

In Carolina's mental outlook, the stereotypical expression "being full of the devil" anticipates and explains certain innovative choices made in moments of crisis, such as the decision to marry without her father's permission, the wish to work in the factory even after the birth of her son, the call for a different division of labor in the home. The self-image of the rebel-born can be of great help in transforming reality, particularly in the processes of cultural transformation linked to the new experiences many women went through in the first decades of the century. Myths and stereotypes could be employed to mediate between traditional and new, between reality and imagination, between individual and collective.

Carolina's remark about "being full of the devil" reminds us of Mary

Douglas's observations on the greater salience of women in the cults of possession: it is the very marginality of women with respect to the social divisions of labor which means that they are less involved than men in the fundamental institutions of society and which pushes them into a symbolic state which allegorically represents their social position. This is something to keep in mind in order to explain the preference, certainly not absolute, of women for representing themselves as rebels rather than using the self-image of good worker privileged by men of the same age and social condition. But we'll come to this later on. Now let us briefly enlarge our considerations on the recurrent theme of irreverence and rebelliousness present in so many of the oral autobiographies of older women workers.

The theme appears both as a self-image and as a tradition received from previous generations. A typical form it takes is that of stories about women who run away after marriage and go back to their mothers, sometimes for a short period, perhaps as a means for negotiating better conditions with their husbands. Two women, Albina Caviglione Lusso (born in 1903) and Lina Villata (1896), who both were factory workers for long periods of their lives, enjoy recalling stories of women in the family who tried to run away before the marriage:

> Albina: My aunt, my mum's sister, was born in 1873.
> Lina: Bloody. . . .
> Albina: So it's a hundred years or so ago, she married this fellow because my grandmother made her marry him. She ran away from home the evening before the marriage, and went to my aunt's, to an aunt who was already a great-aunt. "I'm not going, I'm not going home. I won't marry him, I won't marry him, I won't marry him." And so my grandad went again to the house in the evening and said: "You have to marry him."
> Lina: You marry him then!
> Albina: "You have to marry him." And she married him, she married him. . . .
> Lina: But she got to the point of marrying him?
> Albina: Yes, she got to the point of marrying him . . . and then direst misery, direst misery. Look, I've seen misery because I've always lived as a worker, I've lived in factories where . . . but the misery there was in that house I've never seen the like of.

The women follow up this story with an older and formal version of a similar lesson, the song "Bel uselin del bosc" (Nice little bird of the wood):

> Albina: It's a song sung by my grandma, at the time it was a love song (she refers to the fact that during the Fascist dictatorship it came to be sung with political connotations), wait, I'll sing it for you, all right:
>
>> Dov'a saralo vola, dov'a saralo vola? Hohoho!
>> Sla fnestra dla mia bela.
>> Dov'a sara vola? Sla vnestra dla mia bela.

Cosa a l'avralo porta? Coas a l'avralo porta? Hahaha!
Na letra sigilela.
Cosa a l'avralo porta? Na letra sigilela.
Cosa a-j saralo descrit, cosa a-j saralo descrit? Hehehe!
La bella si marita.
Coas a-j saralo descrit? La bella si marita.
Son maridame ier, son maridame ier. Hehehe!
Ancheuj son gia pentija.
Son maridame ier, ancheuj son gia pentija.
Fuissa da maride, fuissa da maride. Hehehe!
Mai pi 'm marideria.
Fuissa da maride mai pi 'm marideria.
Viva la liberta viva la liberta! Ha ha ha!
E chi la sa tenila.
Viva la liberta e chi la sa tenila!

Where will it have flown?
To my beauty's window.
What will it have carried?
A sealed letter.
What will have been written therein?
The beauty is getting wed.
I was wedded yesterday, today I have already repented.
Were I to wed, never more would I wed be.
Long live liberty, long live liberty
and who knows how to keep it.

According to Costantino Nigra, the great folklorist, the song was sung throughout northern Italy: a version was recorded by him in 1855, but the song is certainly older.[3] Its transmission is therefore the example of the passing from generation to generation of a formal tradition that changes its uses and meanings according to the social and cultural conditions.

If, on the one hand, autobiographical material and family traditions are selected out of the necessity to legitimize new forms of behavior, on the other hand, they echo older, conventionalized stories. The narrative tradition is thus grafted onto the present and illuminated by the new forms of behavior with which, however, it is not to be confused, even though it changes meaning and function in accordance with them.

The oral testimonies also bring into the open already existing areas of particularly feminine social life involving the passing of experiences and stories, from mother to daughter, grandmother to grandchild, and between neighbors, friends, and relations. In this context the areas of discourse are distinctive in nature and value—they constitute family stories, conventionalized traditions of long standing, personal narratives. These three levels, and perhaps other ones, interplay with each other. Areas of women's discourse are discernible and seem endowed with cultural and symbolic autonomy. The resulting fields of discourse have different relationships with forms of social reality: for example, gossip can generally influence behavior more directly than a personal mythology or song, which are less "functional" and possess greater autonomy and symbolic meaning.

All this draws attention to the impossibility of making direct use of oral memories as immediately revealing facts and events. Rather, they reveal a tension between forms of behavior and mental representations expressed through particular narrative guises. Interpretation should aim at identifying the patterns in the contradictions between the content of the stereotypes, on one hand, and the information which emerges through in-depth interviews and participant observation, on the other.

WORK

It is striking to notice that the oral autobiographies of men, in the group of interviews that form the basis of the project, insist in many ways on the idea of the good and capable worker, using it as a privileged self-representation. The same idea appears repeatedly in women's life stories, but in a more complicated and contradictory form.

Women's narratives often begin with an emphasis on the importance of work, which is not always indicative of the identity that will be dominant in the overall autobiography. Maria Coletto (born 1913) begins by saying: "Oh my life! Work, work, and more work!" Ludovica (1907): "I began working when I was ten and a half in a woollen mill." But these are only the starting points for more articulate representations of self as joker, rebel, or impulsive character. Maria Coletto, for instance, proceeds in her narration recalling her experience as a worker in a chocolate factory:

> The first week I was there . . . I saw all that lovely chocolate. . . . They put a forewoman over us to supervise. And when we saw the forewoman we were on our best behavior, and when she went away we did everything under the sun. And then one day, as a result of eating hazelnut chocolates, I got indigestion. You know I spewed up—if you don't mind my saying—whole nuts like this? If I wasn't at death's door that time, well, I'll never laugh again! My sister went white as a sheet, a bundle of nerves! Because the owner, the late signora Rina: "But how come—she said—she's been sick? You can see she's eaten too much chocolate."

In other instances, work is not thought worth mentioning unless as a means of emancipation. Thus, Carolina Griffanti (whom we have already met) asked about how hard work at Fiat was, replied "Not hard! because we say: 'We were born to work! We were born to work!'" Work was taken for granted. Carolina mentions her job at the factory only in passing, recalling her wish to continue working after having a child.

Female identity often seems based on work only thanks to an instrumental approach to it. Luigia Varusco (1890) follows a precise narrative line in recounting the story of her life: "Let's follow a thread," she declares, and the thread is her move from one job to another (contrast this to Carolina's method of narrating by associations, leaps, and repetitions). Luigia insists that factory work meant for her an improvement with respect to house-work and domestic service (although she is perfectly aware of the exploita-tion involved in waged work); but she values factory work as a means for independence, not for its contents as basis for self-esteem.

This is not to say that women did not devote themselves utterly to their jobs when they had the opportunity. Albina Caviglione tells how she stayed behind many evenings in the factory to work alone at learning the more skilled jobs of upholstery. Lina Villata expresses pride in the quality and quantity of her work at the Manifattura Tabacchi: "I learnt to do five jobs at the tobacco factory and I never refused any job they gave me to do, never. I left as a highly skilled worker. Anyway, I did 36 years and 6 months of service, a bit more than just a day, you know." But such capacity for work does not seem to constitute in social terms a primary narrative identity; what is true in actual life does not necessarily have a direct correspondence on the symbolic level. There are—this is the hypothesis—male stereotypes that women's narrations can eventually use, but more seldom, with a sense of transgression, of challenge. In the words of Luigia Varusco, who is aware of the presence in her life story of masculine stereotypes: "I should've been born a man."

The most obvious thing to note would be that women's work is charac-teristically less skilled and given less recognition, or lacks security, making it less suitable as a basis for an identity. But this observation is in a certain sense saying too much and too little, because identity and self-presentation could be connected to work even in these circumstances, as it happens in men's oral autobiographies. Furthermore, even highly skilled women who sometimes express pride in their skill do not present themselves as dis-tinctive because of this.

The effects of self-presentations of social values linked to certain forms of work rather than to others should be called to mind. This becomes evident through comparison with ongoing research using oral sources from middle-class women born between 1890 and 1915, and who in the first thirty to forty years of the century chose to work as clerks or teachers. For them, work seemed to offer not only material independence but also the primary basis for a psychological and social identity, and sometimes even a justification for not marrying. Such attitudes are affected by contem-porary choices: women who have established their identity through work, even at great cost to their options in life, are encouraged to present this choice in the light of many young women's current tendency to see work, of whatever kind, as an indispensable stage in their emancipation.

These tentative observations find some support in other researches. Catherine Rhein, in her work on French unskilled women, has found that work is a central theme in almost all their oral autobiographies, but is referred to in terms of "absolute necessity and constraint," "duty assumed to last a life-time." On the other hand, in their collection of testimonies of working-class and lower-middle-class women, Jean McCrindle and Sheila Rowbotham have noted that "work has taken on greater meaning" for the younger women and those in receipt of further education; for them "work has been an important aspect of their identities as independent people."[4]

Certainly we need more research and reflection on such themes. A first general observation can be that if the history of the idea of work is extended to include women, the usual scheme of a steady decline from pride of skill to refusal of work does not stand up. In contrast, waged work over the past fifty years has become an ever greater component of women's cultural and social identity. It is true that this has not been due to its intrinsic contents, with the result of establishing split identities. The consequent lacerations of historical forms of female identities are indicative of the contradictions unleashed by the processes of liberation and self-affirmation, whether material or cultural. It may well be, at the same time, that there exists today, in a number of cases and situations, still another tendency: how many women of the younger generations, that are today, let us say, between forty and fifty or between twenty and thirty, would base their self-image on work, and in which way, with which undertones (apology, pride), and which contradictions?

FINAL OBSERVATION

We have analyzed a group of seventy oral autobiographies, collected with the method of eliciting narratives that are as "spontaneous" as possible in a constructed situation like the interview. Major differences in the narration of women and men (present in equal number in the group) have appeared especially in the presentation of self-images. Women and men choose different narrative resources—by and large, not in an absolutely determined way—and combine them in different strategies of recounting their lives.

A primary assumption is that the symbolic and the factual levels do not coincide, that the narrating subjects are perfectly aware of this difference. The distance and sometimes contradiction between one's own image and one's own life in terms of events can be a powerful utopian force. The dialectic between myths and experiences is fruitful and alternatively stirs up or is fed by the energy of emotions and affections. All this leads up to a recognition of the stratification of oral narration—all, but particularly the autobiographical one—which is not static and given once and for all, but moves and changes according to the strength of feelings as they are influenced and formed by ongoing processes.

Gender is not a mere variable in the complex architecture of narration about oneself. Far from being a causal determinant, it acts as a pole of reference along a continuum, where male and female stereotypes can be chosen and combined. The choice is influenced by personal experience and imagination, collective pressures, social conventions and values, past and present interests and desires. Women's areas of discourse, with different meanings and functions, can be discerned within the general social sphere of speech.

Interpretation should be able to recognize the various levels of expression and eventually find through other sources, as well, the historical contexts wherein they make sense. The guiding principle could be that all autobiographical memory is true; it is up to the interpreter to discover in which sense, where, for which purpose.

It is evident that different disciplines are necessary in order to allow such interpretation to take place; even in the brief notes that this paper has presented, we have relied on the suggestions of history, literary analysis, folklore, and women's studies. Further light could be shed on the subject if more systematic comparisons between researches of the same kind, but on different areas and times, could be planned for the future.

Notes

1. A larger version of this paper appears in a book published by Cambridge University Press (1987) under the title *Fascism in Popular Memory*. Most of the present version is based on a translation from the Italian done by Bob Lumley.

2. M. Douglas, *Natural Symbols* (Harmondsworth: Penguin, 1973), A. Jacobson Schutte, "Trionfo delle donne: tematiche di rovesciamento dei ruoli nella Firenze rinascimentale," *Quaderni storici* 44 (1980); O. Niccoli, "Lotta per le breche, La donna 'indisciplinata' nelle stampe popolari di ancien regime," *Memoria* 2 (1981); M. Perrot, "La popolana ribelle," *Nuova Donna-Woman-Femme* 15 (1981); N. Zemon Davis, "Women on Top," in *Society and Culture in Early Modern France* (London: Duckworth, 1975).

3. C. Nigra, *Canti popolari del Piemonte* (Torino: Loescher, 1888).

4. J. McCrindle and S. Rowbotham, eds., *Dutiful Daughters* (Harmondsworth: Penguin, 1979); C. Rhein, *La vie dure qu'on a eue* (Paris: C.O.R.D.E.S., 1980).

PART FOUR

Narrator and Interpreter

WHOSE VOICE?

Personal Narratives Group

Working with personal narratives raises questions about authorship: Whose story is to be told? Whose voice is to be heard? This section addresses the complex issues of power and authority involved in the production and ultimate use of personal narrative texts.

None of the authors represented here is comfortable with the traditional scholar's assumption of the voice of authority in the creation or interpretation of life stories. They ask us instead to consider the implications of a shared ownership and control over various kinds of personal narrative texts. In the essays presented in this section, there is an emphasis on the collaboration between the two parties involved in most studies concerned with personal narratives—the original "narrator" who tells her life and the "interpreter" who records or analyzes various dimensions of the relationship between narrator and interpreter.

Our choice of this terminology was deliberate. Other common pairings, such as "researcher-subject," replicate the very inequalities that the authors question here. The terms *life historian* and *producer,* which Marjorie Mbilinyi employs in her contribution to this section, work well for life histories but are less meaningful when applied to other forms of personal narrative such as autobiography or journal. As Julia Swindells pointed out in her essay in part two, similar political dilemmas can arise in the appropriation (or misappropriation) of extant narratives as well, although all of the essays in this section do in fact discuss life histories.

Scholars working with personal narratives have sometimes assumed an objective stance in their work, claiming that it was possible and desirable to be impartial observers and recorders of their subjects' lives. Feminist scholarship points to the distortions that result from such a stance, and insists that the perspective of the researcher—in terms of gender, class, culture, disciplinary orientation—be taken into account and acknowledged. In this spirit, each of the essays here recognizes and assesses the impact on her work of the author's own perspective and of the quality of her relationship with the narrator.

Each of the contributors to this section recognizes that the interpreter is an active participant involved in distinctive ways with the shaping of a personal narrative. Marjorie Shostak, for example, states that her work was influenced by the fact that she was twenty-four, newly married, and seeking an answer to the question of what it meant to be a woman. In her essay,

"What the Wind Won't Take Away: The Genesis of *Nisa—The Life and Words of a !Kung Woman*," she notes that Nisa's narrative "reflected a finite contract between fifty-year old Nisa and twenty-four-year-old Shostak; any other combination, no doubt, would have produced a different result." In "The Double Frame of Life History in the Work of Barbara Myerhoff," Riv-Ellen Prell explores Myerhoff's interest in studying such diverse groups as the Huichol Indians of Mexico and a community of elderly immigrant Jews in California. Prell discusses Myerhoff's participation in Huichol ritual, and the way Myerhoff describes both the ritual and her own involvement with it, thereby undermining "the authority of the invisible recorder so often asserted by anthropologists." Marjorie Mbilinyi stresses her active role in interviews with Rebeka Kalindile, and refers to several sessions as "intense debates." She speaks of the need to relay not an exemplary life but rather all the contradictions which came out in the interview.

When the interpreter's involvement in the process of creating a personal narrative is explicitly acknowledged, the nature of the relationship between the interpreter and the narrator affects the text that they create. This relationship reflects the individuality of both narrator and interpreter, and differs from situation to situation. Myerhoff, for example, worked with two key individuals, Ramon, a Huichol Indian, and Shmuel, a Jewish immigrant. She recounted that Ramon was a patient teacher, whereas Shmuel was impatient with her lack of knowledge of her own heritage. Myerhoff allows us to hear his chiding voice throughout her text. Mbilinyi noted that Kalindile was a full partner in their exchanges: "Kalindile never allowed her own narrative to become subordinated to my own agenda of questions."

Both interpreters and narrators approach the process of creating a personal narrative with their own agendas. These, too, affect the shape and focus of the text. The authors here stress the need to be sensitive to one's own motives, as well as to the purposes the narrators bring to the exchange. Shostak realized that her wish to know what it meant to be a woman set a certain pattern for the questions she asked Nisa, and therefore shaped the story which Nisa told. Mbilinyi makes clear that her interest in Kalindile reflected her broader motive "to support oppositional voices which challenge the dominant ideologies of the present" and "to portray women as active makers of history, not passive victims." Being aware of her own purposes allows an interpreter to shape the story without imposing unnecessarily on the text.

Narrators who participate in interviews also have their own motives for doing so. Both Ramon and Shmuel agreed to work with Barbara Myerhoff in the hope that she would help preserve their cultures. While Kalindile wanted to preserve Nyakyusa culture, she was particularly eager to document the oppressions women experienced in the context of family and community. In order to understand the configuration of the story—what it emphasizes, what it omits, what it may exaggerate—the interpreter must be sensitive to the narrator's purposes for telling the story. This sensitivity demands a profound respect for the narrator and what she says. Rather than labeling any story as true or untrue, interpreters need to look for the reasons *why* narrators tell their stories.

When the creation of a personal narrative is perceived as an exchange—a dialogue between a narrator and an interpreter—this dynamic extends to the actual production of the text itself. In the past, few scholars questioned the assumption that the interpreter ultimately had final authority in the formation and publication of a personal narrative. While the interpreter may have thought of herself or himself in some sense as a student during the exchange with the narrator, that role changed dramatically as soon as the actual production of the text began. In this group of essays, however, a sense of collaboration again is evident in terms of the creation of the text itself. Myerhoff wanted to transform the usual subject-object relationship into a subject-subject relationship. The corresponding authority she gives to her narrator results in the presence of two distinct voices in the text. Ramon edited his tapes, playing them over and over until he was satisfied. Mbilinyi also maintained two distinct voices in her work. During the process, she read the entire transcript aloud so that Kalindile could approve of its content and tone. While Mbilinyi had originally planned to retain "the final power of decision-making as producer," when there was disagreement between herself and Kalindile, she ultimately decided that doing so would distort the story. Shostak did assume authority in terms of the format of her text. She decided to put the material in chronological order, and arranged it by theme in order to make the text more accessible to a Western audience. However, she also recognized the importance of explaining to Nisa what she was doing with the text and how the book would be used, and to see that Nisa benefited from the profits.

When the relationship between a narrator and an interpreter becomes a subject-subject relationship, interpreters have tended to want that relationship to be symmetrical. Shostak had hoped to become Nisa's friend, but it was clear that Nisa never saw her fully as that. She was a small part of Nisa's life. In another instance, Ramon's indifference to Myerhoff's family and personal life led her to question the dynamics of that relationship. She concluded that the nature of collaboration "was not mutual in any simple sense."

All of these essays address the actual and appropriate relationship between interpreter and narrator. They each raise questions about issues of power and privilege; all point to the complexity of this relationship. Yet they also suggest that this complexity need not be limiting or paralyzing. What we hear is not a single voice, but a continuing dialogue about possibilities.

"I'D HAVE BEEN A MAN"
Politics and the Labor Process in Producing Personal Narratives

Marjorie Mbilinyi

In this article, I wish to analyze the process of production of a personal narrative which is based on the life of an elderly peasant woman named Rebeka Kalindile, and the political and ethical issues which have arisen in our work.[1] Ours has been an intense working relationship that has led to "true" and creative results. This is partly a result of the method adopted, whereby I continually challenged Kalindile's memories and narratives, and vice versa. The article emphasizes the development of this relationship and its impact on the knowledge jointly produced. I have used tape transcripts of our discussions as well as my Rungwe journal entries of 1985 and 1987 in the text.

The first section briefly describes Rungwe, the area in southwest Tanzania where Kalindile was born in 1914 and where she has spent most of her adulthood. In the second section, I analyze the organizational and institutional context of "Mbilinyi's world." The third section includes a brief summary of Kalindile's life history and an analysis of her objectives for the personal narrative. The changing nature of our relationship and our "crisis of perspective" is presented in the fourth section. In the fifth section I discuss issues of authorship, ownership, and format.

KALINDILE'S WORLD

When Kalindile was born in 1914, the war between the British and the Germans was just coming to an end on Tanzanian soil. The British took over the territory in 1919 and held onto it until 1961, when the nation became independent. Our narrative focuses on the period of British rule. Kalindile's story is more than a story about one peasant woman in colonial Tanganyika, however. Her story reveals the kinds of struggles which occurred during that time over the creation and maintenance of the three colonial labor regimes (migrant labor, casual labor, and peasant labor), with a special focus on the struggles underlying colonial systems of marriage. At the same time, it is a history of the culture of the Wanyakyusa people.

The inhabitants of Rungwe were collectively named the Wanyakyusa by colonial authorities, and actually included several different groups with reportedly separate origins. After their armed resistance against the invading German army failed in the 1890s, the Wanyakyusa adopted a variety of forms of accommodation and resistance in order to combat colonial hegemony and sustain themselves as a people and a culture. A high degree of local cohesiveness has developed, in contrast to those areas of Tanzania which suffered centuries of slavery and international slave trade prior to the European conquest. Their identity as a people and, indeed, a "nation," according to Kalindile, is extremely strong today. It is expressed in the strength of the local national language, Kinyakyusa, and the relative weakness locally of the official national language, Kiswahili. Local pride has often been interpreted by others as arrogance and conceit, including the former colonial authorities who labeled Wanyakyusa a "fractious" and difficult people to rule.[2]

The British set up barriers against African accumulation in farming and business, partly in response to the demands for cheap labor emanating from mining and plantation companies and settler farmers. Denying Africans the possibility to build up a strong economic base as commercial farmers reduced market competition over land, labor, farm inputs, and state support systems while at the same time ensuring a supply of migrant and casual labor. The British also created a color bar in employment, residence, education, and other social services which restricted African women and men to poorly paid, menial forms of work in both waged and unwaged employment.

Forced labor, male taxation, and low prices for African produce were among the many measures adopted to force men either to engage in market-oriented crop production in Rungwe, or to seek waged employment on nearby farms and estates or in the more distant employment centers of Tanganyika, South Africa, or the Rhodesias. By the 1950s, most Rungwe men had worked as miners in South Africa or the Rhodesian Copperbelt. Local employers in Rungwe paid such low wages that most men refused to work for them. They increasingly relied on local women and children for their casual labor requirements. Kalindile and her co-wife were among the many who spent some time of their lives picking coffee and later plucking tea for foreign companies. The two women took turns: while one worked for wages on the coffee estate, the other worked on their household farms, cooked, minded the young children, and did all the other countless tasks which were required of women to keep a peasant household going.

Despite the fact that Rungwe wages were the lowest in the entire colony, Kalindile stressed that they were worth more than today's wages. This is because of the rising costs of living, the worsening terms of trade for agricultural crops on the world market, and the decline in real wages and real producer incomes. She constantly raised the point that "the Tanzanian shilling was worthless." By the 1970s and 1980s, Rungwe women provided a substantial portion of the cash requirements of their households. This is partly the result of the growing cash nexus and the diversification of the local economy after independence. The provision of more social services and better roads and transport systems stimulated market demand for goods and services while increasing the need for money. Women's cash incomes also became more important after the independent government abolished labor migration to the Rhodesias and South Africa. Falling coffee prices further reduced male incomes (most coffee was, and is, controlled by male household heads). Women have acquired alternative sources of income in the off-the-books sector, such as the production and trade of bananas and homebrew beer.[3] They have also successfully struggled to win a share in the proceeds of the tea crops that are grown by many peasant households, including Kalindile's sons. Wives, daughters, and other women refuse to harvest tea for their male household heads and go to work for wages on neighbors' peasant farms until proceeds are shared.

The World Bank-funded smallholder tea scheme in Rungwe has contributed to the proletarianization of peasants and the differentiation of petty commodity producers and traders with sometimes paradoxical outcomes. It led to the opening up of the entire district to permanent all-weather roads, which stimulated the booming banana industry and has led to expanded local market activity in general. Banana is preferred to tea as a cash crop by many men and women, because of the higher rate of return, the lack of successful state regulation, and the fact that it is a traditional food staple. The smallholder tea scheme has also stimulated organized collective action. Tea growers, often led by women, have carried out successful strike actions against the state tea authority since 1983, over such issues as pay deductions, marketing timetables, and authoritarian relations between the management and the peasants.[4]

There is no doubt that Kalindile's "memory" of the past has been affected by her critical conceptions of the present. Both she and her daughter, Tusajigwe Sambulika, are highly critical of present reality and, as a result, tend to portray the past as a better time economically. This illustrates the dynamic nature of life-history making and what it can teach us about the present as well as the past. The fact that memories of the past may not always be "factual" does not represent a problem of validity or reliability, because of the nature of the research methodology which I have adopted. Based on the study of participatory research and popular memory,[5] I have used the personal narrative process to critically examine Kalindile's ideological understanding of life history and to engage her in this critique. The ways in which she transformed her memories of the past are in themselves significant.

Kalindile dwelled a great deal on the "politics of marriage" or "marriage politics."[6] Hers was the last generation of Rungwe women who were married off as young girls, "carried on my mother's back to my in-laws" at the age of four or five years. Whereas Rungwe women had previously enjoyed a relatively high degree of freedom in choice of marriage and sexual partners after their first marriage, by the 1920s and 1930s, the colonial government had begun to implement specific measures to restrict women's freedom of sexuality and of physical residence and movement. The powers of colonial chiefs over women were strengthened via "native" courts in marriage, adultery, and divorce cases, whereas criminal cases—including wife murders—were handled by the district and provincial commissioners' courts. Women therefore found themselves in the contradictory position of being "protected" from battering and murder by white district officers, and having fundamental freedoms restricted by local colonial chiefs and male elders. This contradiction was reflected in Kalindile's ambivalent feelings about national independence and the demands made by local nationalist leaders that African men should resume the power they once had at the local level and chase the white men away.

MBILINYI'S WORLD

I wish to present here some of the more significant organizations and institutions which have affected this work. The University of Dar es Salaam, where I have been working since 1968, has been a major center of progressive thought in Africa. I have been privileged to participate in its debates on socialism, education reform at all levels, development, the agrarian question, the state, the relationship between class, nation, and gender, and methodology in historical materialism. One of the predominant issues which challenged Tanzanian and other intellectuals at the university was their role in revolutionary change and the relationship between theory and practice.

The mood of the *Arusha Declaration* era from 1967 to the early 1970s also encouraged intellectuals who worked in other institutions to critique their institutions and themselves. One result was the development of two formal programs based on participatory research under the separate umbrellas of the Christian Council of Tanzania (Rural Vocational Education Programme) and the Ministry of Youth and Culture (Jipemoyo Project). A loose network of people engaged in participatory research evolved into the Tanzanian Participatory Research Network and the African Participatory Research Network (APRN).

A major influence on the development of participatory research in the mid-1970s[7] was derived from experiences in Central and South America. Intellectuals in Tanzania were challenged to identify with the interests and struggles of oppressed laboring classes in Tanzania, and to promote a new kind of research which sought to break the division of mental and manual labor. It critiqued the 1960s developments in grounded research and phenomenology by asserting that theory and politics were crucial aspects of the research program. The middle-class researcher had a responsibility to share his or her knowledge with the knowledge of the oppressed in the process of production of new knowledge. Democratic relations were sought between intellectuals and other participants, and the knowledge produced was to be returned to the participants and the wider class community. This meant an ongoing process of sharing information as well as the reproduction of written and visual products in accessible form and accessible Kiswahili and other local languages. This production process was not supposed to be detached from action to "change the world"; the researcher was a full participant in political action. Or almost—one of the major criticisms of participatory research in Tanzania was that it tended to take place outside of grassroots and other political organizations. This meant that the insider/outsider problem remained among Tanzanians as well as foreigners, since both could participate today in local developments and leave tomorrow for the university and other places of work.[8]

I became involved in the mid-1970s in the Christian Council's vocational education program based on local grassroots research and education groups, and later in the Jipemoyo Project. These two programs, which were situated outside of the university, provided me with vital reference points for accountability as well as learning.

Toward the end of the 1970s, I and three other women created an informal women's study group outside of the university. The group rapidly expanded and institutionalized itself through formal arrangements with the university. It eventually became the Women's Research and Documentation Project (WRDP) in 1982. Most of the members are Tanzanians, many work outside of the university, and its activities center around research, communications, and documentation. Among its achievements are radio programs on women's issues in Kiswahili and English, and the production of an occasional Kiswahili newsletter and of working papers and other documents in Kiswahili and English. WRDP partly responds to the needs felt by Tanzanian women for a supportive context in which to carry out women's studies. The university lacks a formal women's studies program, and study groups such as ours have provided an alternative.

My local history project in Rungwe is a part of a history program that WRDP initiated in 1984. WRDP held a series of methodology workshops[9] in Dar es Salaam and organized three workshops at the Nairobi 1985 Forum, one of which was entitled "Women's History." In WRDP we have also held our own debates on participatory research, and concretized them in the process of carrying out research in rural areas.

I began to work in Mbeya Region in 1981, when I was invited by regional officials to carry out a consultancy on "women and development" in the context of its five-year development plan. I discovered the incredible amount of past research about Rungwe District at this time. The most fruitful part of the work was the women's speaking-bitterness sessions at public village meetings which my colleague, Mary Kabelele,[10] and I were able to organize in ten different villages. Regional, district, divisional, and village authorities found themselves faced with up to one hundred or more angry and vocal women speaking directly about their experiences of exploitation and oppression.

In 1983 I returned to Isange Ujamma Village in Rungwe, to carry out research on women's participation in village economic and commercial activities.[11] The struggles at the local and national level which centered on Isange and the interpretation of its experiences have taught me to avoid the simplistic peasant-state model of understanding reality. The latter's reduction of all politics and economics to peasant-state relations has become so acceptable now that even the World Bank has adopted it. I wanted to study the capital accumulation process, capital-labor relations, and the operations of international capital in "the concrete." This experience fostered my later analysis of the development of transnational agribusiness in Tanzania and the development of migrant and casual labor and peasant labor regimes.[12]

In 1984, I decided to carry out a local history project in Rungwe, in order to find out more about women's responses to colonial rule and the migrant labor system. I lived for two months in Katusyo Village, Pakati Division, in 1985, and returned for another ten days in early 1987. I was introduced to the village, and more especially to the life historian Rebeka Kalindile, by one of its educated "children," Mwaiseje Polisya. He was a former graduate student who carried out his master's thesis under my supervision[13] and sympathized with my aims. He encouraged his stepmother, Rebeka Kalindile, and me to work together and has provided valuable critical feedback at each stage of the research. He and his wife, Florence, have also provided me with a home base in Mbeya, the regional headquarters where they both are teachers.

The entire Mwaiseje extended family has sustained the project from its beginning. The family is built around the three cowives of the now-deceased head, the father of Mwaiseje Polisya. Rebeka Kalindile, the life historian and coauthor of the personal narrative, is the senior wife of the homestead. Her daughter, Tusajigwe Sambulika, was born in 1932 and currently lives with her mother in Katusyo Village with her youngest daughter and a grown brother, Browni. Sambulika participated in the narratives from the first taping session, providing impromptu explanation, elaboration, and translation. Shelter and most meals have been provided to me by the family of the second cowife's son, Cornel Mwaiseje, within the same homestead.

The Moravian African Church of Rungwe has provided another framework. In Rungwe they say, "If you want to know the women, go to the church." Women have used the church to organize themselves from colonial times, in women's groups, in prayer meetings, in income-earning activities, and in many other ways. The Moravian Church's structure extends from village catechists and village churches to higher-level assemblies, and a parallel structure exists for women's groups. The support of the local Katusyo church as well as that of the Bishop of Rungwe and other officials greatly facilitated the research.

Here I wish to summarize my main ideological and theoretical objectives for the overall history project, which includes archival and oral histories as well as Kalindile's life history. One of the main ideological objectives has been to support oppositional voices which challenge dominant ideologies that support the intensification of global state intervention in Africa today. A related objective has been to increase the awareness of gains made in the past which were due to past struggles and which are now in danger of being lost in the context of structural adjustment. This includes the recognition of women's contributions to the shaping of colonial and postcolonial society. I wish to portray women as active makers of history, not passive victims, but also to increase our awareness of the way that women's actions and consciousness were limited by objective conditions beyond their control.

The main theoretical objective has been to analyze the way in which class relations are embedded in relations of nation, race, and gender, as a result of class struggles which have a specific form and content in specific circumstances. One of my approaches to this pursuit has been to examine specific moments of women's struggles and resistances and/or accommodations to oppressive relations, and to query what and how they resisted/accommodated (or both), and how they perceived their own actions and the responses of others (including the state). I have also tried to broaden the focus of attention in studies of migrant and casual labor systems so as to include the labor reserve (i.e., the site of reproduction in the peasant household and family and the community at large) as well as the "workplace" (e.g., the site of production on the plantation or mine). This has political implications, given the numerous examples of local oppositional actions which have been situated within the class community and not a separate "workplace."

The overall project has involved a mixture of methods which have enriched each other: archival research in Tanzania and England, oral histories and interviews, and the production of the personal narrative based on the life history of Rebeka Kalindile. Three end products are planned: a slide show, a personal narrative in Kiswahili and English, and a longer book which analyzes the situation and struggles of women in colonial Rungwe and the responses of the colonial state.

REBEKA KALINDILE: HER LIFE AND AIMS

Rebeka Kalindile was born in Masoko, Rungwe, in 1914, and is a member of the Mpata clan. Kalindile is named for her father's mother, Kalindile,

Rebeka Kalindile with her two younger sisters, Elizabeth and Maria.
Photograph by Marjorie Mbilinyi.

according to Nyakyusa custom. Her father was not a Christian; he had four wives and many cattle. She was married with her first cowife at a very young age, as noted already. A catechist or church educator of the Christian religion taught her to read when she was a young girl, and her husband taught her to write at her own urging in 1951 after her daughter Tusajigwe had married. Kalindile taught herself to read in Kiswahili when she went to stay in Tanga with her first son's family at the end of the 1960s.

Her husband, Mwaiseje, was an extremely clever and authoritative man, who taught his children to be self-reliant in artisanship and not to "enslave" themselves in farming. He would not allow his wives or children to work more than three hours daily on the farm, on the grounds that there were better ways of using time. He married a third wife, who was the same age as his older children, and he died in 1970. The two older cowives now live in the homestead with some of their grown children and grandchildren, while the third cowife moved to Mbeya Town and lives near her eldest son, Mwaiseje Polisya. Kalindile lives an austere life now, and would be poorer if it weren't for remittances from grown children and the assistance of those living with her or nearby.

Kalindile rarely talked directly about her deceased husband and their personal relationship. She chose to dwell instead on the oppressive nature of Wanyakyusa men and polygamous marriage *in general*: wives were "donkeys" or "slaves." Wanyakyusa men sought to rule women, and like women in other areas of Tanzania, Rebeka referred to this as "male colonisation."[14] Kalindile's seeming reticence about directly personal matters is not unusual in Tanzania, where people in principle do not indulge in private confidences for public audiences. Alternative modes of communication are adopted which require sensitivity and subtlety on the part of both speaker and listener, author and reader.

Kalindile became a leader and adult educator in the local Moravian church. She joined others in creating short skits which dramatized "good" and "bad" women. She acted the roles of the "bad" husband (to the good wife) and the "bad" wife (to the good husband). She traveled to other villages in order to promote women's groups' activities, and was locally renowned for her preaching ability among women. Kalindile was and is also an expert storyteller, a cultivator, a traditional midwife and healer of some forms of illness, and a local historian. She is what Karen Sacks (in this collection) calls a centerwoman, one of those who are relied upon by others to get things going. Whereas she formerly played this role in the church, she has shifted her energies in old age to family networks.

When Polisya first recommended that I work with Kalindile, he explained that she was a spirited and articulate woman who had traveled a lot and spoke fluent Kiswahili. Her knowledge of the colonial days and of women's issues was extensive, and she was very critical about women's oppressed position in society. In 1987, I asked him to explain again why he encouraged us to work together. In addition to the above points, he said that she knew how to read and write, and because of her travels and general enlightenmnent, she could relate to strangers with confidence. He had foreseen that her critical perspective and cultural background would facilitate our understanding of each other and of the project. He pointed out that everything was significant to Kalindile; she was intense about everything: "If she was educated these days, she would have been very daring and courageous."

What were Kalindile's perceptions of the work and my choice of her as the life historian? When we began, I explained that I had come to learn about the past, and especially about the history of women in the colonial days. I said that most of the history writing in Tanzania had ignored women, and that it was time to learn from our female elders. I did not formally state at the beginning that I wanted to produce her life history. My intention all along had been to use the life historian's personal story of her life and perceptions of colonial society as the frame through which we could better understand the personal and the social. As our relationship developed, our work was defined more clearly as the production of a narrative about women in Rungwe which would be based on her stories of colonial Rungwe and of her life.

She was enthusiastic from the beginning, and never had the "Who, me? You want me to tell you my life history? Me?" kind of reaction which I had expected (indeed, very few people in Rungwe responded this way). She understood the significance of her knowledge of the past as well as her central role in the local history of church women and was perfectly aware of her personal skill as a storyteller. My choice seemed to be taken for granted by her and other members of the village. We were both more introspective and communicative about our interpretations of the work and our relationship in 1987. Kalindile seemed surprised that there was more work to do when I returned in 1987, even though I had said in 1985 that I would try to return for joint revision of our work. She exclaimed several times to me and to others during our first meeting, "Everything that I said is true." She agreed to revise the tape transcripts with me after I told her that our book would come back to the community in Kiswahili. I showed her a model for our future book *Miradi ya Wakina Mama Matetereka* (Women's Projects in Matetereka),[15] which is written in Kiswahili with large photos of village women engaged in work and other activities which concretized the point: "There may be some things you said that you don't want others to know about."

Kalindile devoted as much time as she could to our work for the next four days, in spite of the tragic circumstances in which I found her in 1987. Her elder sister was fatally ill, and both she and her daughter Sambulika had moved several miles to the sister's homestead to take care of her. The family of the ill sister and the dying woman herself accepted our work, and created temporal and physical space for us to proceed. All of us were aware of the pressure of time. Throughout this period until the sister's death on the fifth day, I followed Kalindile's direction, and she kept us going: on the fourth morning, for example, she changed her mind about postponing our work till afternoon and said, "Why don't we continue our work?" while we were all shelling beans out front. That afternoon we worked in between several family visitors: Kalindile said, "Let's use every little opportunity."

We taped most of our discussions in 1985 and 1987; Kalindile insisted on regular checks to make sure that the batteries were working (a real problem in tropical weather). I was startled to discover while transcribing our tapes how many times she had asked me whether I understood what she was talking about. She would patiently illustrate the meaning of her words with dramatic gestures. Or she would tell Sambulika to teach me what I failed to learn. Sometimes Sambulika independently understood that a given presentation was beyond my powers of understanding, and would say, "I'll tell you later what she means."

During revision, we went through the transcript together, word for word, with me reading it slowly aloud until a question was raised by any of us (113 pages of script). We ended up discussing each episode together, and in every case, Kalindile wanted to add further elaborations. She also corrected possibly offensive language, such as her original description of the Katumba villagers with whom she organized a women's group. Kalindile stopped me toward the end of that script: "This book is coming to Katumba, isn't it? To the children of those people. Their children would be extremely angry with me for saying that." The three of us found a substitute phrase with the same but less disparaging meaning.

On the fourth day of revision, Kalindile asked me if I was revising all the other people's scripts that I had made in 1985. I explained that I wasn't, because she was the only one with whom I would be coauthoring a book; I hadn't spent so much time with anyone else; and the other stories would be combined together in a different book. Her question left me uneasy, however. Why don't survey researchers return to every interviewee to make sure that they have properly recorded and interpreted their remarks? I know that I lack the time and means to do so, but then, I hadn't considered such a possibility before.

The elder sister died on the morning of the fifth day, and we were all flung into an intensive mourning and funeral process for several days. On the ninth day, however, Kalindile returned to sleep at home for one night after having a tooth pulled. We spent hours together visiting, and in the middle of that day we revised the final part of the script. Afterward she told me, "I'm happy now. I was sorry that you had come at such a bad time." When I replied that I was glad that the work was finished, she said, with a mischievous twinkle in her eye, "This tooth brought me here to finish the work. If we had done it at the mourning, they'd have said, 'Stupid. She drops her mourning to do something so stupid!!'"

Then Kalindile seemed to be answering an implicit question, "Why me?" She remarked, "I didn't used to sleep. I used to lie awake, thinking about my life. . . . Because I know that some women don't know as much. . . . [Polisya] always praised me for my brains."

I have presented my own objectives for the personal narrative. What were Kalindile's? I gradually realized that she perceived the narrative as both a testimonial about the oppressions experienced by women in the context of family and community, and a way of preserving Nyakyusa tradition and culture and handing it down to others.[16] The overwhelming theme to which she returned time and again was that of gender relations in marriage and family, including the present as well as the past. There were three major subthemes: her personal struggles against "male colonization" or "female slavery"; self-improvement of local women individually and collectively; and the theme of being a woman, a midwife, a daughter, and a wife in Nyakyusa society. These themes and the gender relations she was presenting were all embedded, however, in a class and national context. Her stories were often about traditional customs and arts that had died out by the 1950s, like some of the artistic work she did in conjunction with the Katumba group which had amazed the young men back then: "They'd never seen such things before." She explained her approach to women's activities to the Katumba women in this way: "We poor Nyakyusa women should do what we do best, and not imitate the richer [Nyakyusa] women with their embroidered cloth and dresses—we are Wanyakyusa, we are not whites."

She and Sambulika were constantly instructing me in old skills and arts and customs, like eating ugali with a traditional forklike object that reportedly predated the white conquest: "This is how we Wanyakyusa do." The book and I became a vehicle for Kalindile to pass on the culture of her people to younger members of Wanyakyusa society and to the rest of Tanzania (and the world).

The third objective was to protest against current conditions. She and others talked constantly about the decline in their standards of living and the inability to provide adequately for their needs because of low prices for crops and high prices for the items they wanted to purchase. The returns for their work were unbearably low. In our lively debate on "independence," she also challenged me to prove that the conditions of women had improved after the end of colonial rule. As far as she was concerned, men still ruled at all levels.

Kalindile was not interested, however, in discussing the drudgery of women's work on the family farm and the tea estate, or the sexual division of labor. She never spoke about the specific white women and men that she had known in the mission, the tea estate management, or the colonial administration. Nor did she simply bemoan male rule. Kalindile stressed the daily struggles of survival and self-improvement and the positive achievements of her life. I think this resembles Mamie Garvin Fields's approach when she wrote her narrative with her granddaughter, Karen Fields:[17]

> My grandmother dealt in actual people and places, in the choices that she or her neighbor confronted, in what a man or woman did given a particular circumstance. . . . She was not trying to convey "how black people fared in Charleston over the first half of this century," but "how we led our lives, how we led *good* lives."

Most of her narrative is a positive representation of herself and her people—not in opposition to whites, company managers, or colonial administrators, but in the context of a coherent, Nyakyusa society. This also parallels Zora Neale Hurston's work:

> I am not tragically colored. There is no great sorrow dammed up in my soul, nor lurking behind my eyes. I do not mind at all. I do not belong to the sobbing school of Negrohood who hold that nature somehow has given them a lowdown dirty deal and whose feelings are all hurt about it. . . . No, I do not weep at the world—I am too busy sharpening my oyster knife.[18]

However, Rebeka Kalindile did wish nature had played her a different hand: "If I could have, I'd have been born a man."

I believe that Kalindile persisted with this work, in spite of the tragic circumstances of our most recent meeting and her earlier ambivalence about our relationship, because of her own objectives. I also realized while writing this article that her objectives for the book corresponded to the aims of her life's work. Kalindile had a mission, which was to teach other women how to safely navigate the troubled waters of "male colonization" without being brutalized or murdered, and to save the traditions and skills of her people from dying.

"THIS CHILD OF MINE—WHY DOESN'T SHE UNDERSTAND? SHE'S GOT NO BRAINS!"

I wish to focus this section on the development of the relationship between Rebeka Kalindile and me in order to deepen our understanding of the character of the labor process in the production of personal narratives. I think the most creative stages of the process are those in which the producer and the life historian directly interact with and confront each other. This is particularly powerful if the producer has engaged in an honest intellectual and ideological dialogue with the life historian. To do this, the producer must have confidence in her own outlook as well as respect for the integrity of the other partner in the dialogue. The dialogue can become an invitation for each to reexamine the life history, as a story, and to produce a clearer, more critical understanding of the past and the present.[19]

Our work began in August 1985; we worked together intermittently until early October 1985. Polisya introduced me the first day to the family members and requested permission for me to live in the homestead and to work with Kalindile. This was granted, and I returned the following day. I think that break allowed space for Kalindile to take stock of the project. Certainly she took my breath away in a literal as well as a figurative sense on that second day. She and her second cowife showed me around the homestead, including the burial place of their husband and the sites of their former homes. While taking me up and down steep mountain slopes, she began the first of her narratives. Her opening line was, "We women were slaves," while pointing out a neighboring homestead to me which had a cluster of huts encircling one in the middle. "He's built himself a city down there, you see?" (a polygamist peasant surrounded by several wives, each with her own home). It was soon apparent to me that Kalindile had her own set of significant issues and themes to match my agenda of questions. I wanted the narrative to follow the themes which she thought were significant, and realized that I would not be able to pursue all of my preliminary questions.

We had a total of seventeen interviews in 1985, most of the longer ones taped, in addition to daily encounters in the homestead. The interviews averaged one hour. The topic was sometimes initiated by one of my questions, but Kalindile usually shaped her narrative according to the themes of greatest interest to her. The timing fit her work and rest cycle, and her state of health. We usually met in the evening and talked until after nightfall by her fireside, while she roasted some maize or plantain, or while Sambulika prepared supper. We had other listeners who sometimes passed by and would occasionally contribute their ideas.

Storytellers are performing artists. Kalindile chose stories to tell and the style of her telling with an audience or audiences in mind. As I've said already, she would stay up all night, thinking about what to say about her life. The stories were neither spontaneous nor innocent responses to a structured interview schedule, nor were they solely the product of an attempt to speak "the truth" about the past. The storyteller entertains and the historian instructs. While listening to Kalindile's stories that "my fathers told me," I recalled Kabira's analysis of the components that make up an artist's skill: "a question of memory, organization, creation and understanding of the audience."

> A good narrator uses his skill to develop and embroider the skeleton of the available plot with subsidiary details. His own vivid descriptions and songs, his actual style of delivery, gestures, mimicry and use of dramatic repetition are also skillfully interwoven. The way he presents his characters, his variation of speed and tone, vocabulary, persuasion of his listeners, vehemence and drama, are all knit into an aesthetic whole.[20]

Kalindile used these skills when telling stories about her "real" life as well. Much will be lost in the written text, not only because of the translation from Kiswahili (sometimes via Kinyakyusa) but also because reading the written page can never be the same experience as watching a live performance with all of its particular nuances and audience participation. Her narrative was interspersed with traditional and Christian songs which she sang in Kinyakyusa and again in Kiswahili. She acted out little skits; one for example, dramatized the agony a wife feels at night when she hears her husband laughing with his other wife and knows that she is not the beloved.

Certain themes emerged from our talks, which have now formed chapters of the manuscript: "Childhood and Stories of the Past Told by My Fathers," "Puberty and Marriage," "My Work as a Midwife," "Leadership in the Moravian Church," and "Adult Educator in Katumba Village." They were narratives told by Kalindile in one or more sessions; I sometimes stimulated their telling, and always probed for more information and elaboration. These narratives often led to or were built around intense debates on the slavery of women, polygamy, equality, national independence, the role of the church in pacifying women, and bridewealth. We had strong disagreements on the last four topics, which were sometimes painful and always intellectually exhausting. At various times one or the other of us was, I believe, frightened by the crisis of perspective aroused by the views of the other.

For example, I was thunderstruck when Kalindile spoke about her opposition to the removal of white colonial administrators and their replacement by Africans, and challenged me to prove that the position of women,

Rebeka Kalindile dramatizing a song used in church.
Photograph by Marjorie Mbilinyi.

and, indeed, any of the poor, had truly improved as a result of national independence. I found it difficult to accept what looked to me like completely contradictory positions about life and society. I was looking for "exemplary lives," as Karen Sacks calls them in this collection, and felt that Kalindile had let me down. I gradually accepted the fact that there was no one outlook, that Kalindile represented a set of contradictions (similar to the lives reported on by M. J. Maynes and Luisa Passerini, for example), and that somehow I was going to have to "present all the contradictions."

With hindsight, I realized, of course, that her position on independence was not inconsistent after all. I was the problem: I had to learn to listen more carefully. She had told me about the brutality of husbands toward wives, in general, and once dramatized a man screaming at his wife, "You're conceited, aren't you? You think that I can't beat you, or kill you, because you'll run to the white man and get me hung!" The protection that colonial rule had offered women was endangered by national independence as she understood it at that time. (Independence *was* defined locally in racial terms, as the substitution of African men for white men.)

On the first morning after my return from the one-week break, I was informed by one of Kalindile's sons that she had spoken about me at the Friday women's church meeting. He began by telling me, "I think I see the impact of your research now. You are trying to get people to think about the place of women and their rights." (I had given Kalindile a mimeographed copy of the Kiswahili version of our book, *Women in Tanzania*.[21] He said that she preached that "I feel like I am being tested, like Jesus. She talks about human equality. God made women and men different. He put women under men. I do not agree that women are the same as men." She also told them that it's "better for me to talk to her—I can handle her—but I get very worried when I think about her visiting many of you other women around here."

While listening to his story, I recalled one of our last intense debates—the one on national independence. I also recalled that we had moved on to talk about religion. I criticized her teaching then by saying that the church taught women to "turn the other cheek" and be subservient to men. According to my Minnesota conference paper, which was written before the 1987 revision work,

> In reflecting back on her years of preaching and teaching women in different villages, the life historian agreed that, yes, she had contributed to their enslavement. "I agree," she said. "We are God's children. Jesus said 500 men, without counting the women. Paul wrote, 'Women should not speak in church.'"

I couldn't have been further from the truth about her supposed compliance with my views, as I found out during our first revision session in February 1987. We had never discussed this episode in 1985—she wouldn't bring it up, and I felt I couldn't tattle on the tattler. We held more sessions together, and I left with deep unease. In 1987, I had requested that we use our first revision to go over questions about items in the transcripts that I hadn't understood, and to raise key issues or differences that had emerged in our 1985 work. Kalindile initiated the issues in a kind of reflex reaction to my query about labor migration of relatives "before independence." She told me that maybe *we* women got independence, but in Rungwe the men still ruled. I responded by asking how she had coped, given her well-known outspokenness ("msemaji sana"). That was all the encouragement that she needed to speak about the way I had angered and worried her all these days. She repeated the gist of her instruction about how to handle a drunk or angry husband: "Agree with him, leave him alone, and after he's relaxed, ask him what he was talking about. Otherwise, if you talk back, you will fight." She always had physical violence on her mind, including murder.

At this point, I said, "I didn't use to know this. We used to quarrel all the time [my husband and I]. He's Mgoni, and I'm a New Yorker. Very dangerous." Rebeka said, "You know, we want you to live together safely. . . . Can you be tough enough [i.e., to 'handle' your husband]? . . . It is better to endure."

Then Kalindile accused me,

> Yes, and you said that I spoiled the young women. You told me off. I'm speaking the truth. . . . I heard you. You said I taught them to be slaves.
> I'm saying, *don't be slaves*. . . .
> What do you do if he beats you? . . . You told me, "Why not take him to court?" Is the court a woman? Will you accuse him to his fellow male?

It will be clear below that Kalindile had never advocated complacent submission to male rule or what is often called "domestication." Hers was a form of accommodation and resistance based on a strategy of retreat and advance, advance and retreat—not open warfare but guerrilla tactics. There is no doubt that Kalindile perceived the Nyakyusa world that she knew as a war. Moreover, she had no illusions about the gender and class characteristics of the court systems. When I queried this, saying, "So you don't mean that you should agree with everything, except as a tactical move?" she replied, "Exactly! You *fool* him." She went on to stress the need for women to be superintelligent in dealing with men: "Nataka ujanja" ("I want slyness/cleverness"). The need for ujanja was emphasized throughout her narrative.

Kalindile was aware of our misunderstanding and my misinterpretation of her work in 1985, and described her analysis of the situation in this way:

> I said at the time, "We don't understand each other." I said, "My goodness, this child has no brains!" I told her, "Speak false words just to please your husband," and she says, "Accuse him in court or to a local party leader." . . .
> Will you accuse him to a woman? All you can do is be clever.
> Have you understood?

It was only while sharing a meal later on of *ugali* (stiff cornmeal porridge eaten with stew) that Kalindile told me how close she came to withdrawing from our project because of my criticism of her work. She did not tell me straight off; and she had to contradict Sambulika's sugar-coating of the situation to do so. I had begun by probing the reasons for her anger or anxiety during some of our 1985 work, especially on the subject of male and female equality. I suggested that perhaps one reason she may have become upset was that we had produced some astonishing ideas together. New ideas could be frightening, especially when they contradicted strong assumptions that had been relied on for years.

Initially, Kalindile rejected outright the idea that she had been angry with me. Then she began to speak in Kinyakyusa and had Sambulika translate everything I said from Kiswahili into Kinyakyusa, which was not our normal practice. It was clear to me that Kalindile considered this to be an extremely important matter about which she wanted no possibility of misunderstanding. She told me that in 1985, she thought that I was angry with her because of the way that she "domesticated" women (according to my interpretation). She told me that there had never been a question of being afraid to speak her mind, then or now. In Sambulika's translation:

> One thing before you talk anymore with your mother, your mother is telling you that she is only telling you the truth. What she opposes, she opposes to you directly, but she doesn't know anything about fear. Because if you are angry with someone without explaining why, you are not able to teach that person.

However, Sambulika was also trying to hide the fact that Kalindile had been angry with my interpretation of her work as "domestication." She kept assuring me that Kalindile had never been angry, and when she finally said, "She [Kalindile] says, 'Do not be worried, we will tell stories without anger,'" Kalindile directly contradicted her. She said in Kiswahili, "Let me tell her the truth. We said, 'Let's stop the talk.'" Then she turned to me and said, "*You* said, 'Mama, you're teaching the children wrong!'"

She didn't withdraw from the project then, but the strain was there. It was resolved only when I returned with the transcript for revision in February 1987 and Kalindile chose to correct me, that is, to engage in countercriticism. I accepted her criticism, and had to reexamine my mechanical notions about "feminist" behavior in the context of the contradictions existing in "Kalindile's world" and mine.

Why had my interpretation of her work made Kalindile so angry? She had correctly perceived that my criticisms of her teaching called into question the purpose of her life as she understood it. One way that she had coped with the pain and humiliation of being a woman, a wife, and a mother in Nyakyusa society was by being an organizer and teacher of women in the church. She perceived that work to be a way of improving women's lives in multiple ways that are described in the narrative. I had come along and dismissed her life's work as the furthering of women's enslavement, whereas she had committed herself to the loosening of those bonds. Moreover, for Kalindile the narrative was a form of autobiography over which she exerted a great deal of control. Luisa Passerini has pointed out the significance of autobiography as a means of giving meaning to the autobiographer's life. Kalindile had been extremely proud of her work with women and gave special emphasis to it in the narrative. My critique in the context of this narrative was an invalidation of her and her life's mission. It must have been doubly infuriating when I assumed that she had agreed with my indictment.

When we saw each other for the first time in February 1987, Kalindile told me, "My child, you have given me a hard time." I asked her, laughing, "What hard time?" She replied, "I think about you all the time."

Now I understand the multiple meanings of her words: happiness in the context of the strong nonkin-kin relationship that we had developed,[22] and downright anger and pain. So far as she knew, I was telling the world stories about her that were not true and that she had not corrected. My return provided her with the opportunity to do so, and she lost no time in doing it.

I have also gradually acknowledged that, yes, I *was* angry with Kalindile in 1985 and had denied it to her and to myself. I was angry not with her work but with her denunciation of me—as I initially interpreted it—in the women's prayer meeting. My first reaction to the "tale" was shocked betrayal, and then anger. Kalindile undoubtedly empathized with that anger as well as with the pain that followed.

She's never volunteered to me the story of her preaching about me in the prayer meeting, and I have never directly asked her—it is simply not appropriate to do so. However, it gradually became clear that she was partly responding to criticisms from others of our work and her participation in it. Our relationship together had been somewhat controversial in the village as well as in the Mwaiseje homestead; there is envy, and Kalindile is herself a controversial figure, as is her daughter, Sambulika. A woman living "alone" without a man, as Sambulika is doing, is not accepted, not even by kin. It is therefore likely that Kalindile has faced intermittent criticisms for engaging in the personal narrative and is probably held responsible for any misconduct on my part. Her apparent denunciation was one way of distancing herself from me while at the same time protecting my right to be there, in the village and in her homestead, and her right to work with me.

Pain and anger seem to be inevitable aspects of open, critical narrative production, which requires appropriate coping mechanisms. One is to structure the labor process from the beginning so that the life historian knows that she will be a full participant in later stages of the production process: in transcribing, editing, and organizing the material. Then she will know that she will have ample opportunity to correct any misunderstandings or misinterpretations of the producer, and to offer a "true" presentation of herself. Another is to create a supportive network locally, a kind of formal or informal local history group which has regular supportive contact with the participants. This would provide support but also accountability.

The 1987 transcription stage of revision reinforced my belief in the correctness of the critical approach adopted and in the need for honesty on both sides.[23] If I had chosen to remain silent in 1985 about my views of Kalindile's work, I'd have represented her narrative later as an example of the "domestication" of women by Christianity. This is the common interpretation in feminist work. It was only because I spoke my mind that

Kalindile was able to correct me in this and other instances. Moreover, Kalindile has also reevaluated her ideas and assumptions as a result. She has taught me that reality and human agents of history are more complex than we often realize, and that we must learn to understand and respect the contradictory ways in which women have coped with oppression.

AUTHORSHIP AND FORMAT

Who is the author of this work? In 1985 it became clear to me that we were jointly responsible for what was produced, and that it would be dishonest not to acknowledge us both. However, the transcripts also underlined the significance of Tusajigwe Sambulika's input in both supporting the work and clarifying points of misunderstanding or ignorance. Early on in the revision stage of the transcripts, I spoke to Kalindile about the possibility of having just us two authors, or having all three, or having us two with acknowledgement of Sambulika's assistance (Rebeka Kalindile and Marjorie Mbilinyi with Tusajigwe Sambulika). She initiated the topic at our last revision session, and said she preferred the last form. She explained that sometimes what Sambulika said was not true, and besides, "she wasn't there."

After my departure from Rungwe, I decided to reexamine other works of a similar nature. A variety of methods have been adopted by producers of narratives who apparently share similar methods of production. All produced the text jointly with the life historian, using taped interviews which were sometimes supplemented with other materials. Other tasks, such as organizing, editing, and revising, were shared differently. Some named only the producer as author,[24] others named themselves as editor and held the copyright.[25] In the case of *Lemon Swamp and Other Places,* the life historian, Mamie Garvin Fields, was named as the author *with* the producer, Karen Fields, and they both shared copyright. A similar pattern was adopted by the authors of *Let Me Speak!*[26]

The producer as editor and/or sole author is probably a derivative of the academic context in which social science is usually carried out. A life history is actually defined by anthropologists as "an *extensive* record of a person's life told to and recorded by another, who then edits and writes the life as though it were autobiography."[27]

All of the first set of producers cited above made note of the intensity of their relationships with the life historians, and the trust which became the basis of their working relationship in the reporting stage, the stage when the life historian spoke about her life. They shared the realization that the life historian often initiated topics, and some also realized that she had her own agenda. For most, however, the relationship was completely altered afterward, in that the life historian no longer had a voice in transcribing, revising, and editing. A contradiction thereby developed between the nature of the work process in the reporting stage and in the later stages. I think this has had two effects. The producer feels morally correct about naming herself as sole author or editor, but it leads to ambiguity about the character of the work relationship and the integrity of the finished work vis-à-vis the purpose and outlook of the life historian. I think that that ambiguity is one source of the unease about producing life histories that several producers reported at the 1986 Minnesota conference.

Another issue to resolve was *format*. How could we present the contradictions which arose between us and our views in the labor process? Or were we to remove our differences from the final text? At the Minnesota conference I argued that if we did have major differences of opinion over parts of the narrative, I would retain the final power of decision making as producer. However, I also expressed my unease with this solution:

> The ethics of the above situation are not obvious to me. The stories are not personal property. They are the collective product of the exchange which occurs in the speaking/recording period. New ideas emerge for both as a result of exchange and debate. That is the very task of popular memory, to challenge the life historian to rethink her life story, to critique and change it. This creates new possibilities of changing reality as well.

Sounds good, but I wasn't entirely convinced. At a public seminar at the University of Copenhagen, I received the suggestion to present all of our views, more or less verbatim. If we were having differences, show them. A model was presented to me, Crapanzano's *Tuhami*.[28] Several different formats were adopted by Crapanzano: the producer speaking in the third person about the life historian, the life historian speaking in the first person, and both speaking in interview sequences. Kalindile and I examined *Tuhami* together in February 1987, and I translated portions of it in order to illustrate these different possibilities. It was agreed that the first-person life-historian voice would be used for most of the narrative. Where Kalindile and I did have substantially different views, however, we would present an edited version of our debates, and include Tusajigwe Sambulika when she was a participant.

Mwaiseje Polisya then suggested the idea of bringing the debates together as a concluding chapter. There would then be no need for a third-person analytical voice to explain the background to the debates. I had expressed my dissatisfaction with inserting this voice into an otherwise coauthored work. The exception would be in the postscript on methodology, which provides background to the production of the narrative. Polisya also noted that the presentation of all of our voices in debate would correct misconceptions that people might have about Kalindile's ability to sustain an intellectual debate with a "university professor." Her strength of conviction, intelligence, purposefulness, and power would be directly visible. The same device could be used to show how Kalindile initiated, sustained, blocked, or corrected different lines of argument.[29]

Our narrative remains an open text which is still subject to further joint revision. It has been argued that autobiography is a closed form, whereas in fiction you can rearrange things. However, I learned from Kalindile that life historians (and probably autobiographers) also rearrange their stories. The rearrangements may reflect the objectives of the narrative and interpretations of their lives, and are a way of protecting oneself against the dangers of self-revelation. My writing of this article could be called, I suppose, an act of "intellectual autobiography," "making visible what is normally, usually, conventionally, hidden to readers: the shifts, changes, developments, downturns, and upturns"[30] in the working relationship of the producer and the life historian. I am subject, therefore, to the dangers of self-revelation, but I believe that this story had to be told.

Notes

I am grateful for comments received from participants at the conference on Autobiographies, Biographies, and Life Histories of Women at the University of Minnesota (1986) and from the reviewers for this collection, and at subsequent presentations at the University of Copenhagen (1986), Women's Research and Documentation Project (1987), Dar es Salaam (1986), and Centro di Documentazione Ricerca e Iniziativa Delle Donne, Bologna (1987). I especially acknowledge the feedback and support received from Rebeka Kalindile, Tusajigwe Sambulika, and Mwaiseje Polisya in our lengthy discussions of the issues raised here, to Susan Geiger and Janet Spector, and to Women's Studies and the Center for Advanced Feminist Studies at the University of Minnesota for having provided me with a congenial place for reflection. I was born in the United States and became a citizen of Tanzania in 1967.

1. I gratefully acknowledge the assistance provided to this research project by SIDA, IDRC, WRDP, IDS (Sussex), Dartington Hall Trust, Fund for Human Need (Methodist Church, London), and Leonard Cohen Fund.

The final editing of this article occurred in December 1987 at IDS (Sussex), following my return from Rungwe, where we revised the manuscript together in August 1987. I have not included additional material based on this work except for an occasional note.

2. More detailed analysis of the struggles referred to here and Rungwe's political economy is found in Marjorie Mbilinyi, "Agribusiness and Casual Labour in Tanzania," *African Economic History* 16 (1986), and "Runaway Wives: Forced Labour and Forced Marriage in Colonial Rungwe," *International Journal of Sociology of Law* 16, no. 1 (1988).

3. For a detailed analysis, see Mwaiseje Polisya, "Banana Trade and Position of Women in Rungwe District" (University of Dar es Salaam, Master's thesis, 1984); see also Marjorie Mbilinyi, *"This Is the Big Slavery": Agribusiness and Women Peasants and Farm Workers in Tanzania* (Dar es Salaam University Press, 1987, in press).

4. Ibid.; for further analysis of Tanzanian peasant women's resistances against

capital and the state, see part 1 of Ophelia Mascarenhas and Marjorie Mbilinyi, *Women in Tanzania: An Analytical Bibliography* (Uppsala: Scandinavian Institute of African Studies, 1983).

5. See below.

6. Mbilinyi, "Runaway Wives"; for discussion of "marriage politics," see Ann Whitehead, "The Effects of Political and Socio-economic Change on the Politics of Marriage in North-east Ghana" (paper presented to Association of Social Anthropologists, Cambridge, 1983).

7. Yusuf Kassam and Kemal Mustafa, eds. *Participatory Research* (New Delhi: Society for Participatory Research in Asia, and International Council for Adult Education, Toronto, 1982); and Popular Memory Group, "Popular Memory: Theory, Politics, Method," in Richard Johnson et al., *Making Histories* (London: Hutchinson, 1982); a detailed analysis of several of the concepts used here is found in Marjorie Mbilinyi, Ulla Vuorela, Yusuf Kassam, and Yohana Masisi, "The Politics of Research Methodology in the Social Sciences," in Kassam and Mustafa (1982).

8. See Conclusions of IDS Regional Workshop on Research Methodology in Kemal Mustafa, ed. *African Perspectives on Participatory Research* (Toronto: Participatory Research Group, 1982).

9. Susan Geiger introduced the work of the Popular Memory group to WRDP when she spoke on life-history methodology at these workshops.

10. Marjorie Mbilinyi with Mary Kabelele, *Women in the Rural Development of Mbeya Region* (Dar es Salaam: Mbeya RIDEP Project, Tanzania/FAO, 1982).

11. Marjorie Mbilinyi, "Cooperative Organisation in Isange Village," in Mbilinyi et al., *Women's Initiatives in the United Republic of Tanzania* (Geneva: ILO, World Employment Programme, 1987).

12. Mbilinyi, "Agribusiness and Casual Labour in Tanzania" and *"This Is the Big Slavery."*

13. Note 3.

14. Mascarenhas and Mbilinyi.

15. Rustica Chengelela et al. (Dar es Salaam: Taasisi ya Elimu ya Watu Wazima, 1985).

16. This assessment of Kalindile's objectives was confirmed during our revisions of the manuscript in August 1987.

17. *Lemon Swamp and Other Places* (New York: Free Press, 1983), pp. xix–xx.

18. "How it Feels to be Colored Me," cited in Alice Walker, *In Search of Our Mothers' Gardens* (New York: Harvest/HBJ, 1983), p. 115.

19. Popular Memory Group.

20. Wanjiku Mukabi Kabira, *The Oral Artist* (Nairobi: Heinemann Educational Books, 1983), p. 16.

21. Mascarenhas and Mbilinyi, translation by Patricia Mbughuni, "Mapambano na Mitaala ya Wanawake Tanzania" (University of Dar es Salaam Press, 1987, in press).

22. During her sister's three-day funeral, Kalindile stated publicly, "I didn't know that someone from so far away could be my child. I have learned now. I lost children. It's as if this one has come to replace them from inside of my womb." In August 1987, kin and villagers referred to me as "Kalindile's child."

23. During the final revision of the manuscript in August, we revised the postscript, which includes a description of this "crisis" episode. Kalindile agreed with my conclusion. At one point she exclaimed, "Oh yes, it is necessary to always speak your mind. I don't like the people who just sit and agree, 'yes, yes' with nothing to contribute." This chapter is now part of the entire coauthored text.

24. Fran Leeper Buss, *La Partera: Story of a Midwife* (Ann Arbor: University of Michigan Press, 1980); Vincent Crapanzano, *Tuhami: Portrait of a Moroccan* (University of Chicago Press, 1980); Marjorie Shostak, *Nisa* (London: Allen Lane, 1981).

25. Elisabeth Burgos-Debray, ed. *I, Rigoberta Menchu* (London: Verso, 1984).

26. Note 7; Domitila Barrios de Chungara with Moema Viezzer (New York: Monthly Review Press, 1978).

27. L. L. Langness, *The Life History in Anthropological Science* (New York: Holt, Rinehart and Winston, 1965), pp. 4–5, cited by Susan N. G. Geiger, "Women's Life Histories: Method and Content," *Signs* 11, no. 2 (1986): 336.

28. I am grateful to Susan Whyte and her husband (who made this suggestion) and to Ilse Kirk, who shared Crapanzano's work with me.

29. Polisya read the transcripts as well as the manuscript.

30. A term created by Liz Stanley, "Biography as Microscope or Kaleidoscope? . . ." *Women's Studies Int. Forum* 10, no. 1 (1987):21.

"WHAT THE WIND WON'T TAKE AWAY"
The Genesis of *Nisa—The Life and Words of a !Kung Woman*

Marjorie Shostak

This essay about personal narratives is something of a personal narrative in its own right. It explores questions I have asked myself for eighteen years, since I first collected life histories in the field—questions I have never formally addressed in print, or perhaps even fully answered for myself. How best to handle the material, how to present it fairly, and how to find forms suitable for publication—these are some of the problems, both practical and ethical, that I have grappled with. My solutions have been compromises, at best, idiosyncratic constructions bound by the material and by my individual experience. Nevertheless, I offer them here in the hope that they may help clarify these problems for others working in similar ways.

First, some background about me and my research. Armed with the life histories of Cora Dubois *(The People of Alor)* and Oscar Lewis *(The Children of Sanchez)*, I went, in 1969, to the northern fringe of Africa's Kalahara Desert in northwestern Botswana to begin a twenty-month stay with the !Kung San (Bushmen). My goal was to collect life histories, a vehicle through which I hoped the people's experiences, thoughts, and feelings might be expressed. I returned again five years later and stayed five months, continuing this line of research along with others.

What fascinated me about the !Kung was that, although their ways had begun to change, people still maintained much of their hunting and gathering tradition: wild plant foods composed about 65 percent of the diet, and wild game meat the rest. People were seminomadic and lived in groups that fluctuated in composition, usually numbering between fifteen and thirty. Social life was essentially egalitarian, with minimal differentials in wealth, and with no formal status hierarchies or social classes. Work was hard, but there was plenty of time for leisure: women gathered about two to three days a week, and men hunted about three to four days a week. Food was usually more than adequate, sometimes abundant, and only rarely scarce. Children, adolescents, and the elderly were not regularly enlisted in the food quest.

This way of life is similar in many ways to that of our remote ancestors living tens of thousands of years ago, long before the advent of agriculture. This was the context in which our humanity formed and flourished, nourishing the remarkable breadth of human abilities as we know them today. How reasonable or difficult this way of life was is lost in the past, its shadows sketched in archeological sites, on the walls of caves, and in the very presence and persistence of humans on earth today.

The !Kung are one of a very few human groups who have lived in recent times as hunters and gatherers. They are fully modern people, in no sense remnants or leftovers from the past—physiologically, psychologically, or intellectually. All have also had some degree of contact with outside cultures, some for hundreds of years. Nevertheless, even in the most marginal areas—the only ones in which hunters and gatherers now remain—a pattern of life prevails that is likely to be similar, in many ways, to ones followed by hunters and gatherers of the past. Even modern hunters and gatherers living in diverse locales—Australia, central and southern Africa, South America, and the Arctic—share many organizational features.

I was fortunate not to be one of the first anthropologists to study the !Kung San—fortunate because by the time my first field stay was completed, a large body of data collected by other anthropologists and medical scientists was available. Without this work, my own ability to interpret, make sense of, and relate personal narratives—singular voices within a highly varied range—to a more generalized whole would have been compromised.

The life-history interviews were extensive and intimate and were conducted without interpreters. The first hurdle, of course, was learning the language—replete with clicks and tones and bearing no relationship to anything I had ever heard before. I launched my first "interviews" after about six months. I asked pregnant women which sex child they preferred, polygynously married women what it was like to share a husband, and a handful of women and men—those most likely to tolerate my intrusive questions—their thoughts about marriage.

The results? At this distance it does not seem surprising, but at the time it felt quite devastating: my ambitious questions coupled with still-too-rudimentary language skills led to failures dismal enough that had I had the inclination to pursue other lines of research, I might have adopted a new stratagem with embarrassing speed. But I didn't (of course), and by the end of the next six months, things had begun to look brighter: my interviewing skills and language ability had improved to the point that a "research protocol" was developed, one that lasted until the end of my stay.

That protocol was the interview itself. My initial approach was to include anyone willing to talk to me about his or her life. After conducting a number of what turned out to be fairly tense interviews with men, I realized that they felt uncomfortable talking with me about intimate subjects—much as I did with them. Subsequently, I turned my attention solely to women.

By the end, I had invited eight women to work with me. Each set of interviews was introduced in the same way: I explained that I wanted to learn what it meant to be a woman in the !Kung culture so that I could better understand what it meant to be one in my own. I previewed the topics I hoped to discuss: earliest memories, feelings about parents, siblings, relatives, and friends, childhood play, marriage, relationships with husbands and/or lovers, childbirth, parenting, feelings about growing older, and thoughts about death. The women were encouraged to discuss anything else that they felt touched the core of their lives. An interview lasted about an hour, was conducted exclusively in the !Kung language, never included other people, and was tape-recorded. Each woman was interviewed eight or more times.

I tried to elicit specific incidents rather than generalized statements. Discreet memories were more likely to capture the texture of the women's experiences and to highlight the variations among the different women in their life stories and in their interpretations of these stories. The tape recorder was used not only for detail but to enable the reconstruction of how memories followed one another and how words were used; the goal of the final translation was to reflect a sense of the !Kung language, to preserve its nuances, beauty, and subtlety of expression.

There was considerable variation in the women's willingness to be drawn into this process, but overall, the interviews were successful: each woman opened a piece of her life to me, and each piece reflected on and deepened my understanding of the experiences of the others. Of the eight, one woman stood out: Nisa.

Perhaps because she was emotionally vulnerable at the time of our interviews, or just because she took pleasure in the process of reviewing her life, Nisa put more effort into our work than did any other woman. She also had exceptional verbal gifts and articulated her story by reaching more deeply into herself and by choosing her words more deliberately than did the others. While I ordinarily was directive with them, Nisa quickly grasped the requirements and took charge; the momentum was often hers. We completed fifteen interviews during my first field trip, and six more during my second. Her story is the one I ultimately translated, edited, and published.

The result is *Nisa: The Life and Words of a !Kung Woman*. A short outline of its structure reflects the way I resolved the questions raised by the material. As I saw it, three distinct "voices"—or points of view—needed to be incorporated. The first was Nisa's. Presented as first-person narrative, her voice was translated and edited from the taped interviews and chronologically ordered into fifteen chapters, from "Earliest Memories" to "Growing Older."

The second voice was the "official" anthropologist's, putting Nisa's story into cultural perspective: the ethnographic background to topics Nisa discussed was reviewed in headnotes preceding each chapter of her story. The third voice was my own, not primarily as anthropologist but as a young American woman experiencing another world. This voice was sandwiched on either side of the fifteen chapters of narrative and ethnographic notes. A personal introduction set up the overall framework of Nisa's story, and an epilogue summarized my second field trip, including my final encounter with Nisa and my closing thoughts.

Finding an acceptable balance for these three voices was problematic: it took many drafts before that balance was arrived at. Along the way, I confronted and tried to resolve a number of methodological and ethical questions, which can more generally, perhaps, be understood as questions about the uses of personal narrative, especially those conducted in cross-cultural settings. Five of these questions follow.

1. *Can personal narrative be used as ethnography? Since no person is ever truly representative of a culture as a whole, how should an informant's personal biases and distance from statistical norms be handled?*

One of the first issues I struggled with was how to deal with Nisa's representativeness, or lack of it. Nisa's life experiences were different in many ways from those of most other women: she had no living children, she had been married five times, and she was unusually uninhibited, if not an outright extrovert. I wanted her individual voice to be presented clearly, but other women's experiences were needed to balance it.

The interviews conducted in an identical manner with seven other women provided the broad base I needed: Nisa's experiences were compared to theirs. The base became even broader when material collected by other fieldworkers was included. My position, ultimately, was quite favorable: when Nisa said she first married at age nine, I looked up the age curve of first marriage for girls in one publication, the marriage ceremony in another, and the economic and political considerations involved in a third (Lee and DeVore 1976; Marshall 1976; Lee 1979; Howell 1979; I found out, for example, that although on average girls first marry around age sixteen, some, especially in Nisa's generation, married as early as age nine). The headnotes summarized this perspective, enabling the reader to place in context Nisa's sometimes unusual experiences in her own unencumbered narrative.

2. *Can a personal narrative be used even as a true account of the person who is relating it? How dependent is a personal narrative on a particular interviewing relationship?*

Here, a class that I audited, taught by Vincent Crapanzano at Harvard University in the late 1970s, provided guidance. He noted that personal narratives do not exist independently of the collaborative process involved in their collection. People's stories are not in final form, shape, and content, waiting patiently for a glorified mechanic (i.e., biographer, anthropologist, or the like) to open their "verbal tap," allowing the preformed story to escape. Instead, an interview is an interaction between two people: one, with unique personality traits and interests at a particular time of life, answers a specific set of questions asked by another person with unique personality traits and interests at a particular time of life.

In presenting Nisa's story, I therefore took care to describe our relationship as best I could: an essentially practical one which we both thoroughly enjoyed but which did not involve significantly more time than when we actually were working together. There was no doubt that Nisa, aged fifty and experiencing a difficult adjustment to menopause, filtered her life story through her then-current perspective; there was also no doubt that Marjorie Shostak, aged twenty-four, recently married, a product of the American 1960s, asked questions relevant to a specific phase of her life. I asked Nisa to tell me what it meant to be a woman; her answer was her narrative: selected memories retained through time—real, embellished, imagined, or a combination of all three—which best served her current definition of self. Her narrative thus reflected a finite contract between fifty-year-old Nisa and twenty-four-year-old Shostak; any other combination, no doubt, would have produced a different result.

3. *Can personal narratives be used freely in our own work for our own purposes? Is the collection and publication of personal narratives a boon for researchers while being a thinly disguised "rip-off" of informants? Where does our ultimate responsibility lie?*

It was less clear for me, not working toward an academic degree, than for most graduate students and faculty what I had to gain by working on Nisa's narrative. Indeed, had I not been personally "hooked," feeling almost a sense of responsibility for publishing it, the course of my life during the past eighteen years would have been very different. But I *was* hooked, although never without ambivalence.

The first time its value was impressed upon me was soon after I returned from the field and passed around some preliminary translations; they were met with tremendous enthusiasm and encouragement. An article I subsequently published was followed by a call from the Harvard University Press, inquiring about my future plans for writing a book.

It took ten years before *Nisa* was finally published. Work on the book was only one of the reasons it took so long; I was also intensely involved in other projects. By the time I made a firm commitment to completing *Nisa*, I had translated her twenty-one interviews twice: once after my first field trip, and again after my second. Having become more proficient in the !Kung language, I felt I could render more subtle and accurate translations from the original tapes.

However smoothly or roughly my life might otherwise have gone, I have nevertheless clearly profited by having published the book. But what did Nisa gain? The actual interview process seemed a positive one for her, and in some small way, it may even have helped her. Our initial work took place during an emotionally stressful time: the recent onset of menopause was bringing home the finality of her childlessness; by that time, all of her four children had died.

Talking about her life, reviewing the births, the deaths, the marriages, the many additional loves, the highs and the lows—all while "teaching" me about life and womanhood—Nisa also took pride in her skillful handling of the situation. She reveled in the knowledge that she was teaching me the "truth" about life, while others, she would explain, often taught me "lies." She benefited in other ways (as did the other women), with presents and with an agreed-upon payment. Status also accrued to her among the !Kung for being involved with "anthropologists' work."

But there was more. Nisa responded to our talk as though she appreciated the chance to contribute to something "bigger" than what was typically asked for by the anthropologists. She was well aware that I planned to bring the verbatim material I collected back to the people with whom I lived. They, I had explained, would be interested in learning about !Kung women's lives. She approached the tape recorder as an ally, one with tentacles reaching out to worlds beyond her own. She jokingly referred to it as an "old man"—a symbol, perhaps, of a wise, experienced presence that could receive the full import of all she hoped to say. During the very first interview, she expressed this concern directly: "Fix my voice on the machine so that my words come out clear. I am an old person who has experienced many things, and I have much to talk about."

She was also aware of the fragility of talk—and of experience. Reflecting on the interview process itself, she once said, "I'll break open the story and tell you what is there. Then, like the others that have fallen out onto the sand, I will finish with it, and the wind will take it away." Perhaps she recognized that with me there was a chance that the wind might *not* take *all* of it away.

Indeed, during the last interview of my first visit, she spoke about my taking "our talk" with me when I left. She said she would collect more talk and "save it for me." When I returned four years later, she reminded me of this: she said she hadn't forgotten her promise and collected things to talk to me about. This and other responses to the challenge of our work suggested that the interviews were a welcome outlet for her, a satisfying and otherwise unavailable avenue for self-expression.

What about more material rewards? When I returned to the field, I spoke to Nisa about my desire to publish her account—something that would not, in fact, happen for another six years. I likened the final book to products for sale in stores, a parallel with which she was already familiar. If it sold, I told her, she would get something out of it. If it didn't, she might not.

Her initial response was, "If this is what you want to do, that's good. But you're the one who has to do it, not me." I explained that, indeed, it would be years of my work, but that it was her story. Concerned about her privacy, we agreed that I would use pseudonyms. Together we settled on "Nisa" and other names. Giving her consent, she said that if the book sold, she would like some cows. I reviewed with her the most problematic stories—those involving violence, and others that might be seen as personally compromising—and asked if she wanted any of the material excluded. She answered without hesitation, "all our talk, all that this 'old man' [the tape recorder] has heard, wants to enter the talks."

Nisa has received her cows and continues to receive gifts from me. As a result, she has become one of the people with wealth and stature in the changing world of the !Kung. I have contributed additional time and money helping the community she lives with. But where my ultimate responsibility lies in relation to her is still somewhat unsettled. L. L. Langness and Gelya Frank in *Lives: An Anthropological Approach to Biography* discuss some of the subtleties of the interview relationship. They point out that informants sometimes harbor "unexpressed expectations" of anthropologists. In the process of receiving attention from outsiders, usually from those with higher status than their own, informants may become vulnerable. They cite the claim of cross-cultural psychologist David Guttman that "[informants] too often experience our transient gestures toward equality as massive seductions," and recommend close supervision of anthropologists not only by experts in their particular field but by—and here they may overestimate the wisdom of these practitioners—clinical psychologists or psychiatrists as well.

These concerns are legitimate, but they can also be exaggerated and even patronizing to informants. In Nisa's case, I think the seduction worked both ways. I didn't enter Nisa's life until she was about age fifty, and when I did, it was for a very short period of time. When I returned four years later, her life in the interim had clearly been fully lived, although she had not forgotten to "collect" stories for my return. Even if my impact on her was larger than I recognize, my belief now, as then, is that—except for the later financial rewards—I have played an essentially minor and positive role in her life.

That does not justify my shirking from what I see as a continuing responsibility toward her and her community or underestimating what she gave. She offered weeks of her time, telling her story with gusto, courage, imagination, and humor, along with thoughtfulness, occasional sadness, anger, and longing. For me, "talking her talk with me" and trying to make sense of it involved many years of my life. The ultimate gain for either of us can hardly be considered to be financial. Nisa gave her talk; I tried to keep the wind from taking its beauty away.

4. *How does the editing and translation process affect how personal narratives are used? What factors must be considered when translating, editing, and presenting a personal narrative once it has been collected?*

Shaping Nisa's narrative required considerable discipline and attention to detail. A total of twenty-one interviews—representing between twenty-five and thirty hours of tape, all recorded under less than ideal conditions—were translated twice, a process that was tedious and time-consuming. The initial translations were literal, word-for-word transcriptions written in English, but with unusual expressions noted in !Kung. Following a second field trip, I translated and transcribed the initial fifteen interviews again, along with six additional interviews conducted during this subsequent stay.

These translations were broken into segments, usually the length of a story, and were roughly edited. These segments were then grouped, usually by topic, sequenced into loose chronological order, and more finely edited. Details and embellishments from incidents discussed more than once were combined into one account. To clarify the flow from one story to the next, missing or unclear time markers were inserted (for example: "Not long after," or "Some time passed."). All questions of clarification, all diversionary comments, and all directive suggestions on my part were eliminated from the final narrative.

In addition to this editing, an overriding structure needed to be created, a "literary" one that would grab the attention and maintain the interest of American readers. To that end, I experimented with a number of formats. My first approach treated each interview as its own chapter and followed it with ethnographic and personal commentary. This didn't work: the interviews lacked consistent dramatic and emotional integrity; they didn't stand up well on their own. Comments and asides as well as occasional interruptions from the outside frequently disrupted the flow of talk. Or, the conversation jumped around, restlessly, from topic to topic, settling on a clear direction only halfway through. Or, I would introduce a string of interruptions to clarify the flow of details, or merely to have an unfamiliar word or expression defined. The overall progression of interviews did have an interesting character, but ultimately it was not enough to be the most effective form in which to present Nisa's story.

The main alternative was the chronological presentation—the one I chose because it made sense, not just to me but even in terms of !Kung narrative form. Although they had no prior experience with my specific life-review format, Nisa and the other women had no trouble adopting the chronological approach. In Nisa's first interview, we did a "once-over," quickly reviewing the grand scope of her life from her earliest memories to the interview-present. The second interview started at the beginning again. Throughout that one, and the next thirteen, we proceeded again through her life story, this time much more slowly, stopping often, touching events in depth, carefully moving forward in time until we reached the interview-present. At the end of each interview, we would discuss where we might pick up the next day. The next day sometimes began with a review of the end of the previous day's interview. More typically, it would start with a recent dream, or Nisa would tell me that she had prepared her thoughts in a certain direction for our talks that day.

The six interviews conducted with Nisa during my second field trip, four years later, clarified material collected during the first trip: we reviewed stories I hadn't previously understood, went over unclear time sequences, added material in areas that had been underrepresented, and reviewed events in Nisa's life during my four-year absence. For both sets of interviews, no constraints on time or on the total number of interviews existed; we determined the end of each one, and the series as a whole, at the point both of us felt her story had been told.

Nisa had her own sense of narrative style. Most of her stories were told with a beginning, a middle, and an end; some were short, others lengthy. Usually, the chronological, or linear, mode I encouraged prevailed, although sometimes she, or I, would jump to a related topic. If I interrupted to ask a question, she might reprimand me, "Wait, I'm getting to that. Now listen." At times, the process of narration itself became her focus, as when she described the dissolution of one of her marriages and ended her story with, "That's all, and we lived and we lived." An unusually long silence followed. Then she added, thoughtfully and slowly, "No, there is something in my heart about this that isn't finished. My heart is still shaking. The story hasn't come completely out. I'm going to talk more about it until it does. Then, I'll go on to another. Then, my heart will be fine."

The chronological approach also found support in !Kung traditional storytelling. The !Kung exercise sophisticated narrative pacing and sequencing skills in a rich body of oral myths, those describing the time "in the beginning"—when God walked upon the earth and animals were still evolving from people—as well as in their animal tales, stories of character and intrigue, dependent on chronology and an orderly succession of events. Similarly, frequent recountings of hunts and experiences while gathering require subtle verbal cues and accurate time sequencing. It is possible that had I been less directive, a fairly comparable indigenous narrative form would have emerged.

But with few conventions to guide me, each editing decision was guided by my ultimate goal: to present Nisa's unique experience of life—as expressed in her interviews—as a distinct voice within the context of !Kung culture as I, and other researchers, saw it at that time. Because, as "objective" as each researcher tried to be, our collection and interpretation of data were inevitably influenced by the intellectual "umbrella" we shared. (For example, since then, the !Kung's long history of contract with other cultures, which we were aware of but did not emphasize, and the "myth" of their isolation have come much more to the fore.) My headnotes reflect a view generally shared by anthropologists in 1981, and, in some ways, the narrative material chosen does as well.

As described above, questions of clarification were eliminated, duplicate accounts were collapsed, extraneous story fragments were excluded, and a chronological sequence was imposed. In addition, a small number of stories I didn't understand, and anecdotes and minor incidents about people not central to the themes of the narrative (such as customs of or gossip about the neighboring Bantu-speaking people) were also eliminated. Stories that

covered duplicate ground, and that would have impeded the general flow
of the narrative, were also left out (for example, dreams that were similar to
ones included, or secondary stories about lovers—none important or con-
taining details not already in the narrative; even in its published form,
many readers find the narrative too heavily weighted in that direction and
find some of Nisa's numerous amorous encounters tedious). There is no
doubt that I also held subtle and not-so-subtle biases toward the material.

Nowhere were the editing choices more delicate than in the translation
process itself. I would not be honest without admitting that there were
times when I was tempted to "adjust" the narrative beyond what could be
considered justifiable. Nisa, as those familiar with the book know, is a
strong, earthy, sexual, highly self-contained but not always exemplary
character. I was sorely tempted to leave out some of her less appealing traits
to highlight those that ennobled her. A slight shift in the translation, so
subtle that no one but I would know, could also have achieved this end.
How much grander Nisa might have appeared had I translated everyday
idiomatic speech into literal, poetic utterances! "The sun rose" is prosaic;
"The dawn broke open the darkness" is poetry. But if every !Kung child
and adult, dull or witty, described the sunrise in the same standard way,
then, when Nisa used those words, my responsibility was to translate it into
standard English—which I tried very carefully to do as I went along.

Another translation problem was the use of repetition. In a culture with
strong oral traditions, repetition often becomes part of the ritual form. For
example, as one memory ended, Nisa often said, "and we lived and we lived
and we lived." (The phrase might actually be repeated several more times.)
Although a more "literary" expression could have been employed, such as
"a few moons (or rainy seasons, etc.) passed," Nisa used repetition: it
symbolized the passage of ordinary time, bridged two stories or parts
together, and acted as a dramatic device around which to organize her
thoughts—a technique used widely by other storytellers. In translating her
words, such strong strings of repetitions did not work in English, and I
often substituted "and time passed," or "and we just continued to live." In a
sense, this epitomizes the problem of translation: the !Kung expression
conveys a different sense of time than do the English ones—a sense of the
past that is more immediate and continuing. Instead of losing that completely, I left some of it in, trying to retain its flavor, but substituted words
or reduced the repetitions drastically to make it work on the printed page.

My editor at the Harvard University Press once asked in jest, but with
telltale nervousness in his laugh, "You do have interviews with Nisa on tape
. . . don't you?" Ultimately, Nisa's narrative and the assumption of my
having edited our work responsibly and professionally have been accepted
on faith. Not that this faith has been misplaced; it has not. Nevertheless, the
handful of people who could have checked my translations never have. I
suppose they never felt the need; most of them had worked with me in the
field, had evidence of my language abilities, had heard many similar stories

themselves, and had heard enough gossip about the personal nature of my work from the !Kung themselves that they trusted that I did what I claimed to have done. Above all, they knew enough about the !Kung to know that Nisa's narrative, even when it surprised them, rang true.

5. *Can personal narratives be used as a mirror or guide to our own lives?*

If they could not, most of us would probably be much less keen on doing them. After all, they are difficult to obtain (especially in foreign contexts), laborious to work with, and tricky to present. Methodological obstacles are vast: becoming proficient in another language, developing rapport, learning interview techniques, insuring reliability of data, adopting appropriate sample size, maintaining objectivity, and recognizing one's own biases. Ethical issues are no less complex: protecting an informant's privacy—within the community as well as without, educating informants about the collaboration so that they truly can give informed consent, recognizing the informant's sensitivity toward us and ours toward her or him, and translating, editing, and presenting the informant's "true" voice in such a way that the idiosyncratic and the generalizable can be distinguished.

The impetus for surmounting these obstacles came, for me, from the realization that if I didn't do it, no one else was likely to. After all, fewer and fewer !Kung remained connected to their fast-disappearing hunting and gathering traditions, and the other anthropologists who worked with them had different research interests. While a well-told story of any person's life is of value, one that came from a culture which reflected a most ancient form of human organization—a form in which all our human potential originally became manifest—seemed potentially to be of great significance. When I devised my project, I hoped I would learn from the !Kung what it meant to be human.

The impetus for collecting personal narratives, however, came from an overlapping but distinct set of issues: recently married, living in the field with no other outsiders, I found fieldwork much more isolating than life as I had known it before. I learned much about the !Kung language, their !Kung way of life, and who they were as a people. Setting aside, as best I could, involvement in my own world, I nevertheless remained an outsider, there to interpret and bring back pieces of another way of life. In truth, I was drawn to interviewing people because I felt lonely; I hoped, perhaps, that "structured friendships" would allow me to share in people's lives and feel part of the community. After initial difficulties, they did just that.

A few years before *Nisa* was published, my literary agent sent part of the manuscript to numerous publishers. At one house it was rejected because, it was claimed, Nisa's voice wasn't interesting enough; she sounded as if she could be "the woman next door." Despite the rejection, I was elated. That was, after all, what I had been hoping for. Nisa—at home in the Kalahari Desert, part of a society with no chiefs, no status hierarchies, and minimal inequities of wealth, semi-nomadic, small-scale, and minimally materialistic (each person's possessions weigh about twenty-five pounds)—was being mistaken for "the woman next door"! Her experiences must reflect something universal, after all.

My desire to find a guide, someone to mirror my own life, had been realized. Nisa's voice reverberated not only within me but within others. Considering her story, perhaps it is not so surprising: a woman living in one of the most remote areas of the world, facing life with courage, humor, spirit, and dignity, who, despite repeated tragedy, carried on with a sense of entitlement to enjoy what was yet to come. She had told this story with care and generosity, a story with echoes of an ancient time, reflecting themes tens of thousands of years old.

CONCLUSION

One of the people Barbara Myerhoff interviewed for her study of a community of aging Jewish immigrants in California was Shmuel. He had come to the United States from Eastern Europe early in this century, at a time when pogroms against Jews were rampant. Speaking about life in Poland before it was all "wiped out like you would erase a line of writing," he said about death: "It is not the worst thing that can happen for a man to grow old and die." He continued, "But if my life goes, with my memories, and all that [the knowledge of a way of life destroyed by Hilter] is lost, that is something else to bear" (Myerhoff 1978, pp. 73–74).

It is for Shmuel, Nisa, and the silent others they represent, as well as for ourselves, that we should continue to record these lives and memories. The ethical and methodological problems may be formidable, but they are small compared to the goal. Indeed, the most important ethical message regarding life histories is not a restriction but an obligation: we should make every effort to overcome obstacles, to go out and record the memories of people whose ways of life often are preserved only in those memories. And we should do it urgently, before they disappear.

No more elegant tool exists to describe the human condition than the personal narrative. Ordinary people living ordinary and not-so-ordinary lives weave from their memories and experiences the meaning life has for them. These stories are complex, telling of worlds sometimes foreign to us, worlds that sometimes no longer exist. They express modes of thought and culture often different from our own, a challenge to easy understanding. Yet, these stories are also familiar. It is just this tension—the identifiable in endless transformation—that is the currency of personal narratives, as they reveal the complexities and paradoxes of human life. As we cast our net ever wider, searching for those close as well as those far away, the spectrum of voices from otherwise obscure individuals helps us learn tolerance for differences as well as for similarities. What better place to begin our dialogue about human nature and the nature of human possibilities?

References

DuBois, Cora. *The People of Alor*. Minneapolis: University of Minnesota Press, 1944.

Howell, Nancy. *Demography of the Dobe Area !Kung*. New York: Academic Press, 1979.

Langness, L. L., and Gelya Frank. *Lives: An Anthropological Approach to Biography*. California: Chandler and Sharp, 1981.

Lee, Richard. *The !Kung San*. Cambridge, England: Cambridge University Press, 1979.

Lee, Richard, and Irven DeVore. *Kalahari Hunter-Gatherers*. Cambridge, Mass.: Harvard University Press, 1976.

Lewis, Oscar. *The Children of Sanchez: Autobiography of a Mexican Family*. New York: Random House, 1961.

Marshall, Lorna, *The !Kung of Nyae Nyae*. Cambridge, Mass.: Harvard University Press, 1976.

Myerhoff, Barbara. *Number Our Days*. New York: Dutton, 1978.

Shostak, Marjorie. *Nisa: The Life and Words of a !Kung Woman*. Cambridge, Mass.: Harvard University Press, 1981; New York: Vintage, 1983.

THE DOUBLE FRAME OF LIFE HISTORY IN THE WORK OF BARBARA MYERHOFF

Riv-Ellen Prell

In discussing the work of anthropologist Barbara Myerhoff, I will consider the life historian rather than the life history, the ear rather than the voice, and the pen rather than the tape. By reading, as it were, from the recorder to the text, we learn that a life history is the product of two active participants who formulate one life. The anthropologist helps to shape the life history that she records just as the subject's ideas about person and culture will be reflected in interpretations of the life. In her work, Barbara Myerhoff consistently violated conventional scientific norms for life history and theory by introducing herself into the life of her subject, and introducing her subject into her theorizing. She maintained multiple and contradictory voices in all her work. Hence, she transformed the subject-object relationship of the traditional life-history interview into a subject-subject relationship. Life histories were of interest to Myerhoff because through them she learned how people lived in relationship to a culture which provided models for constructing a meaningful life. This very process drew her attention to how people created meaning in their lives, a process which was inevitably innovative. Myerhoff recognized that the settings for eliciting a life story were as much occasions for "showing" or reflecting on a life as ritual or other conventional cultural events. Hence, she understood the mutuality of two subjects' presence in a life history. With this realization, Myerhoff expanded the life history from a technique for recording life events to a method capable of reconceptualizing the relationships embedded in research. Self reflection and revelation became central to her view of culture and life history.

At the time of her death in 1985, Myerhoff had produced two life histories and a series of articles about the reflexive nature of culture. She had collected many more life histories and was working on an as yet unpublished work, *Tales of Fairfax,* a collection of stories and life experiences of Russian immigrant Jews in Los Angeles combined with a discussion of the place of narrative in culture. She did not label her first work a life history, and it was not one in a conventional sense. Given her theoretical

241

interests, however, in retrospect it seems quite possible to think of it as such.

The book, *Peyote Hunt* (1974), was an analysis of a religious and cultural complex of symbols of a Mexican Indian group, the Huichol. Her entire interpretation of the culture relied on the relationship she built with a Huichol shaman, Ramon Medina Silva. Following months of work during which the shaman dictated and explained texts concerning Huichol religion, he took Myerhoff and her colleague, anthropologist Peter Furst, along with several Huichol pilgrims, on a pilgrimage to the sacred land of Wirikuta, where they were the first non-Huichol to witness this event. They participated with the Huichol, who in the course of the ritual became the ancient ancestors and gods. The anthropologists saw them "shoot" the peyote, that is, the deer god, consume it, and dream, in the case of the shaman, the cultural lessons and sacred knowledge the gods wished them to know and pass on.

Myerhoff begins *Peyote Hunt* with a chapter she entitles "Ramon and Lupe." Initially it follows the narrative course of Ramon's life, his shamanic ancestry, his own illness and call to shamanism, his marriage to Lupe, and their creating a life as artisans on a crossroad near Guadalajara, where Huichol gather around them, relying on Ramon's leadership. Within this narrative of Ramon's life, and in her introduction, Myerhoff presents Ramon not as an object of research but as a collaborator. She describes Ramon "listening to playback of his songs and chants with delight, of his stories with great attention, erasing a passage here, adding a comment there, until he was entirely satisfied with the finished product" (1974, p. 37). The information Ramon provided was normally forbidden to non-Huichol. He decided, however, to recount the tales and myths for a book he hoped would preserve his culture, which he believed was in jeopardy (1974, p. 38). This wish and collaboration led Myerhoff to write in her introduction that "this work is as much theirs [Ramon and Lupe's] as mine. . . . I have tried to tell it as they told it to me, so that it shall not be forgotten" (1974, p. 24).

Myerhoff wrote of her "parallel interests" with Ramon concerning religion, myth, and symbolism and asserted that the "depth" of her study was due to Ramon's "intelligence and erudition" (1974, p. 17). She described their method of work, in which Ramon moved back and forth speaking Huichol and Spanish, providing his own translations, discussing his word choices with her (1974, p. 20). Their work of recording Huichol religion through his eyes became a portion of his personal narrative. Ramon's narrative and Huichol culture merged in *Peyote Hunt*. Myerhoff included his interpretations of Huichol life as well as their shared cross-cultural work.

Similarly, nowhere is she bolder in asserting their collaboration or parallel interests than in her description of her own experience with peyote under Ramon's guidance. She places this tale in the "Ramon and Lupe" chapter, merging her own experience with his biography. As she enters Ramon's biography, so he enters hers. It is only through her identification with Ramon and, to some extent, Lupe, that taking peyote is meaningful. She understands her peyote-induced experience to challenge directly the scientific model of linear rationality that she brings with her from the West. Under the experience of peyote, Ramon appears to her as a red bird bringing her to a "gnome like figure" whom she asks the question that has preoccupied her throughout her work of recording religious texts: "What do the myths mean?" She receives an answer she suspected all along. "The myths signify—nothing. They mean themselves. They were themselves, nothing equivalent, nothing translated, nothing taken from a more familiar place to distort them" (1974, p. 42). As the peyote wears off, she is frustrated because as she focused on her hallucination of a little creature at the center of a yarn painting (Ramon's art form), she had missed one at the edge of the painting.

> I had lost my lesson by looking for it too directly, with dead center tight focus, with will and impatience. It was a practice which I knew was fatal to understanding anything truly unique. It was my Western rationality, honed by formal study, eager to simplify, clarify, dissect, define and analyze. The message could emerge anywhere. One had to be alert . . . reserving interpretation for another time. (1974, p. 43)

In her rendering of overlapping biographies and collaborative research, Myerhoff questions the conventions of Western science. Though her book is full of interpretations of Huichol symbolism and is a relatively early synthesis of the ideas of symbolic anthropologists, she does not privilege their theories. She maintains the integrity of Ramon's interpretations and introduces anthropological ones separately. Her ultimate rationale for the book evokes Ramon's voice.

> My main goal is to help fulfill Ramon's most cherished wish—that of presenting and preserving something of the power and beauty of his customs, his symbols, his stories so that one can see why, despite all the physical hardships and privations that "it is not a bad thing being a Huichol." (1974, p. 21)

She feels urgency about carrying out this wish because Ramon, as she notes in her introduction, was killed in 1971 during an argument, a short time after she had last seen him in Mexico.

Myerhoff's book is in no conventional sense an ethnography. Rather, it is the story of a man she labels "exceptional." Neither is it a biography. She tells his story of the Huichol at his request. In this sense it is a cultural account rather than the life of one person. She presents herself as a student, referring to Ramon as a "teacher" leading her and Furst through a mythic realm. Her trust is intense enough for her to take peyote under his guidance. She does not follow the ordinary course of anthropologist as student, for she does not move in her book from student to authority, usurping the teacher's voice to become the Western expert.[1] Though the book is an "expert's" account, it maintains the teacher's voice in the text and asserts repeatedly that though the myths and ritual are amenable to "scientific" analysis and dissection, they are not contained or fully explained by them. The method of narrative recording she used in the life history is then reproduced in spirit within the finished scholarly text.

Myerhoff's presence in her book is unusual for a standard anthropological work. She is constantly visible, overstepping the ethnographer's conventional place at the margin of an ethnographic work, describing the "entry" to the field in the work's introduction.[2] Myerhoff records interviews, takes peyote, and participates in the pilgrimage. All these activities undermine the authority of the invisible recorder so often asserted by anthropologists. This mixture of life history and ethnography effaces neither subject of the work: neither Ramon nor Barbara.

Perhaps because her work contradicted the scientific canon, Myerhoff thought about the significance of her relationship with Ramon for her understanding of anthropology for some time. Before the book's publication, she had planned to include an epilogue she had written about Ramon and Lupe's trip to Southern California in 1971 to give performances and show their yarn paintings at both the Science Museum and the University of Southern California. During this time, they stayed with her family. It was a complex tale about her failure to translate what she believed was their "symmetrical relationship" into her own world. At a friend's suggestion, she left it out because "it was his story and I did not want to turn it into mine," she told me. I have seen only one brief reference to that epilogue in print, in which she argued that there were no conventional words for the relationship between an anthropologist and her "key informant." She was perhaps naively disappointed in Ramon's apparent indifference to, for example, her photographs and stories of her family, which forced her to question the nature of collaboration in research. She concluded that it was not mutual in any simple sense. She was led to question the meaning and place of the subject-subject relationship within anthropology, and gained heightened self-consciousness about it (Myerhoff and Ruby 1982, pp. 32–33).

Myerhoff, then, overtly intended *Peyote Hunt* to be the story of a heroic shaman, but the work and the visit led her to think more consciously about the relationship that created it. Before Ramon's visit, Myerhoff believed her most important work was to produce as accurate a translation as possible of Ramon's own words in order to preserve them. She saw the greatness of Ramon's culture, though it remained invisible to the Mexicans around them, who saw only poor and downtrodden Indians. Her work was to make visible what she saw, a matter broadly of translation and reporting. She captured the mutual act of translation in *Peyote Hunt* to demonstrate its impact on her and, by extension, us. Because Myerhoff preserves both voices, she includes us in the act of discovering a personal and cultural story which is capable of enriching our own lives.

SHMUEL'S LIFE: THE OUTSIDER

Myerhoff's second life history, though apparently different from the first, also found its impetus in her apprenticeship to another teacher. This life history is the first ethnographic chapter of her widely read *Number Our Days* (1979), the study of elderly Jews associated with a senior center in Southern California. Life history is not only the book's key methodology but its unifying thread. Each chapter is preceded by a myseh (Yiddish for story) that Myerhoff recorded in a life-history class she organized for the elderly while she was conducting her fieldwork. Week after week, they came and talked about what they had experienced, argued about their perceptions, fought for center stage, and provided Barbara with rich data not only about the events of their biographies but about growing old and living in an alien culture.

One chapter in particular, "Needle and Thread, The Life and Death of a Tailor," is a partial life history of one man, Shmuel Goldman. He is in one sense an outsider to the community, because his boldly voiced atheism and political opposition to Israel provoke anger from and rejection by other members of the center. But he does not abandon the community, telling Myerhoff that the center is the only place he can continue to speak Yiddish. He also admits that he believes that they need him to remind them of certain moral and political truths. This very outsider status, in addition to his erudition and perceptiveness, make him a powerful and eloquent voice to describe his shtetl childhood destroyed by Nazism, his socialist and Jewish values, and his reflections on what his life has meant.

Though this chapter is a more conventional life history than Ramon's, it is neither chronological nor solely focused on Shmuel Goldman. Myerhoff again introduces herself into the life history by making the context for eliciting it part of its content. Not only does she record his words, but she often describes her own responses: admiration, desire to be valued, and fear of disappointing him. Shmuel's wife, Rebecca, moves in and out of the story as well, usually at the beginning and end of the many sessions devoted to recording the life history. Shmuel's death a few days following their last interview is also placed in the chapter to make explicit the connections he drew between the story he told and his consciousness of his life's nearing its end. Myerhoff concludes the life history with his memorial service at the center. Some of his detractors refuse to attend, lingering outside. She reports that she is unable to listen dispassionately to their attacks on Shmuel and walks past them, allowing herself the luxury of not doing research for this day.

Myerhoff makes extensive use of Shmuel's own words in the life history. His descriptions of his childhood hometown in Poland run on for pages. His discussions of how he values work and the meaning he derives from sewing a good garment are presented in detail, as is the ensuing debate between Barbara and Shmuel about the relative value of this passage for the reader. Shmuel understands himself to be Barbara's teacher. He is therefore frustrated by what she does not understand about what is important in life, and wonders at the same time what is the worth of the things he tells her. She explains that his attitude toward work makes his life "infinitely richer than others" (1979, p. 66). When Shmuel chastises her for exaggerating, he asks Barbara if she will include his scolding her in her book. She writes, "I suppose I'll have to leave it in, won't I? To be fair to both of us." Again, Myerhoff weaves the process of creating the life history and her relationship with her subject into the finished product.

Myerhoff is strangely silent about her rationale for the use of the life history. She describes in detail why the other chapters take the form they do, but she does not explain why she wrote the life history as she did. She describes the conversations she records as Shmuel's "intentional lessons" (1979, p. 41). Early in the chapter Shmuel says of himself, "I'm not typical" (1979, p. 42). Rather, Shmuel, as outsider, is made prominent for Myerhoff because he is exceptional, and appears to exemplify what she saw in the lives of the elderly Jews. Their Eastern European Jewish culture provided them values, attitudes, and coping skills that allowed them to transform every day and every moment into a meaningful encounter. The encounters were often painful and contentious, but they vibrated with meaning and significance.

Shmuel's life is remarkable because of his gloss on experience, a gloss Myerhoff believes is Jewish and humanistic. She wrote of him, "He made everything ordinary into something special" (1979, p. 29). Shmuel's life history, like Ramon's, reveals a person who is remarkable because his culture is. Its significance for the larger work is to exemplify the ability of these immigrants who have lost so much to live fully and well in relationship to their portrayals by the dominant culture. If Ramon contended that Huichol life was beautiful because it was theirs, so Shmuel found his hometown special because it was his.

> This little town I loved so much, with all its faults, I have to say we belonged there in such a way that we could never belong in America. Why? Because it was ours. Simple. Not so good, or bad. But altogether Jewish. (1979, p. 68)

Shmuel's life story is placed at the beginning of the book to locate all of what follows—conflict, suspicion, celebration, and loss—within the frame of a relationship to the larger culture which alternatively may denigrate or romanticize the group. The seniors at the center all fight against invisibility and death. The nobility Myerhoff ascribes to Shmuel's life is contrasted with its objective circumstances. What creates the capacity for both Ramon and Shmuel to live remarkable lives is a symbolic/cultural system that makes the construction of such a life possible. Myerhoff presents remarkable persons, but not isolated individuals. Much of what she wants to record about them is the wisdom of their culture, as well as their construction of it.

This life history is again a work of collaboration without a single authoritative voice, although this time Myerhoff presents symmetry as illusory. She describes Goldman as "teacher, guide and critic." He repeatedly accuses her of "ignorance," and chastises her for her inability to understand and her penchant "to exaggerate." Ramon is a patient teacher. Shmuel is constantly appalled by all Barbara does not know about the Jewish culture that they share. His voice is present in every chapter, reflecting on what happened, often in tension with Myerhoff's own assessments. She is, of course, aware that because of certain of her advantages as a native-born American, she had opportunities and attained achievements never possible for Goldman. Though she may judge herself more successful and less deserving, she nevertheless insists on their parallels. She describes her thoughts as she rushes to keep up with him on the way to a taping session in his home:

> Our shadows were exactly the same size—small, compact, heads enlarged by wiry curls. Despite the forty years that set us apart, despite our differences in sex, history, knowledge, belief and experience, we resembled each other. It could be seen that we were of the same racial stock. Shmuel had a way of reckoning all differences between us in his favor, mocking without cruelty, yet in a way that always made me feel somewhat apologetic. I was grateful for all our similarities and read them as signs of hope in the validity of my attempt to comprehend him. (1979, p. 42)

Collaboration, however, also implies dangers Barbara seemed to be unaware of in her work with Ramon. Shmuel's life history begins with his assertion of the potential risk of all such research:

> You cannot tell someone, "I know you." People jump around. They are like a ball. Rubbery, they bounce. A ball cannot be long in one place. Rubbery, it must jump.
> So what do you do to keep a person from jumping?
> The same as with a ball. You take a pin and stick it in, make a little hole. It goes flat. When you tell someone, "I know you," you put a little pin in. (1979, p. 41)

Aware of the illusion of symmetry in the first collaboration, Myerhoff felt her challenge in the second was to maintain the "rubbery" quality of the life and not deflate it. Her method for maintaining the bounce was to continue the collaborative style she developed in the many-voiced *Peyote Hunt,* but to rethink what "interpretation" meant. Rather than viewing herself as she had previously, as a "translator" of Ramon's tests who offers Western interpretations without privileging them, she redefined interpretation. Myerhoff introduces the notion of reflexivity as a "native" act as well as an analytic one in *Number Our Days*. Her subjects self-consciously reflected on themselves and their cultures as an anthropologist reflected on the foundations of society. Because she incorporated the context of recording the lives of others in her accounts of them, Myerhoff maintained that the act of recording and the act of self-interpretation were parallel because both were the product of persons reflecting one another.[3]

THE GREAT STORY

Myerhoff's book *Peyote Hunt* was a fully developed example of what she subsequently called "a great story," a cultural macrocosm that provided a history, a personal story of individual experience, and an orderly interpretive framework for meaning (ms.). The pilgrimage to Wirikuta and the group's cultural symbols articulated the Huichol past and present to living Huichols. Their past as hunters was enshrined in their present life through the deer god and many references to an ancestral homeland. Their difficult present lives as maize cultivators were accounted for in a rich mythology about the maize girl god and her relationship to Huichol, and put in perspective by their access to paradise in their journey of return to their ancestral homeland. Finally, in the private and unspoken periods provided by the ritual use of peyote, Myerhoff argued that an aesthetic dimension to life was always present. The Huichol could assume a future in which a coherent past was always available. Only Ramon had peyote visions that were made public, for his were provided by ancestors and gods. The great story was translated and lived by Ramon in a more intense way than others. He told stories of gods and past shamans in the present tense, for they were his stories as well as the stories of those around him. His training allowed him to mediate between his fellow Huichols and the gods, and in that mediation make them always accessible to one another. Ramon was a culture hero and a fellow Huichol at once.

Myerhoff was clearly influenced by Clifford Geertz's well-known article on religion (1973). In it he laid out the relationship between the "great story" and the individual, demonstrating how religion is a model for reality as much as a model of it. *Peyote Hunt* translated those ideas ethnographically, allowing Myerhoff to argue that Ramon and the Huichol, even in the face of overwhelming cultural change, carried on an ancient tradition precisely because their great story shaped their individual lives. To use Geertz's phrase, their culture gave them meaning. Between the publication of her two books, Barbara wrote to me reflecting on this very process of meaning making.

Yesterday I taught one of the most exciting sessions ever—it began with a

review about Speer's Secret Diaries from Spandau Prison. As you remember, he was Hitler's architect. The lecture was about the possibility of
teaching human values, me telling them that I once thought, "meaning"—
and you know all that includes—symbolism, mythic thought, ritual—the
whole—anyway that meaning was optional, that a person was incomplete
and infinitely poorer without this vision, but that was the limit. It suddenly
came to me that it was not merely unfortunate to live without meaning, it
was a danger to society and one's fellows. It was one of those electric
sessions in which people began to find numinous and eternal struggles in
their mundane affairs. (Personal correspondence, April 23, 1976)

Myerhoff was coming to realize that this extraordinary value of meaning
making she had seen among the Huichol could not be confined only to
those cultures or leaders who appeared to resist change.

When looking for a way to explain how ordinary people found meaning
in life, she often used the ideas of an anthropologist whose impact on her
thinking was significant. American anthropologist Robert Redfield drew a
distinction between the "great tradition" and the "little tradition," a contrast
she used throughout her work (1971, pp. 40–59). The great tradition was
upheld by the literati. It was the written, elite, self-conscious body of
knowledge of an often urbanized priesthood. Redfield had in mind the
Sanskrit tradition of Hinduism. He noted, however, that the little tradition
coexisted with that elite formulation. The ideas of the folk, their beliefs and
practices thought of as superstitious by the priesthood, constituted a little
tradition. Great and little traditions were connected and mutually effecting,
but the force of the little tradition, on a daily basis, outweighed the great
tradition, which was available to "the folk" only through the infrequent
visits of a priest who was needed on specific occasions. In retrospect, what I
suspect Myerhoff found so consistently useful about the idea of two traditions was that they allowed her to explain how individuals continue to place
themselves in a great story even when they alter it, often beyond recognition. Ramon spoke out of his culture, but so did less-educated, less-elite
practitioners of culture whose efforts to fit themselves into a story required
adjusting a variety of traditions to one another.

If all humans engage in interpreting and contemplating the meaning of
their lives, then Myerhoff was interested in learning how culture made that
process possible. The more she was interested in creating life histories, the
more she was interested in finding the cultural settings where people
created their identities. Her work with the elderly convinced her that even
as the great story splinters, as happens with immigration and entry into a
complex pluralistic society, people still frame their lives in relationship to a
culture which generates multiple and rapidly changing "great stories." She
expressed this view in her work on women's journals, written with her long-
time friend Deena Metzger. They explored how a self can be constructed
through a journal, concluding that as a result of journal writing the self is
placed in a larger frame. They wrote:

> The materials encountered in the journal process are dealt with first in their raw, highly individual, utterly subjective state. But once interpreted and assimilated, they are transformed to some degree. Once examined, they are no longer utterly unique; they begin to reveal familiar and even universal configurations. One's own story is thus seen to contain elements of the stories of others, common to humanity. . . . Consciousness is then raised to a higher level, for the self can be seen now as the microcosm for the macrocosm of human experience. (1980, p. 113)

If Ramon represented the participant in the classically great story, and American feminist journal writers represented those whose stories were newly made and elaborated, the Southern California elderly Jews were squarely in the middle. They had a great tradition which they claimed, but which they altered, rewrote, and argued with. On the seaside benches and in their senior center, they lived a great tradition as a little one. The *Peyote Hunt* chapters began with elegant texts dictated by Ramon, but the mysehs of *Number Our Days* revealed fights between great and little tradition, with the little tradition often triumphing. The life history of Shmuel is a story of an ordinary man who lives a culture that exists no more. His memories are moving because he speaks as a member of a moral community, not as an isolate. His culture is not the "high culture" of rabbinic Judaism. Rather, his thirst for knowledge and justice and his joy in tailoring are understood by Myerhoff as expressions of the little tradition of the shtetlach of Europe— an amalgam of traditional Judaism, socialism, and Eastern European Jewish experience. Though Shmuel is a marginal person in the beach community of the elderly, his life reflects the intersection of the great and little traditions.

It was from Shmuel and all of the other people at the center that Myerhoff uncovered an insistent and persistent struggle to create visibility for themselves, otherwise unseen to the outside world. As she watched them fight to keep their childhood culture alive and to find integrity in it, she turned to the idea of reflexivity, the consciousness of the self as a constructor of identity and all categories of meaning. As she moved to the study of people deprived of access to a great story, she became more conscious of how persons make themselves up through improvised stories.

REFLEXIVITY—THE SEARCH FOR REFLECTING SURFACES

The theme of story, then, runs through Myerhoff's work to explain life histories in radically different cultural settings. She asked how the self accommodates to a story, possibly undermining it but certainly developing in relationship to it. For Myerhoff this human/cultural process of finding stories within stories, or storymaking through stories, was an example of reflexivity, the capacity to arouse consciousness of ourselves as we see the actions of ourselves and others. Reflexive events are set off to make actors conscious of both the frame and content of social life. In ritual or cultural events, the self reflects on itself as well as on the underlying cultural system that creates it. Myerhoff, with colleagues Clifford Geertz, Barbara Babcock, Victor Turner, Ed Bruner, Jay Ruby, Don Handelman, Bruce Kapferer, and many others, found reflexive events and experiences fertile field for analysis of how persons, by dramatizing and ritualizing social interaction, are active constructors of their own place in society. Myerhoff learned from the elderly Jews what she came to theorize about the basis of human relationships. They created meaning insofar as they depicted their lives to others, not only in murals and stories about their histories, but on every occasion they could create to maintain their visibility and command an audience (1986). Myerhoff wrote of the seniors, "We see a group of people creating themselves" (1986, p. 165). She meant that because they were conscious of their social invisibility, which resulted from their age, poverty, ethnicity, and many infirmities, they created occasions for their own visibility. In their center, in interactions with Myerhoff, in political fights and rituals, they constantly looked over their shoulders at themselves, measuring their success in persuading themselves and others of their vitality, their usefulness, and the reality of their past obliterated by Nazism.

In *Peyote Hunt,* Myerhoff juxtaposed meaning (relating to the story) and interpretation (explaining what the story meant). She privileged meaning, equating it with Ramon's directly dictated texts. She set her interpretations off from his, maintaining them both. But in her later work she saw her subjects' subjectivity as well as her own engaged in the process of interpreting. Recording gave way to understanding all forms of interpretation. She continued to deprivilege "science" but to emphasize acts of interpretation. Certainly she was an interpreter of conflict, ritual, and stories in the lives of the elderly. But so too were the elderly, particularly Shmuel, as they reviewed their lives and continued to play them out against a variety of cultural stories.

Reflexivity was an important idea for Myerhoff because it may have helped her to resolve the conflicts she must have felt about why the great story did not include everyone, why little stories had to be created and great stories rewritten. Reflexivity allowed her to understand persons as active and self-conscious narrators of their own lives. Though she was interested in how to bring a life story in line with a great story, she surely knew that not all lives would fit in.

This lack of fit raised the problem of gender. Herself a feminist, interested in women's culture and genres such as the journal, she knew that the great tradition often alienated women, who might try to accommodate it but also might abandon it altogether. Clearly she was drawn to Shmuel, the subject of her fully drawn life history, in part because his insights came directly as a result of his total alienation. His relationship to the great story could not make him a full participant. And interestingly, both subjects of her life histories had wives who weave in and out of the life histories but do not stand on their own. They reflect some of the great story, are essential supporters for their spouses, and yet never fully capture her attention. In *Peyote Hunt* she speculates that Lupe, Ramon's wife, will carry on his work after he is tragically killed. Myerhoff describes her as fully adequate, yet, perhaps because of her culture and ours, she did not see in Lupe as complete a spokesperson for the great tradition as was her husband/shaman.

Myerhoff never made gender a central category for her analysis. However, in *Number Our Days* she looked at the differences in the lives of elderly men and women, concluding that women adjusted to aging more easily. She attributes that difference to the fact that these women's lives were more concrete, particularistic, and domestic than men's. Retirement was not as wrenching for them because their particular activities continued in old age. Nevertheless, Myerhoff was drawn to the world of ideas of the men she interviewed. She admired women's ways of coping, but she sought the magic and power of spiritual life rather than domesticity. She did not believe that domesticity or spirituality was intrinsic to either gender. She was aware of what kept women in many cultures within a domestic sphere. She was nevertheless drawn to the great stories and their interpreters, and kept a distant, loving, even wistful affection for the domestic.

Reflexivity in human culture offered Myerhoff more than the idea that outsiders are often reflective gadflies with insight and self-consciousness. Rather, she was after the settings and occasions for staging oneself, particularly for those aware of and distant from the scripts or stories provided by culture or a group. In reflexive events, the subject and object, as well as a consciousness of the process joining them, are present. The symbolic meaning of a story is shot through with a self-consciousness of one's own place in it. She never could give up the idea of culture, broadly conceived, that suggested that human meaning springs from some collective dimension, universal, ethnic, or gendered, carried in humans' stories, making them personal and compelling. Reflexive moments were the richest because they framed the process of meaning making, and made participants aware that they were makers of meaning. Because reflexivity implies a distance and unity at once, marginalization may still be integrated with a yearning for a great story. And stories may grow richer for their retelling from the outsider who claims them even while rejecting them (Myerhoff 1982).

For what was preserved in *Number Our Days* were lives seen and made important by an anthropologist, a witness to invisible lives. And with the center members' heightened visibility, they succeeded not so much in getting someone to find them valuable, as in confirming what they themselves believed all along. They found in Myerhoff someone able to make them subject and object, as they had, on a smaller scale with a smaller audience, made themselves. Myerhoff not only had been a personal reflecting surface

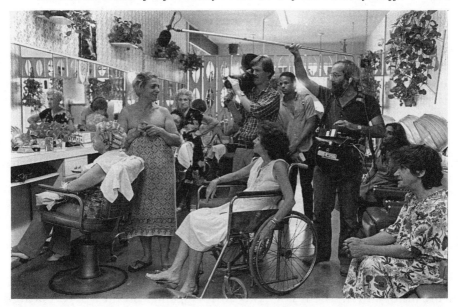

The various frames in which life-history research occurs. Myerhoff, seated in the wheelchair, is interviewing women in a local Fairfax beauty salon. She, in turn, is being recorded and filmed by a crew for the film *In Her Own Time*, about her battle with cancer. The filmmaker, seated behind the crew to the right, is observing both the filming and the interviewing. Summer, 1984. *Photograph by Bill Aron.*

for them, but by making them "famous," she had provided one on a grand scale. They were self-constructors par excellence. The seniors' invisibility grew, in large measure, from living in a modern society that is practiced at marginalizing persons who are different from the mainstream. Reflexive activity does not arise in culture solely to respond to the pain of being distanced. However, it appears from the range of Myerhoff's work that modern society heightens both people's sense of alienation and their occasions for individual, as against communal, reflexivity.[4] Myerhoff's interest in reflexivity seems to have allowed her to stay suspended between an interest in how individuals accommodate to great stories and an acknowledgment that humans often remain engaged in making themselves up, aware of their alienation from stories and framing occasions to reflect on them.

Myerhoff grew more concerned with reflexivity as she grew more conscious of the construction of the story and of the life history. That is, she experienced in her research what she thought was happening in society. She was aware of herself as subject and object and the process that created the consciousness of both. She revealed herself as a subject more, though she never lost sight of the real subject of the research. She more forcefully took the role of witness that the people at the center required of her. She dramatized them dramatizing themselves. As a self-conscious reflecting surface, she found herself rethinking anthropology and culture. As a recorder of the drama at the center and as a participant in that drama, she came to see her own story with theirs, learning from them, and feeling both hurt and approved of by them.

LIFE HISTORY: THE DOUBLE FRAME

In their introduction to *The Cracked Mirror*, Myerhoff and Jay Ruby wrote:

> In more protracted reflexive works . . . the frame is repeatedly violated, and the two stories commenting on each other travel alongside, simultaneously commanding our attention and creating a different world than either represents by itself. (1982, p. 4)

This description of reflexive genres in culture resembles the production of a life history. In the life history, two stories together produce one. A hearer and listener ask, respond, present, and edit a life. The recorder, especially one who casts herself as student, is taking that life in, perhaps assimilating it to her own great story. So as the life history takes shape, it is inevitable that the recorder will enact what Paul Rabinow, borrowing from Paul Riccouer, thought constituted the essence of participant-observation fieldwork: "Comprehension of the self by detour of the comprehension of the other" (cited in Rabinow 1977). One must know oneself through and in light of the other. The subject-subject relationship is itself a reflexive event in which a self is presented with the full knowledge of reporting, or constructing itself. The recorder participates fully in a parallel if submerged frame. In the event of self-construction, the relationship to stories great and small is clearly uppermost. And Myerhoff was willing to merge great stories of one self with her other subject, herself. For it was the way that the stories of others could comment on all lives that she seemed to understand and communicate. She achieved that stance by making herself present, even subtly, in her writing. Watching the other watch herself or himself throws the self into active relief.

A letter Barbara wrote to me about the process of writing *Number Our Days* well illustrates this process of merging of stories:

> I am in Santa Barbara in my retreat, having snatched a few days to work on the Shmuel life history. It goes bloody slowly . . . but the work feels very right. I splurged—spent all my money from a workshop I did last week on journals—to buy the new Howe book [*World of Our Fathers*] and two huge gorgeous books of photographs of Eastern European Jews and Jewish life. I have them open before me and am playing Yiddish and Hassidic music. The environment begins to grow and grow inside me. This is a good way to

do this work. It's raining outside—it's a whole world within. (Personal communication, February 7, 1976)

The world within was created by her engagement with the world without, her participant-observation fieldwork. In order to understand Shmuel's life history, she, as it were, takes Shmuel in and then brings him out in the printed word. This is the single act of two voices which Myerhoff never merges.

Myerhoff argued that seeing oneself in the eye of the other is an essential core of human interaction. In her production of life histories, one is aware of the double gaze of both subjects. They were seen, and she was seen. That mutual respect and witnessing were as apparent in her relationships with subjects as in any normative social interaction. It is apparent from her writing that her informants always felt deeply valued. That was made vivid at her funeral. A rabbi with whom she had worked closely in the Fairfax community was one of her many eulogizers. He was not an easy participant in the event. Forbidden to hear the singing voice of a woman by Jewish custom, he prayed psalms in a hunched-over position whenever one of Barbara's friends sang. But after saying relatively standard things about making her death meaningful by undertaking more Jewish requirements such as lighting Sabbath candles or doing charitable acts, lines provided by his great tradition, he added something else.

> Barbara spent a lot of time with us at Passover. She watched us clean and change our dishes. Barbara, I asked her, why do you care about these things? The Seder I can understand, but why cleaning? She answered, because I see you clean with care that is how I understand you love God.

He was obviously moved by the accuracy of her witnessing, of what she understood as a strange outsider-insider to his Hasidic orthodoxy. That she understood them enacting their lives was for him of equal importance to urging his listeners to achieve greater piety.

BUT IS IT SCIENCE?

Ironically, though Myerhoff was a bold innovator of anthropological work, she remained defensive, often forswearing her writing as a work of anthropology. She refers to *Peyote Hunt* as "personal" and "subjective" and to *Number Our Days* as influenced by, but not a work of, anthropology. The more she yearned to include her voice in the work, to present a full picture of those she studied, and to explore narrative forms in their culture, the more uneasy she became in seeing her work as mainstream anthropology.

She self-consciously and unapologetically incorporated into her life as well as her work precisely what she saw. In Ramon, and Shmuel, the

Russian Jews of Fairfax, and feminists enacting women's culture, she saw an authenticity she longed for in American culture, one that suited her soul and her intellect. She saw how people made the world whole through the sacred, through knowledge, through intimacy with their history, and through sheer invention.

She was seen as a student in that process by every subject of a life history she undertook. I believe that she was seen and wanted to be seen as a seeker capable of understanding what her subject knew. Two weeks before Barbara Myerhoff died, not quite fifty years old, she gave the last interview for a film, *In Her Own Time* (Lynne Littman and Barbara Myerhoff), which documented how she confronted her terminal illness within the Lubavitch Russian community of Los Angeles, where she was conducting fieldwork. Thinned by cancer almost to the point of emaciation, her voice raspy as a result of her disease, she spoke with eloquence and clarity about that fieldwork. "If I can in my work make it clear to others what they are, what they feel, what they do. If I can pass that through me and out to others, then my work is done." It was precisely the use of the life-history method that made it possible for her to stand as passageway capable of presenting her own voice and that of others. Built into the life history is the possibility of maintaining the polyphony that we know characterizes human society. In her commitment to those voices, she anticipated what Marcus and Fischer (1986) have called "experimental ethnography," which they contrast to realist ethnography, the very tradition she was skittish about challenging. As a collaborative effort necessarily focused on interpretation, the life history, at its best, can achieve an interaction that can be translated into written form. Myerhoff's interest in narrative, self-consciousness, reflexivity, and the creation of meaning is inevitably tied to the production of life history.

The life history should bear some resemblance to the complex of ideas and biography that helped shape and interpret it. Two voices produce one, and in Myerhoff's case she never merged them. Story and reflexivity were theoretical constructs that not only led Myerhoff to an interest in the life-history methodology but helped her resolve personal and intellectual conflicts about the place of the individual in the great story, a concept to which she was drawn but which often marginalized the very people she wanted to understand. Because the life-history method actually replicated the very interaction she found at the core of human culture, Myerhoff came to envision culture, and the individual's relationship to it, as the dynamic interaction of frames and stories that produce an innovative perspective on what is inherited and given.

Notes

I acknowledge the generous help I received from the following people who read an earlier draft of this article: Ed Bruner, Sara Evans, Steven Foldes, Shirley Garner, Amy Kaminsky, Elaine May, Pamela Mittlefehldt, and Cheri Register.

1. See Clifford's discussion of student-teacher relationships in fieldwork in Clifford and Marcus (1986, p. 108). Crapanzano (1980) explores an alternative form of relationship in psychoanalytically oriented work that examines the narrator-interpreter relationship in transference-countertransference terms. Two recent books about the life history in anthropology also address the significance of this relationship for the final product (Langness and Frank 1981 and Watson and Watson-Franke 1985).

2. See Pratt's discussion of that placement in Clifford and Marcus (1986).

3. A useful discussion of reflexivity can be found in Babcock (1980). This article introduces a volume including a paper by Myerhoff and Metzger. Babcock's article was influential in Myerhoff's work.

4. Victor Turner draws a distinction between individual and plural reflexivity, associating the former with complex society and the latter with traditional societies (1977).

References

Babcock, Barbara
    1980   "Reflexivity: Definitions and Discriminations." *Semiotica* 30: 1–14.
Clifford, James
    1986   "On Ethnographic Allegory." In James Clifford and George Marcus, eds., *Writing Culture: The Poetics and Politics of Ethnography,* pp. 98–121. Berkeley: University of California Press.
Crapanzano, Vincent
    1980   *Tuhami: Portrait of a Moroccan.* Chicago: University of Chicago Press.
Geertz, Clifford
    1973   "Religion as a Cultural System." in *The Interpretation of Cultures,* pp. 87–125. New York: Basic Books.
Langness, L. L., and Gelya Frank
    1981   *Lives: An Anthropological Approach to Biography.* Novato, Calif.: Chandler and Sharp.
Marcus, George, and Michael Fischer
    1986   *Anthropology as Cultural Critique.* Chicago: University of Chicago Press.
Myerhoff, Barbara G.
    1986   "'Life Not Death in Venice': Its Second Life." In *Judaism Viewed from Within and from Without: Anthropological Studies,* ed. Harvey E. Goldberg, pp. 143–70. Albany: State University of New York Press.
    1982   "Life History among the Elderly: Performance, Visibility, and Remembering." In *A Crack in the Mirror: Reflexive Perspectives in Anthropology,* ed. Jay Ruby, pp. 99–120. Philadelphia: University of Pennsylvania Press.
    1979   *Number Our Days.* New York: Dutton.
    1974   *Peyote Hunt: The Sacred Journey of the Huichol Indians.* New York: Cornell University Press.

ms   "The Ritual Telling of the Great Story That Shapes Individual Lives."
          (Posthumously edited by Mark Kaminsky)
Myerhoff, Barbara G. and Deena Metzger
   1980   "The Journal as Activity and Genre: Listening to the Silent Laughter
          of Mozart." *Semiotica* 30, no. 1–2: 97–113.
Myerhoff, Barbara G. and Jay Ruby
   1982   "Introduction." In *A Crack in the Mirror: Reflexive Perspectives in An-
          thropology,* ed. Jay Ruby. Philadelphia: University of Pennsylvania
          Press.
Pratt, Mary Louise
   1986   "Fieldwork in Common Places." In James Clifford and George Mar-
          cus, eds., *Writing Cultures: The Poetics and Politics of Ethnography,* pp. 27–
          50. Berkeley: University of California Press.
Rabinow, Paul
   1977   *Reflections on Fieldwork in Morocco.* Berkeley: University of California
          Press.
Redfield, Robert
   1971   *Peasant Society and Culture.* Chicago: University of Chicago Press.
Turner, Victor W.
   1977   "Variation on a Theme of Liminality." In *Secular Ritual,* ed. Sally Falk
          Moore and Barbara G. Myerhoff, pp. 36–52. Assen: Van Gorcum
          Press.
Watson, Lawrence C., and Maria-Barbara Watson-Franke
   1985   *Interpreting Life Histories: An Anthropological Inquiry.* New Brunswick,
          N.J.: Rutgers University Press.

PART FIVE

Truths

TRUTHS

Personal Narratives Group

All autobiographic memory is true. It is up
to the interpreter to discover in which
sense, where, for which purpose.

—Luisa Passerini

When talking about their lives, people lie sometimes, forget a lot, exaggerate, become confused, and get things wrong. Yet they *are* revealing truths. These truths don't reveal the past "as it actually was," aspiring to a standard of objectivity. They give us instead the truths of our experiences. They aren't the result of empirical research or the logic of mathematical deductions. Unlike the reassuring Truth of the scientific ideal, the truths of personal narratives are neither open to proof nor self-evident. We come to understand them only through interpretation, paying careful attention to the contexts that shape their creation and to the world views that inform them. Sometimes the truths we see in personal narratives jar us from our complacent security as interpreters "outside" the story and make us aware that our own place in the world plays a part in our interpretation and shapes the meanings we derive from them.

Shared stories provide significant ways of understanding the world. In oral cultures, elders tell life stories for the edification and socialization of children in the community. Knowing how and why such stories are true is part of the process of maturing, and is fundamental to intellectual, emotional, and social development. To understand one's own life in light of these stories is to be a full participant in a particular culture.

Even in our world of printed facts and impersonal mass media, we consciously and unconsciously absorb knowledge of the world and how it works through exchanges of life stories. We constantly test reality against such stories, asserting and modifying our own perceptions in light of them. The significance of these exchanges for women in clarifying social realities and challenging hegemonic oppression has often been profound. Contemporary political movements have capitalized on life stories in their efforts to transform society and women within it. In the course of the Chinese Revolution, women came together to "speak bitterness," recounting lives of pain and persecution at the hands of patriarchal families. In the contemporary Western feminist movement, consciousness-raising groups allowed women to tell each other about their experiences, doubts, and anger—without fear of judgment or punishment. And even when we are not gathered in groups for the explicit purpose of exchanging information about our lives, we do so informally all the time. These exchanges and the knowledge they impart about emotional and physical well-being, communal values, aspirations, or power become part of our reality. They are as true as our lives.

Far from encouraging our ability to think creatively about discovering the truths in personal narratives, our academic disciplines have more often discouraged us from taking people's life stories seriously. Disciplines have mainly done this by elevating some kinds of truth—the kinds that conform to established criteria of validity—over others. Generalizations based on these elevated Truths become norms which are rarely challenged for their failure to consider or explain exceptions. This elevation and generalization serve to control: control data, control irregularities of human experiences, and, ultimately, control what constitutes knowledge. Considered in these terms, the truths in personal narratives cannot stand the tests to which they are subjected, i.e., the tests of verifiability, reliability, facticity, or representativeness. Using such a limited definition of Truth admits only one standard at a time for the perception and interpretation of a small segment of a complex reality. While such a conception may be "safe" in its claim to meet any challenge to its scientific validity, it inevitably excludes certain experiences that require understanding. As appealing as it may be to some to carry out this Cartesian division of the world into discrete and knowable parts, the cost is high. It is devastating for those whose experience, history, and perceptions—whose truths—are obliterated.

Interpreting Women's Lives has explored this dimension of plural truths, the truths of experience, history, and perceptions embodied in personal narratives. We have emphasized the multiple truths in all life stories. Only by attending to the conditions which create these narratives, the forms that guide them, and the relationships that produce them are we able to understand what is communicated in a personal narrative. These angles of interpretation not only provide different perspectives but reveal multiple truths of a life. These truths are essential because they are specific; they are not abstract generalizations about life. While we do not deny the usefulness of some generalizations about women's lives, we realize that generalization without attention to the truths of experience is fruitless. Therefore, rather than focus on the objective Truth, we focus on the links between women's perspectives and the truths they reveal.

Feminist theory seeks to disrupt the most basic, the safest of ideas about Truth—and to force them to stand up to examination against other facts, standards, experiences, and pespectives. Beginning from the point of view of the female "other," feminist theory assumes the fact of difference and asserts that if Truth rests on generalization, it must take into account experience that has previously been ignored, forgotten, ridiculed, and devalued. Feminists have argued that concepts of Truth, embodied in generalizations such as Mankind or the universal "he," typically refuse to acknowledge gender differences and therefore are deceptive. They are generalizations that close off certain questions, and assume a partial reality to be the whole story. The feminist revision of the search for knowledge has sent us to new methods and new places, and has encouraged the hunt for new sources of insight into women's realities.

Women's personal narratives embody and reflect the reality of difference and complexity and stress the centrality of gender to human life and thought. They are, therefore, critical to the elaboration of a more finely nuanced understanding of humanity and to a reconstruction of knowledge that admits the fact and value of difference into its definition. In other words, women's personal narratives provide immediate, diverse, and rich sources for feminist revisions of knowledge. In the face of women's life stories, the search for Truth requires truths—a symbolic as well as semantic revolution by which we both challenge and reconstruct the traditional definitions of reality.

For example, the essays in *Interpreting Women's Lives* have focused on the construction of a gendered self-identity and on the relationship between that self and society. In recognizing that society does not provide an inalterable script for the life course, and that the person does not develop apart from such constraints, we have had to understand the sources of the truths of individual women's experiences. Each essay, therefore, has addressed how reality was constructed for a particular subject of an autobiography, biography, or life history. What supports, generates, or undermines that reality were crucial questions for each interpretation. None of these lives was presented as exemplary of others. Each life required attention to its uniqueness in order to learn how to interpret the truths of women's lives. These essays suggest that truths result from the process of constructing a gendered self.

The interpretation of women's personal narratives also forces us to rethink the division between subjectivity and objectivity. From the outset, feminist theory has been skeptical of the claim of objectivity. Other critical traditions operating in and on the edges of the academic disciplines share this skepticism. But beyond this, inherent in feminist claims and feminist political strategy, is a positive valuation of the subjective. The truths that women's voices express are not regarded as merely subjective, that is, pertinent only to a single individual; feminists also reject the Truth of "objective" fact based on the claim that it issues from a standpoint outside individual experience. The truths of personal narratives are the truths revealed from real positions in the world, through lived experience in social relationships, in the context of passionate beliefs and partisan stands. They recount efforts to grapple with the world in all of its confusion and complexity and with the normal lack of omniscience that characterizes the human condition. It is precisely because of their subjectivity—their rootedness in time, place, and personal experience, and their perspective-ridden character—that we value them. It is in probing the nature of the perspectives revealed in personal narratives that we can begin to experience the power of the feminist revision of traditional disciplinary scholarship.

Each of the lives included in this book is testimony to the significance of gender and to the diversity among women. These testimonies ask us to rethink ideas of social class and culture, to reexamine how literature is produced, and to rethink the meanings of historical activity. Our focus on the person within society, time, social class, and gender norms challenges prefeminist ideas that rested on deceptive generalizations that could not admit alternative truths. In part, what seems "interesting" about the personal narratives in this book is that such stories have frequently been excluded from theorizing about social class, society, literature, and history.

Interpreting Women's Lives has also grappled with the question of who owns Truth. In positing the centrality of the interpretive act, we recognize the possibility that the truths the narrator claims may be at odds with the most cherished notions of the interpreter. Personal narratives cannot be simply expropriated in the service of some good cause, but must be respected in their integrity. What are the rules governing their interpretation? Certainly the essays included here have not provided simple answers, but many do suggest the need to recognize both the agenda of the narrator and that of the interpreter as distinct and not always compatible. And they once again remind us that feminist scholars, by simply criticizing the distortions inherent in disciplinary criteria for validation, have not released us from all institutional constraints upon our own use of these stories or from political agendas that shape our interpretation of them.

While insisting that women's personal narratives reveal truths, we still retain our responsibility as interpreters. These stories do not "speak for themselves," nor do they provide direct access to other times, places, or cultures. They may not always speak with clarity, or precision, or even sincerity. The interpretation of women's personal narratives often entails a cautious juxtaposition of alternative truths and feeds into the feminist project of revising not merely the content of our knowledge of human society, but the very criteria that guide our search for truths. *Interpreting Women's Lives* is the fruit of this search.

Contributors

JOY WEBSTER BARBRE is a graduate student in American Studies and the Center for Advanced Feminist Studies at the University of Minnesota. She is coauthor of "Side Trips: The Illustrated Adventures of Sumner Matteson," *Encounters* 5, no. 6 (July 1982), and is currently working on women's personal narratives and issues of childlessness.

AMY FARRELL, an instructor of composition and a graduate student in American Studies and the Center for Advanced Feminist Studies at the University of Minnesota, is working in the area of twentieth-century American cultural history and feminist critical theory. She also teaches a course on reading and writing women's autobiographies.

SANDRA FRIEDEN, Assistant Professor of German and Associate Director of Off-Campus Institutes at the University of Houston—University Park, is the author of *Autobiography: Self into Form: German Language Autobiographical Writings of the 1970s* (Peter Lang, 1983). Her other publications include articles on Christa Wolf, Elizabeth Plessen, Peter Handke, and Brigitte Schwaiger. She has taught courses on German cinema at the University of Houston since 1982 and is currently coediting a volume entitled *Gender Perspectives in German Cinema.*

SHIRLEY NELSON GARNER, Professor of English at the University of Minnesota, is editor (with Claire Kehane and Madelon Sprengnether) of *The (M)other Tongue: Essays in Feminist Psychoanalytic Interpretation* (Cornell University Press, 1985). She has published numerous articles on Shakespeare and women writers. She is a founder of *Hurricane Alice,* a feminist review of the arts and culture, and is on its editorial board.

SUSAN GEIGER, Associate Professor in the Women's Studies Department at the University of Minnesota, is interested in the theoretical and methodological implications of life-history research and considers the collection of life histories essential to her work on African women's history. She is the author of "Life History: Content and Method," *Signs: A Journal of Women in Culture and Society* 2 (1986), "Life History Research," *Women's Research and Documentation Project* (WRDP Papers, no. 1, University of Dar es Salaam, 1985), and "Women in Nationalist Struggle: TANU Activists in Dar es Salaam," *International Journal of African Historical Studies* 20, (1987). She is currently writing a book on women's mobilization in the nationalist movement in Tanzania based on the life histories of several activists.

FAYE GINSBURG, Assistant Professor of Anthropology and Director of the Program in Ethnographic Film and Video at New York University, has researched and written on grassroots abortion activists, focusing on the relationship between female life stories and political activism. She is the author of *Contested Lives: The Abortion Debate in an American Community* (California) and is coeditor, with Anna Tsing, of the forthcoming collection *Negotiating Gender in American Culture* (Beacon). She has also created two documentaries, "In Her Hands: Women and Ritual" and "Prairie Storm."

KATHERINE R. GOODMAN, Associate Professor of German at Brown University, is coauthor of *Beyond the Eternal Feminine: Critical Essays on Women and German Literature* and the author of *Dis/Closures: Women's Auto-biography in Germany, 1790–1914* (Peter Lang, 1986). She has also written articles on autobiographies of German women and on theories of women's autobiography.

ELIZABETH HAMPSTEN, Associate Professor of English at the University of North Dakota, is the author of *Read This Only to Yourself: Writings of Midwestern Women, 1880–1910* (Indiana University Press, 1982). She is researching the history of childhood during the settlement of the Northern Plains. She edits and has published articles in *Plainswoman*.

RUTH-ELLEN BOETCHER JOERES, Professor of German at the University of Minnesota, is the author of the biographic study *Die Anfänge der deutschen Frauenbewegung: Louise Otto-Peters* (Frankfurt, 1983) and coeditor of *German Women in the Eighteenth and Nineteenth Centuries: A Social and Literary History* (Indiana University Press, 1986). She has also written biographical articles and essays on nineteenth-century German women's biographies and on Luise Büchner, Gisela von Arnim, Marie Luise Kaschnitz, and Marieluise Fleisser, among others.

SUSAN M-A LYONS, a graduate student in writing with emphasis on editing and nonfiction writing in the English Department at the University of Minnesota, has published articles in *Occupational Therapy Perspectives in Cardiac Rehabilitation* (Minnesota Occupational Therapy Association, 1985), including "Psychological Aspects of Recovery after Myocardial Infarction," "Outpatient Cardiac Rehabilitation Programs" (coauthor), and "Sexual Activity and the Cardiac Patient" (coauthor).

SHULA MARKS, Director of the Institute of Commonwealth Studies and Professor in Commonwealth History at the University of London, has written *"Not Either an Experimental Doll": The Separate Lives of Three South African Women* (London: Women's Press, 1987) and *The Ambiguities of Dependence: State, Class, and Nationalism in Early Twentieth Century South Africa* (Johns Hopkins and Ravan Press, 1986). Her current research includes work on the political economy of health and health care in South Africa since the late nineteenth century, with a focus on women's health issues.

MARY JO MAYNES, Associate Professor of History at the University of Minnesota, is coeditor of *German Women in the Eighteenth and Nineteenth Centuries: A Social and Literary History* (Indiana University Press, 1986) and author of several articles on European social history. She is currently working on a book on working-class life course and working-class auto-biography in France and Germany.

MARJORIE MBILINYI, Professor at the Institute of Development Studies at the University of Dar es Salaam, is concerned with personal narratives as a politics pertaining to class, nation, and sex. Her publications include "Runaway Wives in Colonial Tanganyika: Forced Labour and Forced Mar-riage in Rungwe District: c. 1919–1961," *International Journal of the Sociology of Law* 16, no. 1 (1988), and "This Is the Big Slavery," *Agribusiness and Women Peasants and Workers in Tanzania* (Dar es Salaam University Press, forthcom-ing).

NELLIE Y. MCKAY, Professor in the Department of Afro-American Stud-ies at the University of Wisconsin-Madison, has researched and written on black women's autobiography. Her publications include essays and articles on Paule Murray, Gwendolyn Brooks, and Zora Neale Hurston. She is currently working on *Narrative and Identity in Contemporary Black Women's Autobiographies, 1920–1970*, a cross-disciplinary study of identity formation in twentieth-century black American women. *Jean Toomer, Artist: A Study of His Literary Life and Work* was published in 1984, her edited collection *Critical Essays on Toni Morrison* in 1988. She is the Associate General Editor for the forthcoming *Norton Anthology of Afro-American Literature* and co-editor of *Twentieth-Century Afro-American Autobiography* (forthcoming).

PAMELA MITTLEFEHLDT, Assistant Professor of American Studies at St. Cloud State University, is researching the ways that women have used story—both fiction and personal narratives—as a tool for social change. She has compiled and edited *Minnesota Folklife: An Annotated Bibliography* (Min-nesota Historical Society, 1979).

LUISA PASSERINI, Associate Professor of Methodology of Historical Re-search, Department of History, University of Turin, has researched the history of social and cultural movements and proposed new uses of oral sources for historical purposes. She was part of the women's movement in Italy in the 1970s and is now part of the cultural movement on women's research in that country. She is the author of *Storia orale: Vita quotidiana e cultural materiale delle classi subalterne* (Rosenberg and Sellier, 1978) and *Torino Operaia e Fascismo* (Roma-Bari, 1984), and of numerous articles on women's history, oral history, and the history of social movements in the 1960s and 1970s. She is on the editorial board of *International Journal of Oral History, Fonti-orali-Studi e ricerche, Memoria,* and *Movimento operaio e socialista.*

RIV-ELLEN PRELL is an Associate Professor in the Department of Anthropology at the University of Minnesota and former Chair of Women's Studies. She is the author of *Prayer and Community: The Hauurah Movement in American Judaism* (Wayne State University Press, 1988) and of many articles on gender, community, and change in American Judaism.

KAREN BRODKIN SACKS, Director of Women's Studies at UCLA, has written *Caring by the Hour: Hospital Workers in an Assembly-Line Age* (forthcoming), a book on the work and struggle of women hospital workers. She is also researching mother-and-daughter relationships. She is on the editorial board of *Signs.*

MARJORIE SHOSTAK, Research Associate at the Graduate Institute of Liberal Arts, Emory University, is the author of *Nisa: The Life and Words of a !Kung Woman* (Harvard University Press, 1981). She has also written articles about her research with the !Kung, and has worked on a film, *N!ai: The Story of a !Kung Woman.*

VIRGINIA STEINHAGEN is a graduate student in the German Department at the University of Minnesota. Her research interests include literature of the German Democratic Republic, adolescent literature, and the writings of foreign workers in West Germany.

JULIA SWINDELLS, freelance teacher at Cambridge University and the Open University, is the author of *Victorian Writing and Working Women: The Other Side of Silence* (Polity Press, 1985; University of Minnesota Press, 1986), a study of nineteenth-century fiction and the autobiographies of working women. She is also coauthor with Lisa Jardine of *What's Left? History, Literature, and the Labour Movement* (forthcoming), and she is currently researching poetic and pictorial representations of pre-Raphaelite women and their place in biography.

MARCIA WRIGHT, Professor of History and Director of the Institute of African Studies at Columbia University, is the author of "Women in Peril: A Commentary on the Life Stories of Three Women of East Central Africa," *African Social Research* 14 (1972), and "Bwanikwa: Consciousness and Protest among Slave Women in Central Africa, 1886–1911," in C. Robertson and M. Klein, eds., *Women and Slaves in Africa* (Madison: University of Wisconsin Press, 1983).

Index

Abortion activism, 59–80
Acceptance, narrative models of, 8
Activism, 62, 85–86, 93; pro-choice and pro-life, 59–80
Activities, range of: among pro-choice and pro-life activists, 71–72
Adams High School (Natal, S.Af.), 41–44, 49, 51, 54
Adamson, Sarah Browne Armstrong, 136–37
African Methodist Episcopal (AME) church, 144, 148–49
African Participatory Research Network (APRN), 207
Afro-American community, 139, 141. *See also* Black American literature; Black American women
Age, 39, 40, 43, 252
Alienation, 48, 251–52, 253
Allen, Richard, 145, 146
Althusser, Louis, 82 n.7
Amanuensis-editor: authority in black narratives, 141
AME (African Methodist Episcopal Church), 144, 148–49
American Board of Missions (Natal), 51
Andrews, William L., 140, 141, 152 n.1
Androcentrism, 4, 6–8, 10
Anecdotes: use in working-class autobiographies, 108–10
Anthropologists, 3–4, 230–31, 241
Anti-family, right-to-lifers viewed as, 69
Artisanal subculture, 111–12
Audience, narrative form as responding to, 99
Authenticity: in Wolf's writings, 173–74
Authority: in narrator-interpreter collaboration, 201, 203
Autobiographical essays: as private writings, 129
Autobiographical mode, 25–26, 29–30
Autobiographical writings: role in German literature of the 1970s, 179–83
Autobiographies, 4, 27–29, 40, 100, 104–107; distinguished from life histories and biographies, 155; popular, 27, 106–107, 112; as viewed in discipline of English, 25, 27, 37–38 n.2, 38 n.6; as viewed in men's history, 24, 25–28; working-class, 26–27, 103, 105–15
Autonomy, sense, of, 146, 150

Baker, Russell: *Growing Up*, 14 n.2
"Ballad of Hazel Miner, The" (Suchy), 133

Band sisters, 153 n.15
Bantu Education Act (1953), 55 n.12
Bantu Purity League, 49, 57 n.46
Behavior, new forms of: use of narrative tradition to legitimize, 193–94
Bellevue, Kay, 67–69
Benedict, Ruth, 160, 168–70
Benjamin, Anna Starck, 133–34
Benning, Carol, 136–37
"Beyond Autobiography" (White), 25–26
Bible: desire to read and interpret, 145–46
Biedenbach, Mieze, 113
Bildungsroman, 105, 109
Biographies, 4, 6, 22, 100; distinguished from autobiographies, 155; fictionalized, 173, 176
Biographies, overlapping: interviewer-narrator collaboration as, 243
Biological rhythms, 105
Birmingham Popular Memory Group, 27
Birth control (Contraception), 70
Birth stories as personal dramas, 65
Black American (Afro-American) literature, 140, 142, 153 n.11
Black American (Afro-American) women: in 19th century, 149–50, 154 n.19; significance in Afro-American community, 139, 142; spiritual autobiographies of, 139, 141–52
Blessing of perfect love, 144, 153 n.15
Bonnet, Rene, 107
Bourgeoisie, emergent: autobiography as genre of, 104, 106
Bouvier, Jeanne, 110
Brocher, Victorine, 112
Bromberg, Pamela S., 140
Brookes, Edgar, 56 n.25
Bruss, Elizabeth, 186
Burckhard, Mary Anna Albrecht, 131–32, 135
Burgel, Bruno, 109
Burke, Peter, 106
Bushmen. *See* !Kung San

Cagliostro (conjuror), 126
Callahan, Daniel and Sidney, 82 n.8
Campaign autobiography, 99; Leakey's as, 165, 166, 168, 170
Capitalist patriarchy, 29, 30
Caretaking. *See* Nurturance
Caring by the Hour (Sacks), 85
Cassandra/Conditions of a Narrative (Wolf), 172, 177–79, 181
Casual labor (colonial Tanganyika), 204

269